# Innocence, Power, and the Novels of John Hawkes

**Penn Studies in Contemporary American Fiction**
A Series Edited by Emory Elliott,
University of California at Riverside

A complete list of books in the series is available from the publisher.

# Innocence, Power, and the Novels of John Hawkes

Rita Ferrari

**PENN**

University of Pennsylvania Press
Philadelphia

Permission is acknowledged to reprint excerpts from published works. A complete listing can be found following the index to this volume.

Library of Congress Cataloging in Publication Data

Ferrari, Rita.
    Innocence, power, and the novels of John Hawkes / Rita Ferrari.
        p.   cm. — (Penn studies in contemporary American fiction)
    Includes bibliographical references and index.
    ISBN 0-8122-3341-7 (alk. paper)
    1. Hawkes, John, 1925–    —Criticism and interpretation.   2. Power (Social sciences)
in literature.   3. Innocence (Psychology) in literature.   I. Title.   II. Series.
PS3552.A82Z66   1996
813'.54—dc20                                                                              96-21425
                                                                                               CIP

# Contents

# Acknowledgments

Joseph Fradin and Leslie Fiedler read an early version of this book, and I remain grateful to them for their support and encouragement. I am particularly indebted to Marcus Klein, whose insights on Hawkes and on American literature provided inspiration at this project's beginnings, and whose responses to my work were always gracious and illuminating. Patrick O'Donnell's extensive work on Hawkes, his consideration of my own work, and his advice and professional generosity have been sustaining and invaluable to me. My colleagues Georgia Johnston and Raymond Benoit at St. Louis University gave me the benefit of their time and knowledge, which I greatly appreciate. St. Louis University's Mellon Fund provided me with research grants as I completed the manuscript, for which I am also very appreciative. The majority of my discussion of *Virginie: Her Two Lives* and *Whistlejacket* in Chapters 6 and 7 first appeared in *Arizona Quarterly*, which has kindly allowed me to reprint this material. I am very grateful to Jerry Singerman for his efforts in bringing this book to print, and also to the efforts of the University of Pennsylvania Press's staff; I am particularly grateful to the advice of the Press's readers.

My family and friends have helped me in innumerable ways. And I am thankful to Jim Schlemmer, for so much.

John Hawkes has seen little of the material in this book, but has given me the pleasure of his kind encouragement. I hope that this book can be a pleasure to him, and that it helps bring new readers to the unique rewards of his novels.

# Introduction

Since the late 1940s John Hawkes (born 1925) has consistently created fictions remarkable for their stylistic beauty and narratological experimentation and for the resoluteness of their visionary engagement with memory and anxiety, violence and eroticism, desire and imagination. The power of Hawkes's extraordinary language to unfold the darkest inclinations of individual psyches and to reveal the horrific failures of culture has been highly praised by critics; Joan Didion, for instance, wrote of *The Lime Twig* (1961) that its power comes from the fact that "the action takes place exactly on the *brink* of nightmare: it is not quite hallucination, and therefore nothing from which you can wake up; it is every waking wish carried to its logical extreme" (22; Didion's emphasis). Yet in his introduction to this novel Leslie Fiedler could validly refer to Hawkes as "the least read novelist of substantial merit in the United States" (viii). While Hawkes has been widely and deeply admired by critics from the start of his writing career, his work, often considered inaccessible, has had an audience in the United States mostly in universities; it has suffered a lack of public attention that other challenging contemporary novelists have received. Conservative critics have responded negatively, rejecting Hawkes's style as unnecessarily difficult and his vision as perverse and unpalatable; they further accuse his privileging of style and his aesthetic concerns of covering over moral emptiness. Perhaps the most scathing comment about Hawkes's work came in Roger Sale's review of *The Blood Oranges* (1971), which he began by calling the novel "the work of a contemptible imagination" (3). Stanley Edgar Hyman, reviewing Hawkes's career through *Second Skin* (1964), says that his novels "do not make the slightest concession to any reader—their vision of life is shattering and their forms are shattered" (24); he sees Hawkes's unconventional creation of form as formlessness. Jack Beatty claims that *Adventures in the Alaskan Skin Trade* (1985) "refers to nothing outside itself" (9).

Yet the generally highly favorable reviews of *Adventures in the Alaskan Skin Trade*, well formulated by Bob Halliday's calling it "the most moving and accessible novel yet from one of the most distinguished of American writers" (6), suggest the persistence of the critical praise from those who have attended to the demands of Hawkes's writing and acknowledged the significance of his body of work to American letters. Fellow writers, among them Donald Barthelme, Gail Godwin, William H. Gass, John Irving, Thomas McGuane, and Robert Coover, have been among Hawkes's most emphatic admirers: Susan Sontag in 1964 called Hawkes "one of the half dozen authors of the first rank in America today" (5); John Barth in 1978 called Hawkes's fictions "outrageous situations and unforgettable scenes refracted through a lens of rhetoric that transfigures them into something as strange and as beautiful as anything I know of in our contemporary literature" (*NYT* 7); Patrick McGrath in 1988 called Hawkes "the most consistently interesting writer, in terms of formal inventiveness, intelligence and the sheer grace of the prose, at work in the United States today" (11). And Hawkes is widely acclaimed, even revered, in Europe, particularly in France. French critics and scholars have produced illuminating examinations of Hawkes's work (including Pierre Gault's *John Hawkes: La parole coupée: anatomie d'une écriture romanesque*), just as there has been steady and acute attention from American academics. There are several American book-length studies of Hawkes, the most wide-ranging and finest being Patrick O'Donnell's *John Hawkes*, published in 1982.

It was the critic and novelist Albert Guerard who first "discovered" Hawkes when Hawkes submitted a manuscript for admission to Guerard's writing class at Harvard in the fall of 1947. Guerard announced on the first day of class that this manuscript "was certainly going to be published and published soon" (O'Donnell 111).[1] The manuscript was *Charivari* (1949). As a twenty-two-year-old anticipating marriage in the summer of 1947, Hawkes satirized himself, his fiancée, and their parents, and more broadly the institutions of marriage and parenthood in this short novel about fearful forty-year-old newlyweds anticipating the birth of a nonexistent baby while a house party of grotesques performs absurd rituals of mock celebration. *Charivari* weaves a dense web of dreamlike, dislocated images that portray the ordinary made monstrous as dream gives way to the anxiety of nightmare. The self-parody of this early work initiated Hawkes's sustained interest in parodying not only human fears and desires, but the genres in which literature has sought to formulate them; his novels thus foreground the textuality that parody necessarily implies. His subsequent work parodies the conventional novel and the authorial role, and, more particularly, the war novel, the picaresque novel, the detective novel, the Western, the pastoral, the *récit*, the erotic tale, and the adventure narrative. By shifting the emphasis from the progress, causality, and resolution encoded in traditional plot to the texture of vivid and recurring images, *Charivari* inaugurates the concern with language and form that dismantles generic expectations and produces fictions of startling stylistic innovation and psychological resonance. In a 1964 interview with John Enck, Hawkes says that he "began to write fiction on the assumption that the true enemies of the novel were plot, character, setting, and theme, and having once abandoned these familiar ways of thinking about fiction, totality of vision or structure was really all that remained" (149). Hawkes, of course, does not do away with the conventional elements of fiction; he simply subjugates their importance and reenvisions their expression.

Hawkes's early interview with Enck remains one of his most important and most frequently quoted, but he has been a generous granter of interviews throughout his writing career. These interviews, particularly those with Heide Ziegler (1982) and with Patrick O'Donnell (1983), provide intriguing insight into his novelistic concerns and intentions. According to Hawkes, "the poles of the authorial self, or of the self that creates something out of nothing, are precisely these: cruelty, or ultimate power, and innocence" (Ziegler 177). It is this combination of cruelty and innocence informing all of Hawkes's novels that constitutes their unremitting tension as self-indicting celebrations of the imagination. For Hawkes, the writing of fiction requires "absolute detachment" and the attempt "to create a world, not represent it. . . . [T]he creation ought to be more significant than the representation" (Enck 154). Such a statement seemingly privileges the authority of the writer and the autonomy of the work of art in contradistinction to more traditional mimesis. Hawkes's fiction is mimetic insofar as he wants "to imitate the interior journey," which for him means finding "all the fluid, germinal, pestilential 'stuff' of life itself as it exists in the unconscious" (O'Donnell 125). Applying Hawkes's aesthetic formulations to his work suggests that it is the bodying forth of inner reality that releases cruelty in his fictional worlds and that the language that creates this reality is innocent. Yet innocence so conceived remains abstract, if not obscure, and, indeed, Hawkes's many formulations of innocence within his corpus—and in his interviews—are themselves often elusive. It is the purpose of this study to explore the ways in which the broad ideas of innocence and power disperse into a multitude of thematic and textual concerns in Hawkes's novels. These concerns are both shifting and constant throughout his work; they include an engagement of violence, sexuality, transgression, transcendence, and mastery, all integral to what his works express about the function of the artistic imagination and the practice of writing.

The coexistence and even simultaneity of innocence and power in the authorial act suggest the obsession with paradox that shapes Hawkes's aesthetics. Paradox, what Hawkes calls "the existence of what does not exist" (Scholes 198), is, for him, the very condition of language: "For me, everything depends on language. The beauty of language is that in its very utterance it is nothing but intelligence being turned into sound, so that in one sense it doesn't exist at all. In another sense, it's the most powerful kind of actuality, so that the paradox of a man behaving through language means the behavior both exists and does not exist" (Kuehl 176). This concept of the paradox inherent in language can be supplemented by Roland Barthes's distinction between the work, with its status as object, and the text, which "is held in language, only exists in the movement of a discourse . . . *is experienced only in an activity of production*." Barthes claims that the text challenges limited and classificatory ideas about writing: "the Text tries to place itself very exactly *behind* the limit of the *doxa* (is not general opinion—constitutive of our democratic societies and powerfully aided by mass communications—defined by its limits, the energy with which it excludes, its *censorship?*). Taking the word literally, it may be said that the Text is always *paradoxical*" (*Image/ Music/ Text* 157–158; Barthes's emphasis). Labeling writing a criminal act (O'Donnell 126), Hawkes has repeatedly expressed his need as a writer to challenge the *doxa*. He says, for example: "I think of the act of writing as an act of rebellion because it is so single and it dares to presume to create the world. I enjoy a sense of violation, a criminal resistance to safety, to the security provided by laws or systems. I'm trying to find the essential human experiences when we are unhinged or alienated from familiar, secure life" (Kuehl 162). Hawkes's engagement of the process of creating meaning in language becomes the transgressive evocation and negotiation of the unpresentable, the activity of repeatedly rendering the ineffable visible. In their resolute paradoxes and radical fictionality his novels transgress the borders of the known and unknown, the ideal and material, absence and presence, creation and representation, innocence and power, inner life and outer world.

This transgression of borders suggests a postmodern inflection of the Romantic reconciliation of opposition through the inner life, or soul, of the artist joining with the Divine "I Am" in the act of creation. Indeed, Hawkes's aesthetics of paradox, along with his privileging of the visionary imagination over the recording consciousness, links him to a Coleridgean Romanticism. For Coleridge, "human Perception" is the "primary" imagination, "a repetition in the finite mind of the eternal act of creation in the infinite I AM." The artistic imagination is the "secondary imagination," which Coleridge considers "as an echo of the former, co-existing with the conscious will, yet still as identical with the primary in the *kind* of its agency, and differing only in *degree,* and in the *mode* of its operation. It dissolves, diffuses, dissipates, in order to re-create; or where this process is rendered impossible, yet still at all events it struggles to idealize and to unify" (202; Coleridge's emphasis). This paradoxical combination of de-creation and re-creation, passion and analysis, corresponds to Hawkes's insistence in his own art on the imagination combining with conscious will to bring order to the chaos of unconscious life and the welter of the world. The narrator of Hawkes's *Travesty* (1976) summarizes this aesthetics of paradox through his ruling principle that "design and debris" are integral with each other in the act of creation and in the form of the created artwork.

Hawthorne provides another formulation of the combination of opposites in the artistic imagination which further suggests a background for considering Hawkes in a particular version of American Romanticism. The ideal light for "pictur[ing] forth imaginary scenes," Hawthorne tells us, is the light which can be seen as a reflection of the imagination: "Moonlight, in a familiar room, falling so white upon the carpet, and showing all its figures so distinctly—making every object so minutely visible, yet so unlike a morning or noontide visibility" performs a sort of alchemy on the domestic scene. All of the domestic details "are so spiritualized by the unusual light, that they seem to lose their actual substance, and become things of intellect. Nothing is too small or too trifling to undergo this change, and acquire dignity thereby. . . . Thus, therefore, the floor of our familiar room has become a neutral territory, somewhere between the real world and fairyland, where the Actual and Imaginary may meet, and each imbue itself with the nature of the other" (*Scarlet Letter* 44–45). It is just this meeting of the actual and imaginary, the transformation and defamiliarization of our ordinary world, that has made the title of Hawkes's 1969 collection of stories and short novels, *Lunar Landscapes*, such a popular description of his fictions for critics. Hawkes creates fictive worlds of absorbing darkness and shimmering reflections which exert the pull of recognition, of sameness and strangeness; the imagination transmutes and reveals with the clarity of its vision.

While Hawthorne's formulation of creation masquerades in milder language than Coleridge's, his texts intriguingly embody the dark implications of Hawkes's aesthetic that links authoring both to innocence and to cruelty and power. Hawthorne writes in the preface to his late novel *The Marble Faun* that "Romance and poetry . . . need Ruin to make them grow" (3). He is comparing the complex layering of past and present and of moral ambiguity in Europe to the clean slate of America, "where there is no shadow, no antiquity, no mystery, no picturesque and gloomy wrong, nor anything but a common-place prosperity, in broad and simple daylight" (3). But of course Hawthorne set much of his best work in America, exploring shadows and gloom and mystery, as well as the marketplace, and making it clear that there is no such thing as simple daylight. Furthermore, in *The Marble Faun*, as elsewhere, Hawthorne introduces a fiction full of indeterminacy through dramatizing in his prefatory remarks his own act of authoring. The continued presence of the Puritan past for the American Hawthorne breeds an obsession not only with the interplay of divine or human law and passionate nature, but with the world seen as a tissue of signs and with the self-conscious use of language both to create and examine identity. Hawthorne grapples with the implications of his own role as author in the tales he tells—which frequently enough are about artist figures—and questions all authority, or interpretations of authority, including his own. The pull to artistic transcendence dissolves in doubt. And while the Actual and Imaginary meet in Hawthorne's labyrinthine language, each calls the other into question.

Hawkes's commitment to the paradoxes of the imagination corresponds to his own foregrounding of the authorial role. "I'm only interested in fiction," he says, "that in some way or other voices the very imagination which is conceiving it" (O'Donnell 121). (Interestingly, in light of Hawthorne's discussion of European versus American settings, Hawkes makes this remark in the context of explaining why many of his fictions are not set in the United States; the issue for him is not one of place but of distance, or authorial control.) In his examination of the innocence and power exerted by this conceiving imagination, he casts illumination on what Coleridge defines as the imagination's efforts "to idealize and to unify." Coleridge asserts that "[t]he artist may take his point of view where he pleases, provided that the desired effect be perceptibly produced,—that there be likeness in the difference, difference in the likeness, and a reconcilement of both in one" (256). Hawkes, too, dissolves opposition in his fiction as well as his aesthetic statements, yet he makes this dissolution uneasy, problematic. Both Coleridge and Hawkes make paradox the condition of art, but whereas Coleridge foregrounds harmony, Hawkes foregrounds tension and contradiction. The contradiction lies in the authorial desire to idealize and to unify, a desire for transcendence which Hawkes's texts examine in all its complexity, exposing the varieties of ruin and fragmentation that are its double.

The shift in emphasis that can be seen in comparing Hawkes to Coleridge is consistent with Patricia Waugh's view, in *Practising Postmodernism / Reading Modernism*, of postmodernism not as "a radical break with previous Western modes of knowledge and representation" but rather "a late phase in a tradition of specifically *aestheticist* modern thought inaugurated by philosophers such as Kant and embodied in Romantic *and* modernist art" (3; Waugh's emphasis). Waugh traces the movement from the Romantic expression of imagination to the postmodern: "The initial structure of value for Coleridge (as for Kant) is in the subjective mind. However, once mind ceases to exist within the *metaphysical* frame of Romantic thought, once correspondence [between mind and world] comes under strain, the subjectivist orientation of the theory develops into the modes of late Symbolist aestheticism and finally into a Nietzschean radical fictionality" (21; Waugh's emphasis). In the mode of radical fictionality, "the self exists in its ability to work with the fragments available to it and from them to project on to the world new fictions by which to live" (20). Or, to return to Hawkes's words, "everything depends on language," but "the paradox of a man behaving through language means that the behavior both exists and does not exist" (Kuehl 176).

Hawkes's self-reflexive employment of language as its own subject reveals his affinities with contemporaries such as John Barth, Robert Coover, William H. Gass, and Vladimir Nabokov, all novelists for whom Hawkes has expressed admiration. These writers flamboyantly engage self-making, world-making, fiction-making, and meaning-making in texts that frequently operate through paradox, parody, and irony. The forces at work in the often elaborate verbal orchestrations of these authors might be approached through Ihab Hassan's neologism "indetermanence," which he uses "to designate two central, constitutive tendencies in postmodernism: one of indeterminacy, the other of immanence. . . . By indeterminacy, or better still, *indeterminacies*, I mean a complex referent that these diverse concepts help to delineate: ambiguity, discontinuity, heterodoxy, pluralism, randomness, revolt, perversion, deformation" (Hassan's emphasis). By immanence, he means "the capacity of mind to generalize itself in symbols, intervene more and more into nature, act upon itself through its own abstractions and so become, increasingly, immediately, its own environment" (152–153).

History is not absent in these texts; it functions as a shaping force which compels refiguration. Barth famously points out in his "The Literature of Exhaustion" and "The Literature of Replenishment" that literary history impinges on every postmodern authorial act, driving the author to experimentation in order to, as Pound directed, "make it new." The awareness of literary history exists within a larger awareness of history, particularly as it comes into being through language. For Hawkes and other writers of his generation, history is of course history after the Second World War. Hawkes himself worked as an ambulance driver for the American Field Service in Italy and Germany in 1944 and 1945, and the death and destruction he witnessed proved formative for his fictive concerns. Albert Guerard's description of Hawkes as an "antirealist" who offers "a recomposed and terrifying world, essentially unexplained" (57) might also describe the novels of Pynchon or Burroughs, whose visions of insidious technology Hawkes doesn't engage, but whose visions of horror and confrontation with meaninglessness and the search for meaning he does. The concern with linguistically constructed experience in the face of fragmentation and alienation is accompanied by, in all of these authors, a self-conscious distinctiveness of style. Yet whereas the foregrounding of style in the linguistic worlds of Barth, Coover, Gass, and Nabokov, or of Donald Barthelme and William Gaddis, often relies on comic and cerebral wordplay, the palpable textuality in Hawkes's work, while also comic, derives from both the sensuality and the cold precision of his prose.

This sensuality and precision, the words and rhythms that embody intimately detailed scenes crafted through authorial distance, the emphasis on "totality of vision or structure," grant Hawkes's novels, as many commentators have noted, the impact of poetry. Hawkes's admiration for Djuna Barnes's *Nightwood* is telling, since Barnes's novel advances through language more than through plot as characters construct shifting borders of identity through a rhetoric of definition and a visceral poetry of experience. The form and content of Hawkes's own night worlds (his experimental versions of Hawthorne's Ruin) extend from his commitment "to nightmare, violence, meaningful distortion, to the whole panorama of dislocation and desolation in human experience" (Enck 142). For these reasons he associates his fiction with "the comic brutalities of the early Spanish picaresque writers" (Enck 141), and traces this sensibility through "Thomas Nashe . . . Lautréamont, Céline, Nathanael West, Flannery O'Connor, [and] James Purdy," all of whom share "a quality of coldness, detachment, ruthless determination to face up to the enormities of ugliness and potential failure within ourselves and in the world around us, and to bring to this exposure a savage or saving comic spirit and the saving beauties of language" (Enck 143–144). For these same reasons he relates himself to Conrad, saying, "My work is an effort to expose the worst in us all, to cause us to face up to the enormities of our terrible potential for betrayal, disgrace, and criminal behavior. . . . For Conrad, the best of men are never safe from their innermost impulses. . . . I'm interested in the truest kind of fictive sympathy . . . sympathy for the saved and the damned alike" (LeClair 27). Hawkes's texts share with Conrad's the intriguing demonstration that the narrator or author figure is implicated in the betrayal, disgrace, and criminal behavior that he narrates. This implication again recalls Hawthorne; and it also recalls Poe, the resolute aesthete whose narrators unfold tales of horror in which they are also actors, using sinuous prose that peculiarly combines passion and ratiocination.

Poe further suggests an interesting starting point for considering the gothic quality of Hawkes's fiction. In his preface to *The Lime Twig*, Leslie Fiedler memorably proclaims Hawkes a "Gothic novelist," meaning "one who makes terror rather than love the center of his work, knowing all the while, of course, that there can be no terror without the hope for love and love's defeat" (ix). This essentially Romantic interdependence of opposing conceptions relates to a similar linkage of opposites in the merging of inner and outer worlds that Bradford Morrow and Patrick McGrath claim as the core of the gothic in their anthology of contemporary writers whom they group together under the title *The New Gothic* (1991). Morrow and McGrath credit Poe with initiating the shift from a gothic literature dependent upon "props and settings" to a literature of psychological and aesthetic exploration which, while still employing some of the traditional props and settings, transforms them to make "climate, landscape, architecture, genealogy, and psychology seem to bleed into one another until it is impossible to distinguish a figure from its metaphors" (xi). The "outer" world in the "new gothic" may have a different aspect from Poe's, but it equally reveals the potential for horror in the contemporary landscape as a reflection of the "hell . . . located within the vaults and chambers of our own minds" (xiv). Hawkes's texts demonstrate an insistence that "heaven" is also located in our own minds, and that the linguistic and artistic rendering of life shares equally in damnation and redemption, in lyrical light and overwhelming darkness. The gothic label still remains useful as another way of articulating the psychic extremities and their imagistic and narrative embodiments in Hawkes's fiction; and Morrow and McGrath's grouping of Hawkes with other contemporary writers (many of them younger than Hawkes) producing gothic fictions—Morrow, McGrath, Angela Carter, Kathy Acker, and Jeanette Winterson among them—suggests an intersection of aesthetics among an extremely diverse group of contemporary writers.

Indeed, Morrow and McGrath's writing that "[s]everal factors conspired in [the gothic tradition's] birth, among them the aesthetic theory that the Horrid and the Terrible were legitimate sources of the Sublime" (xii) links the gothic to the aesthetics of the sublime that Jean-François Lyotard views as the aesthetics of the postmodern. In "The Sublime and the Avant-Garde," Lyotard cites Edmund Burke's elaboration of the sublime as occuring through terror. Terrors, Lyotard explains, "are linked to privation"; for instance, "privation of language, terror of silence; privation of objects, terror of emptiness." Or, in Fiedler's terms, "the hope for love . . . love's defeat." "What is terrifying," says Lyotard, "is that the *It happens that* does not happen, that it stops happening" (Lyotard's emphasis). The substance of art, its status as occurrence, suspends "the terror-causing threat," allows "terror to mingle with pleasure and with it to produce the feeling of the sublime" (251). Lyotard emphasizes the terror of absence when, in "Answering the Question: What Is Postmodernism?," he defines the postmodern as that which "puts forward the unpresentable in presentation itself" (81). This is Lyotard's representation of the Kantian idea of the sublime which, in Lyotard's words, is "an intrinsic combination of pleasure and pain; the pleasure that reason should exceed all presentation, the pain that the imagination or sensibility should not be equal to the concept" (81). Patricia Waugh elucidates this Kantian conception and Lyotard's use of it as "articulat[ing] that familiar Romantic dialectic of impulse toward a plenitudinous transcendence and recognition, explicit or implicit, of ironic finitude which propels the postmodern modes of self-reflexive fictionality and parody. The sublime transcends every faculty of sense, taunts us with a glimpse of inaccessible plenitude and leaves us with the impossible self-conscious wrestle with words in the hopeless struggle to embody it" (27). Language, in other words, becomes the foregrounded medium for the author self-consciously to engage the play of presence and absence as representation struggles to accommodate transcendence.

It is precisely the simultaneous presence and absence that Hawkes attributes to language that makes sexuality a privileged subject in his writing; and it is this conjunction that is central to his engagement of authorial innocence and power, his textual self-questioning of authority and representation, his exploration of the desire for transcendence inherent in idealizing and unifying. When Hawkes defines virginity as "the negative existence of sexual experience" (Emmett and Vine 169), he also formulates the paradox involved in turning sexuality into language. The encounter of sexuality and the desire, predicated on absence, for its representation (whether this be a matter of production or consumption) becomes the authorial effort of giving shape to the imagination, of conferring form on disparate desires and of investing form with desire's inspiration. Hawkes sees "every man as artist" in the realm of sexuality "simply in the sense that sexuality necessitates a free exercising of the imagination. In the sexual union every person knows the sublimity of art. For me the imagination is always and inevitably erotic; eroticism or sexual experience is inevitably and always artistic" (Ziegler 187). The possibility of sexuality exists as both a metaphor and a manifestation of the generative and regenerative powers of the artistic imagination; but more than a traditional metaphor for creativity, sexuality in Hawkes's texts is that which inspires and exceeds representation, and that which is itself constituted in creation. Furthermore, the imagination in Hawkes's novels always functions as a polemic against a perceived or ignored reality figured as other, so that the inscription of the sexual imagination allows for the examination of what is at stake, and for whom, in the exercise of authorial innocence and power.

Most significant among that which constitutes the "Other" in Hawkes's novels is "Woman." The concern with the role of Woman in the male artistic imagination becomes more pronounced and explicit over the course of Hawkes's writing career. Yet a scene from Hawkes's early novel *The Beetle Leg* (1951) intriguingly phrases the sexual dynamics of a male author figure operating on a captive and unknown woman; the author figure, a traveling medicine man, prepares to pull the tooth of a silent Indian woman who, watching him warily, "generated like an octopus the ink of desire" (148). This vision of the frightening and seductive other-ness of women and of desire crossing into the potentiality of form is com-mon to Hawkes's male characters, author figures, and narrators who themselves draw from the "ink of desire" to make their vision actual. Desire given form in language becomes the sensuous surface that reveals and conceals, simultaneously creating and critiquing the sexual and gen-der relations that inform artistic production.

Vision itself, in its ocular and imaginative sense, is a central metaphor, subject, and operative technique for this self-described visionary writer's fictional worlds. Sharply vivid images accumulate in Hawkes's texts, echo-ing and magnifying each other, weaving and unraveling verbal patterns. This engages the reader in the process of creating meaning, of making sense out of the narrative energies dispersed among the objects and obsessions of worlds in dissolution and formation. And it is the layers of authorial control producing and structuring the images that grants Hawkes's texts a polyvalence able to embody his paradoxical aesthetics.

The early novels experiment with first- and third-person narration, as-serting author figures as characters and as idiosyncratic narrators who provide the informing consciousnesses of the fictive worlds. Beginning with *Second Skin* (nominated for a National Book Award, 1964), Hawkes extends his experimentation with the possibilities of first-person narra-tion by writing novels that, with the exception of *The Passion Artist* (1979), have first-person narrators who enact Hawkes's desire for "whatever one creates out of words to be so clearly something made, so clearly an arti-fice, artificial" (O'Donnell 111); these narrators increasingly explore the role of language, art, and the imagination in creating human identity. By developing the narrators' psychology, the late novels intensify Hawkes's exploration of the imagination's access to innocence and power. In the early novels, psychology is more externalized; the boundaries between the consciousness that would shape or transcend reality and that deso-late reality itself collapse.

The often dreamlike quality and dislocated images of the early novels have led many to call them "surrealistic," and although Hawkes resists this label,[2] preferring Guerard's term "antirealistic," he does describe the work as an expression of "unconscious fears and desires" (O'Don-nell 119). At the same time, Hawkes is quite insistent about the primacy of his detached control of the materials of his fiction, materials which, in the early novels, are particularly dark, violent, and destructive and which, on the whole, lack the alleviation of pure beauty summoned by Hawkes's later first-person narrators. In the early novels, cruelty and power are abundantly evident in images and events as well as in the author figures, while the innocence that is also part of the authorial imagination is besieged. Innocence in the early novels is largely the sort of "sick innocence" (269) later manifested by the puritanical Hugh of *The Blood Oranges*. The innocence is that of characters who will not acknowledge their fears and desires and wind up living them in a world dominated by sterility or impotence, violence, and death. Hawkes says of *Charivari* that "[t]he butt of its satire is innocence, and the same holds true for *The Lime Twig*" (Ziegler 173); he is referring specifically to the sexual innocence of the couples who are the main characters of each novel. But in these novels sexual innocence is not too different from sexual death, which Hawkes sees as "the only conceivable analogue to death itself" (O'Donnell 125). It is not until *Second Skin* that Hawkes, according to his own lights, "for the first time . . . allowed innocence to win out" (Ziegler 173). The six novels and novellas before this, then, constitute the defeat of innocence in horrific worlds, but worlds composed of language so dense, visual, and uncompromising that the texts achieve Hawkes's goal of creating "a thing of beauty, as well as of knowledge and moral meaning" (LeClair 27).

While idiosyncratic first-person narrators dominate *The Cannibal* (1949) and *The Owl* (1954), it is not until *Second Skin* that Hawkes develops a psychologically complex narrator who, furthermore, reflects upon his narrative efforts. Authorial innocence and power thus acquire more deliberate thematic resonance, and the dynamics of authorial identification with and distance from the narration gain dimension and ambiguity. The lyrical *Second Skin* also constitutes a break from the overwhelmingly nightmarish worlds of the six novels before it, and thus on one level seems a triumph of innocence, by virtue of the narrator's desire to redeem himself and his world through "the saving beauties of language" (Enck 144). Yet, even as they assert the innocence of their authorial vision, the narrator of *Second Skin* and the first-person male narrators after him create self-questioning texts that subject innocence to a thorough critique. Hawkes says that each narrator of *Second Skin, The Blood Oranges, Death, Sleep and the Traveler* (1974), and *Travesty* (1976) "exalts and punishes what cannot be tolerated in a banal pragmatic world, namely his innocence" (Ziegler 177). In giving narrative shape to their lives these first-person narrators persistently impose order on experience; yet this very imposition of order only serves to expose more fully the threatening chaos of memory, desire, fantasy, and experience which the narrators attempt to control. The reader must deconstruct the elaborate verbal structures the narrators create to find another level of vision beneath them, a vision of a reality that will always resist shaping and of the compulsion to shape, the compulsion for form and transcendence, as itself violent and threatening.

Hawkes calls the subject of his work from *Second Skin* on "the imagination itself"; with *The Blood Oranges* (winner of the 1973 *Prix du meilleur livre étranger*), the novel that follows *Second Skin*, the subject of Hawkes's work becomes "the relationship between sex and the imagination" (Ziegler 177–178). The repression of sexual life that contributes in large part to the pain and deathly impulses in the earlier novels now achieves expression and explicit examination. The elaboration, in *The Blood Oranges, Death, Sleep and the Traveler,* and *Travesty,* of the desires of male narrators who create and control their fictional worlds, including the women they desire within them, necessarily conflates sexuality and aesthetics and implies a critique of the ways in which gender relations inflect both. In *The Passion Artist,* Hawkes returns to a third-person perspective, making the "artist" of the title a man whose innocence is as deadly as any in the early novels, but who now achieves transformation by crossing over to the world of women; through the perspective of these women he achieves artistry. This introduction of a female perspective points the way to female narration in *Virginie: Her Two Lives* (1982) and *Adventures in the Alaskan Skin Trade.* The female narrators of these novels each view and reenvision the activity of male author figures; when Hawkes returns to male narration in *Whistlejacket* (1988), authorial innocence and power acquire renewed analysis, particularly in terms of the reification and fetishization involved in converting life to image and narration. With *Sweet William: A Memoir of Old Horse* (1993), Hawkes inverts the dynamics of narration by impossibly investing the fetishized object with voice.

The following chapters discuss Hawkes's novels chronologically in an effort to explore the development of the thematic and textual engagement of innocence and power over the course of his career. The consistency of Hawkes's fictive concerns is matched by the variousness of their expression; his experimentation with narrative voice and perspective from novel to novel grants resonant complexity to his exploration of the authorial imagination's use of language and assertion of vision, and thus the permutations of narrative perspective integrally inform the discussion of each novel. With each novel, Hawkes employs more and more intertextual play, so that by considering the novels in succession I hope to suggest the multivocal dimensionality he gives to the variety of issues— including those of authority, representation, gender, and eroticism— penetrated by the concepts of innocence and power. The richness of these concepts and their various incarnations reflects the richness of

Hawkes's poetic prose, the marvelousness of his fictions, where dream and desire become the substance of words and words the sight of the imagination. By studying the paradoxical and provisional qualities of innocence and power as thematic and textual concerns in Hawkes's novels, I hope to illuminate how his championing of the artistic imagination does not rest in valorization but rather works to examine the processes of art and the ends it serves.

# Chapter 1
# Textual Image, Authorial Vision, Narrative Voice in *The Cannibal, The Beetle Leg, The Goose on the Grave,* and *The Owl*

> [E]very loving act of definition reverses the retreat of attention to the word and returns it to the world. The landscape which emerges from the language which has made it is quite as lovely, vast and curious, as rich and prepossessing, as that of the deity who broke the silence of the void with speech so perfect the word "tree" grew leaves and the syllables of "sealion" swallowed fish.
>
> —William Gass, *On Being Blue*

In a 1976 interview Hawkes affirmed his allegiance to the "visionary novel" and went on to define his conception of visionary fiction as "a unique world, separate and different from the world we live in despite surface semblances. Visionary fiction is a fish bowl in which the clarity of the bowl is unique and you see the stream of fish, the gleam of fins—it is a fish bowl different from any other" (Santore and Pocalyko 174). The focus of this language on sensuous surfaces recalls Susan Sontag's formulation of the erotics of literature. Hawkes's identification with the visionary and his metaphoric definition of it also suggest his postmodern connection to the Romantic aesthetic; in Patricia Waugh's words, the postmodern artist "can no longer . . . legislate for humankind in the manner of the Romantic poet-seer or poet-prophet. What is preserved in Postmodernism, however, is a fundamental sense of the aesthetic (derived from Kantian thought) as a form of knowing and presenting which is sensuously embodied, an alternative to conceptual knowledge because, ontogenetically, it realises worlds and experiences for which we had no concepts until they came into existence" (15). Hawkes himself relates his fiction to Romantic aesthetics in his definition of the romantic impulse that is simply another phrasing of his definition of authoring; romance, he says, "means to me nothing more than the desire to create something out of nothing and all the attendant images and emotions that the impulse carries with it" (Ziegler 175). Hawkes goes on to link the romantic to the surrealistic:

I should think that the romantic impulse is in itself a duality, or holds in balance the power of unlimited possibility and the nothingness that is the context of all creativity. The phrase "romantic impulse" makes me think of André Breton's locomotive in the forest. The vine-covered rusted engine that's forever inert, forever immobile, dead, somehow conveys more of "locomotive" than the enormous slick black machine roaring down the track. So that the destructive image posits the ideal, while the romantic impulse is always in a sense self-threatening. (Ziegler 178)

The ability simultaneously to evoke the ideal and its destruction makes of the image a privileged locus for Hawkes's poetics of paradox. "My fiction," he says, "is almost totally visual and the language depends almost totally on image" (Scholes 201). Images, in fact, engender fictions: "I write out of a series of pictures that literally and actually do come to mind, but I've never seen them before. It is perfectly true that I don't know what they mean, but I feel and know that they have meaning. *The Cannibal* is probably the clearest example of this kind of absolute coherence of vision of anything I have written, when all the photographs do add together or come right out of the same black pit" (Graham 452). The use of images as a structuring principle of *The Cannibal* and Hawkes's other early work makes the issue of artistic vision as central to these novels as it is to the later novels when visually obsessed, self-consciously artistic narrators control the fictional worlds. The extraordinary images that make up Hawkes's early work assert the shaping power not only of images themselves but also of the narrative perspective that determines them. It is Hawkes's experimentation with point-of-view in his early novels that creates a textual self-questioning of any transcendent visionary aesthetics.

This chapter will look at the way Hawkes's earliest novels reflect the authorial "absolute need to create from the imagination a totally new and necessary fictional landscape or visionary world" (Enck 141). This authorial need has its locus in the author of the novels but also in artist or author figures, however problematically or idiosyncratically defined. In *The Cannibal* (1949), the effort of the creation of a visionary world reveals itself as complicit with the violence and the destructive power that have engendered the reality it seeks to transcend. *The Beetle Leg* (1951) stages a more ambiguous conflict between a desolate reality and the imagination's attempt at control and transformation. The more indeterminate status of conflict in this novel corresponds to a multivocal narrative that unfolds largely in the third-person but also contains two significant first-person voices. *The Cannibal,* in contrast, has the feel of a third-person omniscient point-of-view narration but asserts a single first-person narrator throughout. *The Goose on the Grave* (1954), narrated from a more traditional third-person perspective, and *The Owl* (1954),[1] narrated from the first-person perspective of a death-driven despot, further illuminate the dynamics of authorial vision and narrative point-of-view in their accumulation of the images of richly imagined and densely bereft worlds.

**I**

Perhaps the most unusual aspect of *The Cannibal* is its narration. Zizendorf, a neo-Nazi who calls himself "the leader," informs the reader in a preface, "I have told our story." The reader then embarks on what for Zizendorf is a fait accompli. "Our story" is the story of death and destruction overcome, of "resistance" to the invader become "a show of strength" (168), of "the birth of the Nation" out of its rubble (195), of the creation of "a garden spot." "Our story" is the story of death and destruction entrenched, of a plot against a motorcycle rider, of a people devouring life to the point of cannibalism, of the endless repetition of senseless dreams of glory that are deeds of violence and the weight of history. These stories are the same story, but Zizendorf, who knows all minds yet is single-minded, seems to believe his story of triumph stands clear of the absurd and horrible events he relates.

The story falls into three parts. Part 2 takes place in Germany in 1914 and conveys the world of this Germany largely through the lens of Stella Snow and her marriage with Ernst; Part 1 and Part 3 take place in Germany in 1945 and concern the broken world and dehumanized people of *Spitzen-on-the-Dein,* which Zizendorf intends to return to greatness. Zizendorf, who is "the Editor" as well as "the Leader," plots to kill Leevey, the American overseer of one-third of Germany, and then to publish a proclamation of the nation's liberation from "Western slavery" (177). In telling of the successful execution of his plot he functions as an omniscient narrator, anatomizing the psychic landscape of the town, relating the thoughts and actions of other inhabitants of *Spitzen-on-the-Dein* in both time periods, and thus creating an authority that is all-encompassing but also tenuous and hallucinated. Hawkes had originally written the novel in the third person, but says that as a "final gesture" he went "through the manuscript changing the third-person pronoun to the first-person" (Ziegler 172). The effect of this improbable narration is interesting for Hawkes "not because *The Cannibal* became a genuine example of first-person fiction, but because its 'narrator' naturally possessed an unusual omniscience, while the authorial consciousness was given specific definition, definition in terms of humor and 'black' intelligence" (Enck 150). Hawkes's deliberate identification with Zizendorf thus paradoxically creates a distance between author and narrator, allowing the narration to reveal the disparity between the way Zizendorf views his world and his position in it and the way the reader views these same things, but also allowing Hawkes to reveal the authoring process as itself paradoxical, as enacting and critiquing its own power.

*The Cannibal* opens with the inmates of "the institution," an insane asylum, walking out into *Spitzen-on-the-Dein*, but most of these inmates, including Balamir, one of the novel's recurring characters, "did not realize that they were beyond the institution's high walls" (5). Insanity is no longer contained, but is instead unleashed in a depraved collectivity, displaying itself most shockingly in that aristocratic character, the Duke, who chases a boy through the darkness of the town to kill and cannibalize him. This particular gruesome goal is not realized until the end of the novel, but images of cannibalism are pervasive. For instance, when Jutta, the mother of the boy, is herself a child, she has a "disease that calmly ate at the calcium in her bones" (109) while she lives in a nunnery with nuns "feeding on their wards" (112). Balamir thinks of the romantic accoutrements of war, of spats and silver braid and a pigtailed donkey, and "the bones of men ground into food" (11–12). The idea of cannibalism is only the most extreme imaging of this dehumanized, self-consuming, war-torn, death-ridden world that "gorged itself on straggling beggars" (7), where the bodies of men clog the town's canal, already clotted with sewage, and where the air is choked with the odor of burnt human waste. And these extreme images of destroyed life echo the psychic destruction of people who have years since "stopped talking, except for fragments of a sentence" (14) and who, if they have memories at all, remember without remorse or repulsion and without insight. In an essay on *The Cannibal*, André Le Vot writes that in the "dismantled universe" of this novel,

paralysis affects every means of communication, expression or transmission: roads are broken up, rails twisted, electric wires torn out, pipes broken. The presses are down. Shops are closed or looted. . . . Even the tables, elementary scenes of conviviality, present the image of an overturned order; "There was nowhere to eat . . . and tables were piled on one another, chipped with bullet-holes" (11). The rhythms of community life are themselves broken. Watches and clocks have disappeared and all that remains is a feeling of undifferentiated duration. (Le Vot 185)

Images of stagnant ruin and defunct civilization accumulate, made more horrible by the repeated perversions that exist among them.

The cumulative power of images such as these illustrates the validity of Hawkes's statement that "[r]elated or corresponding event, recurring image and recurring action, these constitute the essential substance or meaningful density of my writing" (Enck 149). Hawkes privileges "totality of vision or structure" over traditional fictive elements (Enck 149), but the decision to structure the text with vivid and resonating images is not merely a formal one. Reliance on images to tell "our story" reflects the way the people of this novel make themselves into the images their culture possesses, whether they have the illusion of individually projecting these images or whether they partake in the illusions projected by their leader. As "narrator," Zizendorf's vision structures the novel; as architect of the resurrected nation Zizendorf's vision structures the people—or at least the people as he sees them. "From the ruins of Athens rise the spires of Berlin" (177), he ends his proclamation to the people, though he has seen neither Berlin nor, so far as we know, Athens. And there is no need for him to see them; what is important is the image they conjure, the idea of Teutonic greatness they represent.

The prevailing images that are the repository of Zizendorf's neo-Nazi ideology are echoes of the images that inspire the ineffectual Ernst, a representative of the German spirit located in 1914. In his adherence to romantic and heroic codes that urge transcendence, Ernst becomes another victim of a metaphoric cannibalism as his body is lacerated, scarred, and mutilated in the many duels he fights in search of honor. He dreams of how "[he] would sit on a worshipped pile of granite, a small duelist in the hall of kings" (44). His courtship of Stella, the strong, blonde embodiment of Germany's spirit, begins by his chasing after her carriage down *die Heldenstrasse,* the boulevard lined with many worshipped piles of granite, statues of war heroes who each "gave him a word to harden his heart: *love, Stella, Ernst, lust, tonight, leader, land*" (54–55; Hawkes's emphasis). The heroic images presented by the statues spawn the insidious abstractions that embody Ernst's world and that structure Zizendorf's narrative as the titles for seven of his chapters, thus establishing the continuity of a shared hallucination.

Ernst comes to abandon the world where war heroes reign, however, in favor of an alternate imaginary order when he becomes obsessed with collecting carved wooden crucifixes. Yet this fetish does not signal any spiritual enlightenment; instead, it illustrates Ernst's grasping at an image of asceticism that implies reward in another upper, superior world (85) that is simply an alternate Valhalla, and which, furthermore, establishes this world's salvation on a sacrificial body. As he dies, with a crucifix on the pillow next to him, Stella sees a "wooden man and fleshless God" (117), as if Ernst has finally indeed been made in his God's image. Ernst's particular fixation at the end of his life only seems to be an aberration in the world of *The Cannibal*, but the fact that his fixation is very particularly with an image emphasizes the power attached to images, and thus the power attached to those who would exploit them. As the heroic leader of the reborn nation, Zizendorf will be a supreme exploiter of images; he will, for example, reinstate a sublimated image of the war machine, a statue of a horse, in the middle of the town. He will re-erect the horse, whose legs and head have been lopped off, "so that visitors drawing near the city could say, 'Look, there's the statue of Germany, given by the new Leader to his country' " (183).

The seduction of the image has its complement in the compulsions of vision, in both its ocular and imaginative sense. As Editor, Zizendorf's vision is re-vision; he must rework the materials of a defunct civilization into the stuff of legend and triumph in history. In their apathy and abjectness the people of *Spitzen-on-the-Dein* seem to have lost sight of what they formerly assumed as their rightful splendor. The Mayor, who exemplifies this state, "was too blind to tend the chronicles of history, and went hungry like the rest with memory obliterated from his doorstep" (8). He is a man who "had witnessed executions with his eyes closed" (9), including the execution of Pastor Miller. The Census Taker, however, "had been forced to watch, deadly drunk, eyes red, while the Mayor, wretched and awkward, looked the other way and dropped the handkerchief that ended Pastor Miller's life at the stake" (22). The Census Taker is haunted by the image of that dropping handkerchief, even as he, by choice and night after night, is impotent witness to the "vague ordeal" of Zizendorf and Jutta's sexual encounters, their "abnormal passions" (21). Zizendorf enjoys having the Census Taker watch him in his barely—just barely—potent performance. Yet though he repeats the image of the falling handkerchief that troubles two numbed men, he doesn't mention the sight of what must have been horrific for his friend to watch, the sight of Zizendorf himself firing the gun that kills the Pastor. But of course no guilt can attach to the Leader, the savior of the people. Instead, the Leader will eventually set the Mayor's house on fire, glad when the Mayor dies "without recompense or absolution" (190). Zizendorf is the man who will tend the chronicles of history himself.

This tending, in its practical enactment, involves watching through the night for the American overseer in order to carry out his murder (thus becoming the new Overseer), and at the same time making sure he and his henchmen are not observed, by the American or by their townsmen. While Zizendorf desires to literalize his triumphant vision, the text of his narrative stages a play of surveillance and voyeurism; there are other watchers, besides Zizendorf, in the night. Jutta's young daughter, Selvaggia, watches at her apartment window, looking for her brother who is being chased by the Duke. The one-eyed schoolteacher, Herr Stintz, is watching too, and when Leevey's motorcycle approaches, Stintz, along with Selvaggia, sees the light (146). In a predatory lunge that parallels the Duke's after Selvaggia's brother, the pedophilic Stintz sweeps up Selvaggia and bundles her off, inexplicably saying, "we must hurry. It's up to you and me" (146). When she protests, "The moon will see," thereby connecting the moon to the motorcycle light which she has already, inarticulately, associated with the Cannibal, Stintz tells her, "there isn't any moon at all" (146). The man and the girl witness Leevey's murder and the disposal of his body, and as soon as Zizendorf realizes it is Stintz who saw the murder, he goes to kill him, too, for he knows Stintz will inform. Stintz, who enjoys "watching the scenes of other people's accidents and deeds" (172), tells Zizendorf that the moon "sees everything. . . . He watches the lonely travelers, he hangs heavy over demons, terrible and powerful. The just man" (172–173). "Someone always *knows*," he continues, "you really can't get away with anything" (173; Hawkes's emphasis). Herr Stintz is quite right that someone always knows, but wrong in thinking that this time it is he. For Zizendorf sees all and knows all in this world, and will extinguish any challenge to his authority. His sight and knowledge is curiously like that attributed to the moon, impossible and godlike—and a fiction. But Zizendorf's fictive quality is experienced on the level of authorial "'black' intelligence" (Enck 150), not within the fictive world itself. His narration is particularly interesting in relation to Stintz's spying, because he informs us of Stintz's movements and thoughts while he, in the time period of the action, does not know it is Stintz who is the spy. His ability, then, to recount the thoughts and actions of the characters is specifically writerly, part of the process of telling "our story." Within the story itself it functions with somewhat sinister implications as a sort of surveillance without agency, insuring that no thought or action in this community that must become the Nation goes unobserved.

Zizendorf ironically sees all and yet sees nothing, for the birth of the Nation he brings about is no birth at all. When he murders Leevey as the beginning of this "birth," he steals Leevey's watch, as well as his motorcycle, thus acquiring, as André Le Vot points out, "authority over space and time" (189). But the resumption of time as a forward movement in history is belied by the unethical and deadly methods used in the attempt to instigate this movement and the absurd and ideologically deadly proclamation that crowns them. There is no redemption for this horrific world, only unending repetition. The narrative ends with Zizendorf telling Selvaggia, "Draw those blinds and go back to sleep" (195), which is telling the young watcher of the story's events to become blind to them and thus relinquish judgment and opposition. Jutta and Zizendorf "shut [their] eyes against the sun" (195), a gesture that for Zizendorf implies that the symbolic acquisition of the watch signifies his own blindness to the significance of his story in history, that all he has watched or witnessed has taught him nothing about the cannibalism wrought by nationalistic or romantic ideals of transcendence or about the implications of the power he has designated as his.

Writing about the significance of the heroic images of the *Heldenstrasse*, D. P. Reutlinger says, "if the course of German romanticism in the nineteenth century began by celebrating the unique identities of individual men, this *Heldenstrasse* led on through the celebration of the *Volksgeist*, and ended by celebrating only the geographical and historical identity of the State" (33–34). And indeed, Zizendorf proclaims, "The land is important, not the *Geist*" (141). He prefaces his story by glorifying the resurgence of an isolated town, whose progress in civic organization he is "very nearly satisfied with" and of which he can say "all of our memories are there." As Editor and as storyteller he is the keeper of their memories; as the man who claims "the tenant was the law" (130) he knows that, whatever romantic ideology might be spouted, one must be ruthless to gain control. Those who live on the land will be the land; he who sees all and enforces his vision will inhabit history.

The land is important as a symbol, an image in which the people, and Zizendorf, see themselves. Just as he sees stealing the watch as a symbol of appropriating history, Zizendorf sees a murder and a proclamation as the birth of the Nation. Zizendorf's conviction of his world's metamorphosis under his leadership has visual and metaphoric echoes in a striking image of potential metamorphosis embedded in the 1914 section of the story. The Merchant, a man who has had vague and violent dealings with Ernst, "died on his first day at the front and was wedged, standing upright, between two beams, his face knocked backwards, angry, disturbed. In his open mouth there rested a large cocoon, protruding and white, which moved sometimes as if it were alive" (94). The cocoon may be a symbol of dormancy that will indeed spring to life, but what is certain is that the Merchant, standing with dropped trousers "filled with rust and tufts of hair," is quite dead and there will be no metamorphosis for him or for all the others who have died and whose corpses are now part of the debris littering the town, just as there is no metamorphosis for a world that continues bent on war. The cocoon in the dead man's mouth is a vivid, grotesque, and also multivalent image that can be read as life caught in the jaws of death, but also as life parasitically feeding off destruction, or as life triumphing in the midst of death. Finally, however, all that comes to life is the image.

Zizendorf is the purveyor of images but at the same time is himself both an image and subject to the image's seduction. In bed with Jutta, he "was a counterfeit, a transformer for several delicate whims and ex- asperating needs, was an image for the moment made from past respect- able devices" (22). Such is the state of Jutta and Zizendorf's relationship of desperation and convenience in which they use each other for me- chanical and emotionless release. Yet Zizendorf's role in Jutta's bed is quite similar to the one he plays as Leader, for if Madame Snow's joyous reaction to his proclamation, and Fegelein's and Stumpfegle's willing- ness to be Zizendorf's henchmen, and Jutta's apathetic acquiescence in Zizendorf's mission are any indication, the image of the triumphant Zizendorf is a reflection of the people's need for the return of their past, their unwillingness or inability to examine the relation of their past to their present, and their desire to have a Leader. Zizendorf can be their Leader because of his ability to partake in—and assert—an illusion. Again, the dynamics of the "personal" is the paradigm of the political: describing his "lovemaking" with Jutta, Zizendorf says, "I rolled up on my side as if awake, and I saw in her body something that was not there, something that graced, I thought, the nibbling lips of goats" (22). So too will he see a garden spot in a place where people eat children. His pa- thetic, mechanical relationship with Jutta further partakes of collective fantasy when he reveals its motivation as his "need to recreate, with amazing frequency, some sort of pastime similar to my comrades' hab- its, a cyclic affection that had finally, in Paris, become fatal to their health" (23).

Zizendorf's desire to transcend his desolate reality through shared experience occurs in the Census Taker, too, a man who seeks self- transcendence in "the appearance of love in the lives of his friends. . . . He lived the smallest chip of illusion, bearing along his drunk path a recognition of the way, a small dropsy formula that might in the end lead him out, beyond the overt sorrow of his partially thrilled, sitting figure" (23). In trying to transcend his self and his sorrow, the voyeuristic, mas- turbating Census Taker "brushed with one hand at the image of Miller" (24), trying to exorcise the responsibility for the Pastor's death and all the suffered indignities it represents. Jutta similarly tries to get beyond the self, but she does this by inhabiting an image rather than observing one. She turns to Zizendorf, "moving in an artifice, a play she well knew, pursed her lips into an act, an act to rid herself" (21); she relies on an established role to rid herself of her desolate existence, but also to rid herself of the burden of her individuality. The image of love is a spectral panacea in this world which Hawkes describes as sexually dead.

Repetitive, escapist, and parodic sex acts exist as one image of the de- lusive constructions the characters in this shattered world cling to in the attempt to establish their own viability. The confluence of Zizendorf's sexual behavior, such as it is, and his historical aspirations has its parallel in the personal delusions of the insane Balamir, who believes he is the Kaiser's son ("How he sought to be that image . . . how he would be Honor in the land he had become" [18]) and therefore will redeem the public. Balamir and Zizendorf are mirror images of each other, and their fantasies become increasingly convergent. In his hallucination Balamir knows it is "his job and his alone to rebuild the town and make his subjects happy" (185); in Zizendorf's narration this is precisely what he himself has done.

The collapse of the psychic boundary between these two men is consonant with the many merged identities throughout the book; such merging is the necessary end of the political ideology that exalts a national identity in which *all* must become the land. Stella Snow is the perfect exemplar of this: in 1914, singing to the audience in a beerhall, "losing one by one the traits that were hers, [she] absorbed more and more the tradition that belonged to all" (45). The assumption of a common identity is most strikingly seen in the 1914 section when Ernst, running after Stella and Cromwell's carriage, "raced to coincide with Princip in Sarajevo" (54), while Stella and Cromwell become coterminous with the assassinated Archduke and the Archduchess. Every character becomes a mirror image of other characters, as they all partake of the images of heroism, justice, beauty, or power with which their culture provides them and which turn out to be models of monstrosity and victimization.

As Leader and Editor, Zizendorf is in the position of dictating what image of themselves the people will consume. As he prepares to print his proclamation of freedom, he says, "by tomorrow, we will have our public, proclaimed and pledged, every single one of them incorporated by a mere word, a true effort, into a movement to save them. Put into the open, the fools are helpless" (175). As Zizendorf speaks, the Duke is carving up his kill, preparing to dine with Madame Snow on her nephew, literally performing what in Zizendorf's case will be a metaphoric but far-reaching cannibalism, accomplished by the voracity of his language. Zizendorf's perceived ability so easily to incorporate individuals into the social body that he heads through his language attests to the potential his words have for effecting submission to a vision of supremacy, and thus to a repetition of past violence.

The control of language grants Zizendorf his power. However, in a world where people have stopped talking or talk only in fragments and where, if they have memories at all, the memories are disjointed and confused, Zizendorf also initially suffers from verbal impotence, from "words that would not come" (16). At the office of the *Crooked Zeitung,* the town newspaper, "[e]ach letter in the plates of type was butchered into the next, all the plates had been crushed with hammers," and in any case, Zizendorf tells us, "my fingers were too blunt to punch the keys and I had no paper" (15). Yet although violence so debilitates a people that they are bereft of language and communication ceases, language itself has the power to enact violence. Zizendorf describes himself, Stump-fegle, and Fegelein as sentries for whom there is "an unrecognized, un-admitted, unnamed desperation that persisted . . . to give strength to us, the hovering sentries, to bring words to the lolling historians. Poison their camps, if only in a quip or solitary act" (130). Zizendorf will enlarge his quips into an "INDICTMENT OF THE ALLIED ANTAGONISTS, AND PROC-LAMATION OF THE GERMAN LIBERATION" and thus wrest power over history from the enemy Other. His words have few objective referents, but they have no need of them; like the word "Victory" that causes the people to celebrate when Stella's father pronounces it from his balcony, thinking that "the war, which had just begun, was over" (70), Zizendorf's words create their own reality. The birth of the Nation is the birth of "the words of the new voice," the proclamation that issues from Zizendorf "creating on a stick the new word" and that falls on the press's "delivery table" (175–177).

Zizendorf says that the "uprising" he leads "must be successful, in-spired, ruthless" (147), a description that, for Hawkes, could also apply to authoring. Hawkes's aim in writing is to exercise "a quality of coldness, detachment, ruthless determination to face up to the enormities of ugli-ness and potential failure within ourselves and in the world around us, and to bring to this exposure a savage or saving comic spirit and the saving beauties of language" (Enck 143–144). Language achieves beauty through its power to create a meaningful reality in a grotesque and cha-otic world by rendering a vivid and precise vision of that world. When Madame Snow takes in Balamir, "the trenches of the countryside were suddenly seen by the light of her candle" (19), and such is the method of the novel: the narrative comprehensively reveals a modern psychic landscape through the particular images of a town and some of its people. The use of Zizendorf as narrator brings a corresponding illumi-nation to the authorial role, revealing the landscape of the imagination by the light of his prose.

Zizendorf speaks disparagingly of his henchman Fegelein, who "had the memory of a frog, a despicable blind green wart to whom all pads, all words, were the same" (165). All words are not the same to Zizendorf, who must utilize language to effect a transformation of reality. The lan-guage of *The Cannibal* reveals a people who are crushed, defeated by the debris of the material world, and a "Leader" for whom language, em-bodying the idea—of greatness, of renewal—can transcend and transfigure this oppressive materiality. But such desire for transcendence effected the original catastrophe. The complicity of Zizendorf's author-ial power in destruction is suggested by the image of "old unreadable issues" of the *Crooked Zeitung*, a vehicle for his words, on which rests the butchered carcass of a little boy.

## II

The dense patterning of particular and recurring imagery that sustains the text of *The Cannibal* creates not simply a self-enclosed, self-reflexive fictional world, but a text that acquires effectiveness by its reliance on, in the words of Marcus Klein, "knowledge [that] is anterior and historical" ("Hawkes in Love," 69). Hawkes "writes stories about characters who as a matter of primacy are defined culturally and socially" (68). *The Canni-bal* depends, as do many of Hawkes's novels, on the reader's knowledge of "the shambles left by the end of the War," shambles in which "Stella and Zizendorf . . . are seen as intensified but otherwise normal eventu-alities of character in the contemporary history of Germany" (69, 68). *The Beetle Leg* takes place in the American West, far from the palpable historical accretions of Europe, but no less imbued with the circum-stances of a particular time and place.

The characters in *The Beetle Leg* are at once odd and typical. We know their typicality from what we've read, and especially from what we've seen: *The Beetle Leg*, as Klein and others note, is a parody of a Western. Donald Greiner delineates the significance of Hawkes's re-visioning of this cultural cliché:

> part of America's peculiar expression of its own innocence is the Western which reshapes the violence, duplicity, and bloodshed used to settle the western terri-tories into a myth of Good Guys against Bad. In the standard Western the very real ambiguities of our western expansion are simplified until we accept Ameri-ca's growth as innocent progress sanctioned by fate. . . . By parodying the West-ern, Hawkes expresses our distortion of that dream of innocence. He uses descriptions of sterility and images of noxious growth to suggest the reality which punctures the myth of westward expansion—in reality the American dream turns out to be a nightmare. (*Comic Terror* 100–101)

The revelation of dream as nightmare propels *The Cannibal*, too; Zizen-dorf's ruling aspirations signal the perpetuation of power and victimiza-tion disguised as righteousness and beneficence. His story is about the resurrection of a town from its ashes, although his claim to creating a garden spot exists against the counter-claims of history. *The Beetle Leg* is about "a vast irrigation project in the arid American West, designed to transform deserts into gardens" (Greiner, *Comic Terror* 99). Unlike *The*

*Cannibal,* which begins with metamorphosis supposedly accomplished, *The Beetle Leg* begins—and ends—with the failure of an attempted metamorphosis of a landscape. But amidst the tangible sterility of this failure exists the desire to infuse a recalcitrant world with meaning, so that the novel, while debunking the claims of a certain historical mythos, examines and engages the process of creating meaning and asserting an imaginative reality.

The center of this novelistic world is an absence. Mulge Lampson lies buried, "entangled with a caterpillar, pump engine and hundred feet of hose" (17), somewhere in a mile-long "sarcophagus of mud" (67) at the site of a flawed dam on a barren plain. This death-inflicting burial is unwitnessed: "No one saw the Gov City man shoveled under. He died at the drop of a lash, was noticeably absent only after a count of heads" (69). (The use of "lash" here fittingly evokes vision and violence.) But this event, which becomes known as the Great Slide, renders Mulge legendary and mythical. His brother, Luke, spends days sowing flowers over the mile-long mound of his unmarked grave; his widow, Ma, spends nights prowling this same land with a divining rod and calling Mulge's name; his lover, Thegna, has stayed rooted, from the time of the Great Slide, to the town that grew near the dam. These are the people who were "closest" to Mulge, and so it is not unusual that they cling to his memory. But the memory of him is also sacralized in the rest of the community. At the barbershop, Mulge's "relics"—his razor and his shaving mug—sit on display and can be touched for fifty cents; postcards of the relics can be bought at the drugstore (72). Camper, a man who worked on the dam and who has returned as a tourist, speaks obsessively about Mulge's disappearance. When Lou, Camper's wife, tries to find out where her husband has gone by asking the men lounging at the side of the road in Clare, they mistake her comments as referring to Mulge and answer her by speaking of the dead man, treating his return as not unlikely and even calling him Jonah (104). The novel opens with the Sheriff's description of his first view of the inscrutable Mulge, and closes with Cap Leech's poetic reiteration of this description and wish to be where Mulge lies—wherever, exactly, that is.

Mulge's death embodies the death of a dream. The building of the dam that was intended to transform the hostile, desertlike landscape into productive farms and prosperous cities fails to accomplish this miracle. The scattered towns—Clare, Mistletoe, Government City—are shabby, dusty, and enervated, and the land is sparsely vegetated and desolate. Faced with the material, visible reality of this wasteland, the characters fixate on Mulge, thereby fetishizing what is invisible and extrapolating signs from it to transfigure the visible. Mulge's widow dramatically demonstrates this propensity in her nightly activity of walking the mile-long stretch of Mulge's grave with a divining rod. Mulge's grave is sacred ground because Ma makes it so. Her instrument is a common one of pioneers and homesteaders, used to reveal water or minerals and thus determine the land's potential for supporting or enriching life, but in Ma's use of it the divining rod becomes a means for revealing life itself and thereby redeeming her world, making it divine.

Because Mulge's death was sudden and invisible, and therefore tinged with unreality, Ma maintains the hope of finding "the slow and unbreathing, blackly preserved, whole and substantial being of the dead man" (117), a figure in which her self and her world can be reconstituted as complete. For Ma, a parody of the sexless Western woman who is part mother, part workhorse, in her daily existence manifests the terrible emptiness and meaningless persistence that characterize this landscape. "She kept her back to the world and her face toward the red range" (a nice pun that collapses the expanse of the plains into the scene of domestic slavery) where she keeps a skillet that is her "pot, the iron of her life," constantly burning (21, 22). The image of her pot recurs when Ma searches the land for Mulge: "Ma's was not a replenished vessel but an iron pot, not oil but scavenged vegetables, and the creditor had come leaving her few words thrown out, downcast lines in the face, the short, forlorn speech of the lonely woman. Hands figuratively outstretched after death" (118). The image of the replenished vessel perhaps looks forward to Hawkes's later articulation of renewable virginity, his conception of perpetual innocence achieved through the aesthetic and sensual enjoyment of sexuality. Such a conception is foreign to this barren, depleted world which acquires much of its horror from the absence or eradication of sex and hatred or fear of women. In the context of this novel the evocation of oil and a replenished vessel as opposed to scavenged vegetables and an iron pot suggests Ma's distance from a beautiful and mythical world, a distance she works to bridge in her inarticulate attempt to resurrect Mulge. Searching the land of his grave, "[s]he knew, she understood these signs of the young shoots crushed in the darkness, the sudden appearance and whirl of insects" (117); she sees the imminence of his return.

Ma's activity has the repetitive and hortative marks of ritual. Part of ritual is the hope of witnessing its efficacy, but Ma is so mired in the misery her ritual works to exorcise that she is blind to the advent of the redemption she seeks. "I've let him pass me by tonight," Ma moans; "But, eyes staring at the flat of her apron, face buried in stiff fingers, she could not hear the quiet footfall, the close deliberate opening of the earth, the parting of the weeds. . . . She could not see behind her" (120). This suggests that Mulge does rise from his grave, but Ma remains oblivious. The advent of Mulge which she implores ends in the assertion of her own humanity as she inscribes her need upon blankness: "she revealed signs of her striking loss in the furls of the earth" (117).

Apart from the signs she awaits in her nightly ritual, Ma cherishes the signs of Mulge to which she seems to have the clearest access:

> Ma had all the photographs of his effects. It was the best she could do. She wrote on the backs of them:
> "I remember this one, remember it well."
> "Bought in Clare for twenty-five cents. I didn't take to the color. Right off."
> "Cut 1 lb. fish fresh as it buys to four pieces." (72)

Mulge's personal effects—his shaving mug, razor, tonic, and septic pencil—are standard and banal, revealing nothing of the perished man. Photographs of these objects are at an even further remove from the man they honor, and Ma's irrelevant and trivial commentary on their backs makes these monuments still more pathetic and absurd. Their importance is that they are monuments; they insist on the reality of Mulge, and they attest to the significance of his existence even while registering its absence. Luke similarly demonstrates the need for evidence of Mulge when, sitting with Camper in the Buckhouse, where there is "a browned newspaper shot of the [dam] project above the bar" (97), he jumps up, pointing at the project photograph, saying, "See him up there? That's my brother! Mulge, what do you say, Mulge?" (101). But the photograph is of the project, and it is likely that neither Mulge nor anyone else is in the picture, or if they are, that they are antlike workers lost in the expanse of the landscape. The absence of Mulge from the photo would be consonant with his absence from the actual landscape, an absence that compels these characters to articulate his presence and to exhort Mulge's speaking back to them.

The death of Mulge by the dam that was supposed to be life-giving is a manifestation of the project's general destructiveness. The degeneration of the dam itself, however, cannot be seen; it takes a seismograph to detect the downward slide of the hill made by the dam: "the hill eased down the rotting shale a beetle's leg each several anniversaries. . . . But if this same machine, teletyping the journey into town, was turned upon the fields, the dry range, the badlands themselves, the same trembling and worry would perhaps be seen in the point of the hapless needle, the same discouraging pulse encountered, the flux, the same activity" (67–68). The people cannot see this entropic, destructive movement of the earth which has blighted their project or which their project has blighted—it is not clear which—and so stand above ground, blind as the dead Mulge, on a land that will make everyone its casual victim: "the seismograph took down the track of the earth and progress of a blindly swimming man inside, in erratic, automatic writing" (99–100). The application of the term "automatic writing" to this machine's activity of recording chaotic movement suggests a parallel to the automatic writing method of generating surrealistic fiction, which expresses the disruptive unconscious manifesting itself in the world. This comparison is perhaps too neat, but has relevance to Hawkes's stated desire to exercise control over the materials of his fiction: "my fiction has nothing to do with automatic writing. Despite . . . vague originations and the dream-like quality of some of these envisioned worlds, my own writing process involves a constant effort to shape and control my materials as well as an effort to liberate fictional energy" (Enck 148). Within the violent and disordered world of *The Beetle Leg*, the authorial desire to control finds expression in the Sheriff and Cap Leech, two men whose propensities include both violence and ordering that depends on their access to what is normally unseen and who provide the most significant informing consciousnesses of the novel.

The novel begins with words the Sheriff reads from a text about astrology. This text within a text suggests a system that governs the world and that can be harnessed for the benefit, even if this benefit is only foreknowledge, of those who can interpret its signs. Yet while he believes in the governing laws of the zodiac, the Sheriff begins his narrative saying, "It is a lawless country" (7). It is a country that he has "watched" for fourteen years, and what he mostly watches for is sexual activity, that activity that "happened or not depending on whether you arrived five minutes early or five late" (8), that activity that transgresses order and control. For the Sheriff, the signs of the zodiac point to sterility and death, their most positive auguring being favorableness "to the destruction of noxious growth" (7). The Sheriff's desire to squelch any sexual expression of life stems from his perverse interpretation of these expressions. To him, women are contemptible, as are the men who desire them; he exercises the power to break men and women apart and even to arrest them. The perverse voyeurism that grows from his repressive contempt has an appropriate imagistic counterpart in his attraction to "the expressionless genitals of animals" (108).

Cap Leech, the traveling medicine man, is similar to the Sheriff in his exercise of power over life, and in his attraction to death and deformity. His life as a wanderer began when he delivered a child (who would become Harry Bohn, another man attracted to the expressionless genitals of animals) from a dead mother "in an operation which . . . was more abortive than life saving" (121). After this he abandoned his family "for earaches and faeces smuggled in milk bottles when he set out with a few sticks and powders for thirty years practice among those without chance of recovery, doomed, he felt, to submit" (122). Yet even though he shares with the Sheriff impulses toward sterility that seem to be endemic to the environment, Leech has the power to affect the living as the Sheriff does not: "The Clare Sheriff was invested with the office to inspect, whip, or detain any unique descendant of the fork country pale families, was in a position to remember when they settled and how well or poorly they had grown. But before him stood a man concerned even more than himself with noxious growth, who was allowed, obviously schooled, to approach his fellow men with the intimate puncture of a needle" (42). Leech's power exceeds that of the law: "He had the power to put them all to sleep, to look at their women if he wished, to mark their children" (129).

Standing before the Indian woman called the Mandan, preparing to pull her tooth, "[e]ven when he was only thinking of what he would do to her, before the old deftness came into his warty fingers, [Leech] was a man apart, not to be disturbed" (146). The detachment of this man with a "wand hand" (151), the hand of a violinist (146), suggests the detachment of the artist so central to Hawkes's thinking; at the same time, Leech "was the dismantler of everything that flew or walked or burrowed at the base of a tree" (151). He is the novel's artist figure, with all the paradoxes of beneficence and malevolence that entails.

The scene of his operation on the Mandan parodies that of Aristotelian drama, with "a beginning, a middle, and finally a scrubbing down of the wagon" (145). The operation itself illustrates the sexual force with which *and* against which Leech's art operates. Having "passed over the crushed strawberries on her breasts," he fishes around in the mouth of "the Indian with violet pudendum" (147) in a passage which, as Patrick O'Donnell says, reads like "a surrealistic rape scene" (*JH* 71). But he stops in the middle of this operation, "suspicious, listening": "The Indian, in a last bodily defense, slightly bulged some muscles, loosed others, and secreted from licentious scent spots and awakened nodes, a sensation of difference marvelous as anything he had ever seen. The captive, still watching him with unchanged eyes, generated like an octopus the ink of desire. . . . She was waiting to see if he would strike" (148). He does strike, entering the wordless mouth and determinedly extracting the tooth, inflicting pain, but also allowing healing. The scene stands in marked contrast to an earlier scene when the Sheriff's deputy, Wade, stares at a group of Indian women gathered outside Cap Leech's wagon: "In the pack he saw one, two, that were maidens in unbelted dresses. . . . It was a circle he could not enter, never touch those with woodsmoke under their fingernails" (37). Leech's scene with the Mandan illustrates his ability to penetrate the circle that surrounds otherness and difference, while testifying that these qualities persist. For the "emanations" coming from this woman are non-representable, producing a sensation "marvelous as anything he had ever seen" but that he cannot see, so that the language specifically evokes and invokes other senses without being able to capture their elusive reality. This man who is privy to the vision of the inner workings of the body, who "had spread anatomy across a table like a net and crumpled with disgust a pair of deflated lungs into a ball" (144), confronts invisible mystery, "the ink of desire" that compels and defies expression.

Leech "sees" what cannot be seen, whether it is the emanations of the Mandan or the creeping progress of disease. His artist's vision exceeds the constricted vision of the Sheriff which introduces us to this novelistic world. When a little girl calls the Sheriff to come to the river where she and a friend are "holding" someone, the Sheriff expects to see some sexual aberration but instead finds only a man, who he later learns is Mulge Lampson, squatting down with his pants off, staring at the water. The Sheriff cannot find good enough reason to arrest Mulge, "[b]ut he was something to stare at for an hour or two" (14); the body of the Sheriff's narration consists mostly of descriptions of his staring at this starer and learning nothing. The Sheriff surmises that the man probably had a car: "he probably found a hollow and hid it there with all the things he carried and everything that made him what he was inside it. . . . That's where I should have looked for trouble" (15). This supposition is a more mundane version of the belief in revelatory signs that compels his consultation of the zodiac. But the significance of Mulge sitting by the river remains bafflingly opaque; neither the Sheriff's staring nor his later description of what he saw can get beyond a flat portrayal. The only relevance the situation can garner is retrospective, when seen in the light of an historical event.

It is not until the second chapter (if we read the Sheriff's words as a prologue) that the reader discovers that the Sheriff's opening narration—his reading of astrology and description of watching Mulge—is spoken to Cap Leech, who, in addition to being the wandering medicine man, is also the father of the Lampson boys. And it is not until Cap Leech's epilogue (which, in the novel's order of events, occurs in chapter 8) that the reader realizes the Sheriff's words are revelatory for the medicine man who sums up the Sheriff's sighting of Mulge in language that is lyrical and mythic, redescribing Mulge as mummified but vital. Leech's language effects a transformation of the Sheriff's fruitless stake-out and hampered vision. That the ordering of the text places Leech's and the Sheriff's words, which occur in the middle of the story, at the beginning and ending of the text locates these men as the text's informing consciousnesses. The Sheriff's sterile desire for law and order, which he enacts through vigilant voyeurism, has its antithesis in Leech's transgressive intimacy with anyone, from an Indian woman to the Sheriff himself, who suffers the disorder of pain. It is the Sheriff's pain that brings him into Cap Leech's wagon, where Leech drugs him with ether and perhaps performs some kind of operation on him, perhaps pulls a tooth. Leech's control over the body and the psyche allows him to gain verbal ascendancy; where before the Sheriff had begun his speech to Leech by saying, "I'll do the talking" (45), Leech tells the drugged Sheriff, "Now . . . I'll talk" (126). This verbal ascendancy is, of course, mostly suggestive, since the novel has a third-person narrator and the talking Leech does is reported later, in the epilogue. But as the epilogue reveals, Leech's desire to be taken to the place where Mulge rests reflects the desire of the other characters to have access to an invisible source of meaning that lies behind the all too evident starkness of this world.

The mythologizing language of Leech's epilogue, along with the centrality of a dead man to the novel's structure and landscape, has led critics to articulate *The Beetle Leg*'s informing myth. Frederick Busch sees Mulge as a water-god who must be resurrected by the Fisher King to fructify the wasteland. Cap Leech is the Fisher King as well as "a Jehovah-like God"; Ma is an earth mother as well as "something of Mary"; Luke is reminiscent of Christ's chronicler of the same name (40–41). Alan Heineman points to the same myth as does Busch, cast in terms of Mulge as Osiris and Ma as Isis; when the little girl leads the Sheriff to Mulge, who is sitting by the river not far from another little girl, he is interrupting, according to Heineman, Mulge's mummification. Mulge's death is "self-willed or predestined," according to Heineman, and his tomb can be seen as a pyramid (139). In a more productive and convincing analysis than Busch's or Heineman's, Lucy Frost sees the novel as dependent on "the patterning of events, images, and language in terms of the biblical myth of Adam's Fall together with the peculiarly American cultural myth of a new Eden" (65); Mulge, of course, is Adam.

The efforts of these readers to make sense of the prominence Mulge has in this landscape and this text duplicate the efforts of the novel's characters to invest harshness and destructiveness with meaning. There is no formally articulated myth in the novel, merely a general impulse toward myth, the characters' belief in the persistence of Mulge and thus in the persistence of their own human significance and the validity of their projects. At one point, however, a group of characters rebels against the weight of their community-authored hagiography. When a group of men, including the Sheriff, go out to the dam in the middle of the night, they ask Luke to talk about his brother, and he and they go about the business of demystifying a legend: "He was a big baby but a little man" whose mother was ashamed of his size; Ma compared loving him to loving a fence post; "[h]e didn't love animals"; "he's not so mighty. In the house or out he was the same, like he was petting something inside his shirt" (134). But the men say these things like boys flirting with a taboo, and their words only serve to demonstrate the depth of their dependence on the mighty legend of Mulge. In their debunking words "they baited the ghost" (134), for his continued life does extend the possibility of vivifying the landscape, if only in their imaginations. The invisible presence of Mulge signifies the same lure Hawkes attributes to the fictive process: the paradox of what exists and does not exist.

The men have made a nighttime trip to the dam because Camper, the tourist, wants to fish. Fishing has its mythic resonances but is most significant for its use in embodying one of Hawkes's favorite images of authoring. The last time Luke Lampson went fishing, he reeled in "the heavy body of a baby that had been dropped, searched for, and lost in the flood. . . . God's naked child lay under Luke's fingers" (132). (Hawkes refers to this baby as a "fetal baby" [Santore and Pocalyko 182].) Similar imagery describes Leech's delivery of Harry Bohn, "fished none too soon from the dark hollow" of his mother; Leech had "dared to extract the secret of a dead woman" (121). The writer must extract the secret of the self as well as the Other; Hawkes believes that "the writer should always serve as his own angleworm—and the sharper the barb with which he fishes himself out of the blackness, the better" ("Notes on *The Wild Goose Chase*," 788). He describes this as a

figure of speech about what the creative process should be. It's an interesting paradox: separating the artist from the human personality, the artistic self from the human self, then thinking of the artist's job as one of catching, capturing, snaring, using a very dangerous and unpleasant weapon, a hook, knowing that his subject matter is himself or his own imagination, which he has to find himself and which he catches ruthlessly. . . . To me, the most horrifying object to touch would be the fetus, and I would be unable to touch one. But in *The Beetle Leg*, that action is a real paradigm of what the artistic process should be. The writer should undertake to do what he finds most difficult and most threatening, and then deal with these materials in such a way as to re-integrate them within human consciousness. When the protagonist of the novel seizes what he has caught, this aborted, fish-like form of dead human life, and removes the hook from the caul that the hook has actually penetrated, then puts it back into the initial floodwaters of Noah's time—that, to me, is a parable of the artistic process. (O'Donnell 123)

Hawkes goes on to describe the fetus as a container of opposites, representing androgyny and "a terrible conjunction of life and death. . . . And since it is reptilian as well as mammalian, it combines everything there is to be aware of, what is still to me the absolute terrifying inexplicableness of life itself, as well as its grandeur" (O'Donnell 124).

The inexplicableness of life amidst violence, sterility, and desolation in this world that was supposed to be the flowering of the American Dream requires the effort of bestowing meaning on random occurrence.

Out of Mulge's gratuitous death in the construction of the dam the novel's characters try to construct a myth to redeem themselves and the land
on which they live. But the image of the flooded land's "virgin darkness"
(68), while suggesting what is unexplored and unplumbed, also suggests,
because of the taint associated with darkness, innocence that is already
compromised. (It also, of course, suggests the association of Woman with
the land, both the mysterious Other to be conquered and controlled.)
So too is the Eden of these Western plains compromised from the start
by the forcing of an idea on a landscape. And in Hawkes's description of
the writer as an angleworm fishing himself out of the darkness, the innocence he attaches to the beauty of language is compromised by the
imagination's violent proclivities.

Leech, the novel's artist figure, the man whose healing intent is compromised by his interest in pain, whose name suggests his ability to get
beneath the skin, who has power over life and death, "brought something of clear vision and bitter pills to the fields of broken axles" (129).
His ability to penetrate beneath the surface of appearances grants him
power and distinction; "a rootless spectator" (128), his detachment
grants him insight. Sitting with his son, Luke, and with Camper in a leak-
ing boat resting on top of a "drowned farm," Leech, "who by the spoon-
ful or on his handkerchief had shared the opiate slipped to his patients,
felt a sudden unpleasant clearness of the head, faced with the foundling
plainsman. The first man had died in Eden, they pronounced him dead.
And now, with brightening eye, he found himself sitting in the middle of
the washed-out garden's open hearth" (140). Leech discerns the fall
from a myth of innocence to the ordinariness of the personal and domestic. But in the moment of this realization, the ordinary is transformed into an image of as much inexplicable mystery and contradiction
as the dead man in the mountain of earth represents. Leech calls Luke
"Boy," but then his vision transforms this living son into a fetus: "He
stared at the tufted head that never turned, at the nape of soft formed
skull the seams of which were not yet grown together, at the lump of
ending nerves that was his neck" (141). Such dissecting vision recasts
Leech's violent, dismantling tendencies in the form of revelation. The
"cheerless recognition" he experiences at this sight illustrates the un-
sparing clarity of Leech's vision, his ability to see terrifying mystery and
possibility in the mundane, and to acknowledge the darkness around
him as within him, too.

Leech is a man "kept alive by a spirit half stimulant, half sleep" (39) —
a description that images the tension between the artistic consciousness
that would order, and the chaotic unconscious, as well as chaotic world,
that resist ordering. The story ends in disorder, although this disorder is
under the aegis of law. A group of men, including the Sheriff, the Sher-

iff's deputy, the deformed Bohn, and the cowboy Luke, go on a shooting spree against the Red Devils, the parodic but enigmatic figures who wear inhuman rubber masks and ride screeching motorcycles through the dust. "Kill most anything tonight," says the Sheriff, "And after a silence he muttered, 'Bound to. In Saggitarius' " (155). The Sheriff, who exercises his own incarcerating vision in the watch he keeps on people, consigns himself to deterministic forces. The zodiac directs that killing will occur, but the law of the Western determines that this parody of a Western must have a shootout, complete with Red Devils. The "law" represented by the genre of the Western, grown out of, as well as engendering, popular cultural myths, and the law the Sheriff represents are shown to be perpetuators of violence, which takes on erotic allure in a sexually stifled world: "Gasoline, tobacco, death, [Bohn] felt the satisfied warning in his groin" (155).

As the men prepare to go on this shootout, stealing Cap Leech's horse as he performs his operation on the Mandan, "[f]rom beyond the wagon came a sudden soprano quailing, a meaningless 'yip, yip, yip,' the singing scream" (149). During the shootout, Luke accidentally shoots himself in the head, and the story ends: "there came that call to kill, louder and singsong, faintly human after the flight of Devils, the nasal elated sounds of the cowboy's western bark. . . . Yip, yip, yip" (158). This meaningless sound is juxtaposed to Leech's epilogue, which ends the text and which uses the most poeticizing, mythologizing language of the novel. Leech's words, in terms of the story, are spoken thirty-three pages earlier, but their disjointed positioning at the end of the text invites reading them back into what has transpired. Such activity duplicates mythologizing or historicizing, which seek to sacralize the past or to make the past speak by overlaying it with a determined set of meanings. The final words of this epilogue, "Take me there," ironically comment on the text's illustration that there is no "there," that while the dam may be Mulge's grave site, the place where he can be seen wrapped in colorless cloth, with dangling fingers, or lounging on the bank of a river, is imaginary. Moreover, the transformation of this desolate physical and psychic landscape into a place where dreams are realized exists only in imaginative constructions. The epilogue extends the possibility of regeneration through imaginative vision, but this possibility contends with a death-dealing world of senseless violence and human expression turned bestial and meaningless. The horror of this unredeemed world finds judgment in the words of Lou, Camper's wife, who is doubly an outsider as a tourist and a woman: "She whispered. . . . A soft, unfamiliar, lucid condemnation: 'Take me out of here' " (154). Leech's "Take me there," falling just five pages later, ironically echoes this condemnation and turns it into as wishful reclamation of wholeness. But the idea of wholeness is belied by the fragmentation of the text, which the disjointed positioning of the epilogue highlights, and which itself mimics the fragmentation of a world whose only community is in violence and death.

## III

The horrific garden spot and fallen Eden evoked in *The Cannibal* and *The Beetle Leg* reappear, transmuted and intense, in the short novels *The Goose on the Grave* and *The Owl*, published together in 1954. *The Goose on the Grave* takes a warwrecked Italy where "the renaissance has failed" (232) as the locale of its fictive distortions that reflect the perversions of a random and violent world. The novel evokes a world that is a "platoon of broken lances" (203) where the wounded on stretchers fill churches and grapes "twitch" (203) on bare vines, where even sleep is horrific as "the cells that grew randomly" (251) distort the body. After watching three priests, "black-breasts" (200), abduct his mother, the young Adeppi becomes a wanderer and victim of adult cruelty, typified by the scene in which a carabiniere beats him on top of a dung heap between a church and a coffin shop and before an impassive audience. The language of this novel is some of Hawkes's most extraordinary, the realization of searing images—of such things as flagellation, hunger, disease, bestiality—relentless and controlled. Yet the severity of narrative dislocations, the obscurity of motivation, and the elusiveness of structure cause critics to rank this as Hawkes's least successful work. The obfuscations of the novel correspond to a departure from Hawkes's experimentation with narrative voice in *The Cannibal* and *The Beetle Leg*, where first-person voices focus the compulsions to create and destroy, to order and transgress. *The Goose on the Grave*'s narration most closely resembles that of *Charivari*. Both texts locate all authorial control in a third-person authorial voice and lack the multivalent quality that allows the narrative voice of *The Cannibal*, for instance, to masquerade as transcendent while the narrative content critiques this transcendence; or the multivocal quality that allows the ordering and dismantling desires of the Sheriff and Cap Leech to confront each other as well as the intransigent landscape. *The Owl*, set also in a war-wrecked Italy (both novels seem to evoke World War II and its aftermath, as well as a peculiar timelessness that points to a certain constancy of motivations in history), is similar to the regressive world of *The Goose on the Grave* in being a world where "the Renaissance [is] driven from our garrets and streets" (154). But the "our" is all important here: the voice that speaks the textual world is of that world—and makes that world, with all the self-reflexive paradoxes entailed in the Hawkesian aesthetic of innocent and cruel authorial detachment.

Hawkes's belief in authorial detachment is concomitant with his belief that "extreme detachment might be a quality of the extreme authoritarian, the dictator, or the leader of a criminal gang" (O'Donnell 126). In *The Owl* the authoritarian and the author figure merge in the narration of Il Gufo, the Owl, who is the hangman of a provincial Italian town called Sasso Fetore (Tomb Stench). Il Gufo, like Zizendorf, assumes impossible omniscience and totalitarian power. He presides over a town where fathers desperately try to marry their daughters to the prisoner of the fortress or even Il Gufo, the only eligible men; the novel suggests that all the young men have been lost to war. Il Gufo embodies the larger rule of tradition and inheritance, the bulwarks of patriarchy, that keeps the town in thrall. And the town submits to the Hangman, just as the characters in *The Cannibal* submit to fascistic rule. The desperate fathers, in fact, collude with the Hangman in his machinations that will keep their daughters forever virgin. *The Owl*, then, more forthrightly than any of Hawkes's previous novels, reveals the misogyny at the root of the desire for ultimate control of the self and the Other, as well as the paradox of the narrator's rich generation of language and of vivid images embodying degenerative, deathly impulses.

In *The Goose on the Grave*, the description of "frescoes that depicted the creation of the world" leave a character "unmoved" (217); Il Gufo describes the scaffold, "the tall lady," as "simple and geometric as frescoes of the creation of the world" and reveals his cold passion (158). The echoing of images between *The Goose on the Grave* and *The Owl* displays repetition with a difference accomplished by the obsessiveness of a personified narrator. Il Gufo's association of a scaffold with the artistic rendering of creation clearly collapses life and death; what is even more significant throughout the narration is the collapsing of boundaries between distinct entities—between things, animals, people—in a world where transgression is punished, where Il Gufo maintains difference and separation between men and women, between ruler and ruled, between self and other.

The narrative's proliferating conflations paradoxically inscribe a geometrics of deathly sameness and of differences by making words mean simultaneously so much more and so much less than ordinary usage would have them mean: in *The Owl* proliferating chains of signifiers point to an ever smaller number of referents. The world Il Gufo creates resolutely points to denied sex and erotic death. Not only is the scaffold an image of creation, it is "the tall lady," it is the Donna; the Donna is Sasso Fetore's statue of the virgin mother, a statue Il Gufo viciously kicks when its face is smeared with blood; Antonina is "white as the Donna," and tall as the scaffold (177–178). All of life narrows to Il Gufo's all-encompassing vision. Separate from all in what he calls "the absolute clarity of my vantage above" (155), Il Gufo is separate even from himself;

at the same time he inhabits all the words with which he calls forth the world of Sasso Fetore. The narrator of *The Owl* speaks of himself frequently in the third person as the Hangman and as the owl, the bird of prey, of night, of vigilance, that accompanies him everywhere. The conflation of himself and the owl occurs in such striking passages as a paragraph that begins "The owl kept watch on peasant and prefect alike"; it goes on to describe the owl in detail, including descriptions of his beak and armor feathers, and ends "I am speaking of myself, Il Gufo" (139–140). The narrative technique of association and displacement renders Il Gufo omnipresent and omnipotent, his language at once generative and murderous. The verbal collapsing of boundaries paradoxically inscribes a transgression that Il Gufo will not allow when it comes to the bounds of the law he so literally enforces.

In this "bridled province" (140) Il Gufo is wedded to the tall lady, the instrument of bloodless death, as he represses and denies all sexual life. When the beautiful Antonina rebels against her father's effort to trade her to the prisoner, she rejects one trap for another, deciding she loves Il Gufo, the embodiment of death. Il Gufo responds with what masquerades as erotic haste and liberatory flight, climbing to a mountain height with Antonina where he thrusts his hand under her skirts and takes her dowry purse. The prisoner attempts to escape by strapping himself to laboriously crafted wings and flying away, his necessary failure already inscribed in the Icarus myth he parodies. Il Gufo, according to law, has the prisoner tortured and finally ceremoniously hangs him, according to "the book from which their hangman knew the terms and directions, the means and methods to destroy a man" (198). He proclaims that the rest of Antonina's days will be spent with the manual of the *Laws of the Young Women Not Yet Released to Marriage* (a title that suggests a release from one prison to another). And he ends his narrative with an unattributed and altered quotation from John Winthrop, displacing this Puritan's invocation of a people's obedience to a covenant with God with his own iron proclamation of authority that asserts the inescapability of determining inscriptions.

Il Gufo's Sasso Fetore, like the worlds of *The Cannibal, The Beetle Leg,* and *The Goose on the Grave,* reveals, as in a dark and distorting mirror, our own culture to us. Il Gufo seems, for instance, to speak merely the customary life-denying and misogynistic wisdom of Western culture when he says, "the distraction and the gaiety of woman preceded the fall of man" (179). Interestingly, *The Owl* omits Winthrop's exhortation of the pilgrims to New England to (through their preachers?) listen to their God, to "choose life . . . by obeyeing his voyce."[2] It is, of course, Il Gufo's voice that must be obeyed; and it is through the use of such a voice that Hawkes creates a self-reflexive discourse of authoritarian power that comments upon the exigencies of the imagination in the world and in fiction.

Hawkes's experimentation in his early novels with the dynamics of narrative perspective and authorial vision produces texts that enact his conception of his fiction as a combination of "idealism, innocence, and luminous, murderous impulse (LeClair 27). This linking of opposites paradoxically echoes the collapsing of difference—and of opposition—in *The Cannibal* and *The Owl*. Zizendorf is the Land, the Owl is the Law. The psyche and the world merge and mutate each into the image of the other. In *The Beetle Leg* Cap Leech and the Sheriff, along with the other characters, make actual the paradox of absence and presence. The characters that serve as author figures and narrators in these novels wield and weld language and vision in such a way that the images of the dead worlds they evoke pulse with life; the power they exert is both fantasized and real, their innocence as compelling and deadly as their desire.

# Chapter 2
## Plotting Dreams: Fantasy and Representation in *The Lime Twig*

> Even the starry union is a fraud.
> Yet gladly let us trust the valid symbol
> for a moment. It is all we need.
> —Rilke, *The Sonnets to Orpheus*

**I**

*The Lime Twig* (1961) portrays yet another desolate landscape; it continues Hawkes's obsession with the horror of World War II and its dismal aftermath, this time using London as the setting. The very ordinariness of its lower-middle-class characters, the tawdriness of their criminality, the familiarity of their routines of living, make this novel in many ways more disturbing than those that came before it. Like these novels, *The Lime Twig* builds upon vivid, detailed images, but now the power invested in images becomes even more problematic and complex. This complexity corresponds to a multiplication of points of view and embodiments of authorial power. The novel begins with twenty-four pages of first-person narration that provide a historical setting, an informing psychology, and a bank of images. The speaker of this section in turn becomes a character described from a third-person limited perspective, which focuses on developing the experiences and inner lives of both the male and female of a married couple. The activities of this couple are manipulated by a godlike author figure, but an author figure as seen from a third-person perspective and the perspective of the other characters. And commenting on the actions of all these characters, who remain unknown to him, is yet another author figure who exists only as disembodied writing. This proliferation and dispersal of points of view, the shifting of subjectivity and objecthood, produces a multivalent text that reflects the assertion of the imagination that would shape and control experience and that is itself subject to surveillance and control. In the spiritually and sexually diminished world of this novel, the characters attempt to enlarge their experience, to make it exciting and meaningful, by projecting their desires into action. But all action is circumscribed— by violence, by victimization, by accident, by more powerful will and vision, by forces of life that are uncontrollable.

The expansion of narrative perspectives allows Hawkes an increase of his own authorial control of complex subject matter and powerful images. With its creation of a recognizable world and with its increased— though parodic—employment of plot, *The Lime Twig* probingly engages mimetic representation, but this becomes the occasion for a heightened examination of representation itself. The desires of characters to transcend the limits of their selves and their circumstances enacts the paradoxes of the innocent and cruel imagination that would make actual its liberating fantasies, while the text reveals every fantasy's implication in the power schemes of others and in the calcifying, incarcerating power of received representations and cultural scripts.

The novel opens with William Hencher's prologue, in which he evokes the wartime world of nightly fire bombings and his and his mother's grim, lonely, and repeated quest for lodgings. Hencher, both caringly devoted and abnormally attached to his mother, is seemingly innocent because he lacks any independence or active engagement with life, but he is also voyeuristic and given to faintly perverse fantasies. He brings us up to the time of the novel's main events, some years after the war, when, still periodically searching for lodgings, he returns to rooms where he stayed with his mother for a while during the war, now let by Michael and Margaret Banks, a dull young couple living out their banal, routine existence in Dreary Station. They are "innocents" too: perfectly respectable, middle-class, repressed, historically ignorant, and culturally bereft. Hencher insinuates himself in the Banks's lives, joining his need to live through other people to their suppressed fantasies of sex, power, violence, and victimization. The fantasy that serves as the storehouse for all the other fantasies is Michael Banks's dream of a horse, which Hencher maneuvers into becoming a reality, thereby involving Banks in the sordid and demanding world of gangsters and crooked horse racing. The novel thus becomes the unfolding of a dream, the enactment of fantasies, a beautiful and horrific unleashing of desires that are themselves a volatile mix of idealism and crassness, innocence and cruelty.

Through the efforts of Hencher and his criminal contacts, a stolen race horse, Rock Castle, becomes Michael's. But Larry the Limousine, the leader of the gang of criminals, merely uses Banks as a front, entering Rock Castle under Banks's colors in the Golden Bowl at Aldington, a race this seasoned horse is certain to win. The scheme involves monitoring Banks's every move and holding Margaret hostage to insure Banks's cooperation, in the process fulfilling what these two "innocents" have most desired and most feared. As the all-powerful man who is in the position of controlling the dream and the nightmare in *The Lime Twig*, Larry, described as "an angel if any angel ever had eyes like his or flesh like his" (83), is a typically paradoxical Hawkesian author figure. Larry's criminality parallels authorial criminality, his cruelty and power concomitant with creative innocence. "Larry is a diabolical character. My sympathies are all with Larry," Hawkes has said. "In 'real' life, the world's hostility would be leveled against him. He's the superb (though parodied) outcast working on trying to live against the greatest odds. He's exerting himself and his own loneliness to attempt to create a world. He merely appears to be a source of evil in *The Lime Twig*" (Kuehl 165). Larry's "attempt to create a world" echoes Hawkes's own stated effort "to create a world, not represent it" (Enck 154). The tension between creation and representation, central to Hawkes's aesthetic, becomes a significant underlying determiner of value in this novel which concerns the efforts of each of the characters to negotiate the twining of fantasy and reality. The novel engages the characters', as well as the author's, struggle with the paradoxes of trying to achieve the transcendent dream in a material medium.

Larry, who controls the action and the fates of the other characters and who appears, for their adulation, erect and broad-shouldered with light ricocheting off of him, has his double as author figure in Sidney Slyter, who never appears at all, existing only in the language of his newspaper column, which appears at the beginning of every chapter and in which he attempts to penetrate the plot afoot at Aldington. Although Slyter's distance from the events of the novel, compared to Larry's responsibility for them, would seem to make him less culpable, Hawkes thinks of him as "the only character in my fiction that might approach a genuinely damned state" (Kuehl 162). Hawkes calls Slyter an image of "the absurd and lonely author himself" (Enck 155), and remarks that Slyter's

sleazy character and cheap column afforded me perhaps the best opportunity for dramatizing the evil inherent in the world of *The Lime Twig.* Slyter's curiosity, his callow optimism, his lower middle class English ego, his tasteless rhetoric, his vaguely obscene excitement in the presence of violence—all this makes him one of the most degrading and perversely appealing figures in the novel. I would say that in reporting the criminal actions of the novel, Slyter carries degradation to its final end. (Enck 150–151)

Slyter's sin lies in his desire to achieve an accurate representation of the mysterious events surrounding the Golden Bowl, a desire that makes him a purveyor of mass-produced fantasies rather than a creator and explorer of human possibilities. The varieties of authorial power lodged in Larry and Slyter illustrate both the potential for the creative, transgressive freedom of acting on one's own vision and the potential for subjection to the delusive and alienating representations of fantasy, both of which possibilities lie in Michael Banks's pursuit of his dreams of power.

In *The Lime Twig* the boundary between fantasy and reality collapses, and this extends the possibility of reality's enrichment; the boundary between one's own fantasies and those of others collapses, too, and this extends the possibility of intimacy, as well as victimization. These possibilities constitute Hencher as another author figure, for, in addition to his narration establishing the world of Dreary Station, revealing the need to escape the imaginative and cultural impoverishment it represents, it also spins out the image repertoire of dreams and desires that he effectively transfers to Michael Banks. This transference engenders the violent idealism and longing corruption of the novel's action.

The link between Hencher's imagination and Banks's dream is thus one of the ways in which *The Lime Twig* explores fantasies and desires that seem to be personal and transcendent, but instead turn out to be part of culturally constructed collective fantasies and external machinations. This tension between the personal and collective, between individuality and the mass, is one of the ways in which the novel questions not only the ability to know the self but also the very idea of the self, and not only the ability to know experience, but also the nature of experience itself; in so doing it examines the imagination's access to innocence and power in its attempt to realize the substance of fantasy.

**II**

With the aid of Hencher, Michael Banks embarks on acquiring his horse, aware of the animal's enormous significance to him, and aware of the import of his dreams to Margaret: "Knowing how much she feared his dreams: knowing that her own worst dream was one day to find him gone, overdue minute by minute some late afternoon until the inexplicable absence of him became a certainty; knowing that his own worst dream, and best, was of a horse which was itself the flesh of all violent dreams" (33). The language in which the text casts Michael's knowledge of his and Margaret's dreams, however, suggests not just the momentousness of his actions, but a whole complex of issues inherent in both the imagining and the attainment of these dreams. Michael's best dream contains Margaret's worst dream—contains, in other words, Michael's fantasy of terrorizing or victimizing his wife. That he sees her terror as arising from the idea that his absence is inexplicable reveals his desire to

wield power by becoming a mystery. His absence, then, would be a paradoxical assertion of presence, a presence guaranteed by Margaret's attempts to supply the mystery's answer, to respond to the effects of his
imagination with the exercise of her own imagination.

And, indeed, Margaret's best and worst dreams engage her attraction
to mystery, to some locus of potential meaning that would be in contrast
to a meaninglessness and boredom so powerful that she stands alone in
her rooms and says, "I'm dead to the world" (64). At night "she would
dream of the crostics and, in the dark, men with numbers wrapped
round their fingers would feel her legs, or she would lie with an obscure
member of government on a leather couch, trying to remember and all
the while begging for his name" (68). The sinister sexuality summoned
in these dreams suggests not just Margaret's transgressive desire, but also
a longing for meaning: the message achieved in working out the crostics,
the elusive symbolism signaled by numbers on fingers, the name that will
clarify. But just as in Michael's conception certainty attends the presence
of mystery itself and not any answer to mystery, the action of the novel
will frustrate any ideas of certainty or of meaning which its characters
venture.

Of even greater suggestiveness than his conception of Margaret's reaction to his absence is Michael's knowledge that the horse of which he
dreams "was itself the flesh of all violent dreams," for while the sleek
mass of a horse is powerfully attractive to him, its greatest power lies in
its embodiment of other dreams. The horse is a metaphor for sexual
potency, for power over women and among men, for adventure, money,
glamour, and danger; the dream of a horse begets the flesh of a horse
which spawns an infinity of fantasies. But the status of fantasies as representations, and representations of representations, makes their realization problematic, calling into question both the nature of experience
and the representation of it in language and by the imagination.

The Banks's everyday life illustrates the poverty of human relations in
the absence of imagination. In the cheapness and ugliness of their surroundings, Michael's and Margaret's actions are predictable and uninspired, and their relationship lacks depth or intimacy. Margaret spends
her days in the constantly gathering dust of their four rooms, or on shop-
ping excursions during which she buys nothing, returning home with
only "a packet of cold fish in the bag" (30). And when Michael comes
home from work, and "after the sink was empty and her apron off," he
would ask Margaret, "*Feeling lucky?*"; "It was never luck she felt but she
would smile" (65; Hawkes's italics). For them, the presence of the other
holds no enchantment: "When Banks had first kissed her, touching the
arm that was only an arm, the cheek that was only a cheek, he had
turned away to find a hair in his mouth" (68). In contrast to this

untransfigured experience of the self and the other and the brute materiality of their lives, fantasies open the arena of representation in which
nothing is just what it is, everything is something else.

The multiplicity of significations available in dream or fantasy, which
serves as a compensatory alternative to desolate existence, manifests itself from the start of the novel in Hencher's prologue. During the war,
away from the room of his suffocating proximity to his mother, he
watches a bomber crash in the middle of the laundry court—and in the
midst of his narration of the dreary circumstances of lodgers in Dreary
Station. And suddenly Hencher, confronted with the bomber's "shape-
less immensity" (20) and the naked woman, "Reggie's Rose," painted on
its nose, enters the realm of fantasy, approaches the phallic fuselage,
goes into the womblike cabin, and, breathing through the missing pilot's
oxygen mask, can merge with Reggie and Rose and mother all at once.
The polyvalent image of the bomber is a fitting predecessor to the dream
of the race horse, an image of multifarious phallic desire, and even a
metaphorical bomb: as Banks and Hencher work to lift the horse from a
barge with pulleys and chains, Hencher compares their activity to lifting
bombs out of craters (51).

The attainment of his horse leads Michael to Sybilline, the young, attractive woman in Larry's gang, whose arms he sees as not just arms but
as lovely things with "freckles like little brown crystals out of the sea"
(99). In Sybilline Michael finds his ideal Woman who embodies whatever
he imagines will fulfill him. "In Syb's voice he heard laughter, motor cars
and lovely moonlit trees, beds and silk stockings in the middle of the
floor" (120), images laden with romantic and glamorous and sexy significations. He admires the row of pearl-tipped hairpins pushed into Syb's
hair, which make him think "of the faces children model out of bread
dough and of the eyes they fashion by sinking raisins into the dough with
their stubby thumbs" (120). This homey image of child's play converts
Syb, in part, into something created by an innocent Michael. It also, however, effects an evocative comparison of pearls to eyes, recalling Ariel's
Song. For not only has Sybilline become goddesslike in his eyes, Michael
himself seems to have undergone a sea-change, revelling in a world he
sees as grown rich and strange, a world in which he can believe, while he
is with Syb, that he has metamorphosed into the charismatic and powerful figure he dreams of being, transfigured by this "good fun for our
mortality" (163). Set loose in the realm of fantasy, Michael can now experience eroticism, not only when cavorting in bed with Sybilline, but
even when eating eggs in a kitchen, for in fantasy objects and situations
are transformed by the overdetermined meanings attributed to them.
"Don't you know what eggs are good for, Michael?" Syb asks (148), and
even this ordinary food becomes (somewhat grotesquely) stimulating.

The novel's title is itself an indicator of the multiplicity of significations involved in the dream and in the language used to convey this dream. Lime twigs snare birds, and the "innocents" in the novel—Hencher, Michael, and Margaret—are each at some point associated with birds. They are indeed all entrapped, victims of their own fantasies and those of others. But "lime" has other resonances. Rock Castle, bearer of so much metaphorical weight, is entered in the Golden Bowl under Banks's colors, lime green and black (62). And when twice in the novel Michael "was tasting lime" one thinks of the fruit, associated with ease and clean drinks and good times, yet each time Michael tastes lime he is experiencing the realization of his dream as nightmarish. He tastes lime when he actually first has "his" horse, and in an "unidentified black shabby van" endures the discomfort and unpleasant odors of being in the truck's cab with four other men, with a thumping horse behind them, and of realizing, for a moment, the enormity of what he has done by actually having made his dream a reality (54–55). The other time he tastes lime is when he glimpses Margaret, in strange antique clothing, in the crowd at the races, and witnesses her being whisked away, a foreboding sign that there are forces at work insuring that he is not in control of his dream (107). In another taste of the sinister, at the baths where the gang kills Cowles, one of its own members, Michael smells the disinfectant odor of white lime rising at the spread of Cowles's blood. And the man behind all this splendor and horror is Larry, the man who limes all the other characters, and who has a dream of a life away from violence and criminality, a dream of marriage to Little Dora, perhaps a child or two, and of the idyllic Americas full of trees with limes on the branches (166).

Although both Michael and Margaret are limed, the volatile potential for joy and victimization resting in Michael's dream manifests itself most startlingly and cruelly in their separate fates. While Michael lives out the sexual potency of his dreams, spending an orgiastic night of lovemaking with Sybilline and three other women, Margaret undergoes the extremity of sadism implicit in his dream and her own dreams, suffering a beating by the gang's heavy, Thick. Robert Scholes writes that Michael and Margaret, "In their separate beds . . . have explored the world of violence and sensuality. Margaret's excess of pain and suffering has been ironically balanced by Michael's excess of 'pleasure'" (*Fabulation and Metafiction* 186). But the irony here is so severe that any idea of Michael's pleasure and Margaret's pain balancing each other is something of a travesty, recuperating excess—whether of joy or pain—for a distanced, aesthetic ordering, bringing to it the satisfaction of design. The desire for such design to absorb the paradoxes—and injustices—of pleasure and pain is to become the obsession of Hawkes's first-person narrators in his subsequent novels. In *The Lime Twig*, however, the artistic consciousness is diffused among several characters, and the two primary characters, Michael and Margaret, who experience the paradox of pleasure and pain, struggle with the violation of their superficial world, brought about by the realization of their fantasies, by continuing to process experience through the veil of culturally constituted constructions. The scene of Margaret's beating serves to reveal the elision of experience in the impoverished imagination's recourse to received representations.

In this parody of a mystery thriller Margaret's "thrill" is a beating after which "she was like a convent girl accepting the mysteries" (129). Her perverse perception of sacredness contrasts to the mundaneness she acknowledges even in her fantasies of victimization at the hands of powerful men, for while she has exhibited an attraction to mystery, her fantasies, the products of an unoriginal imagination, remain separate from "reality," leaving it unchanged in its banality: "She was Banks's wife by the law, she was Margaret, and if the men ever did get hold of her and go at her with their truncheons or knives or knuckles, she would still be merely Margaret with a dress and a brown shoe" (70). But the actual beating with a truncheon has disrupted her conviction in the ordinary, forcing her into the unknown; "she only wanted a little comfort, a bit of charity; with the awfulness, the unknowable, removed" (126). Thick's beating has exceeded culturally available representations of violence familiar to her, but she still can only "know" the experience in terms of such representations:

She hadn't believed Thick's beating, really, though it put her out for an hour or more. Later, lying strapped to the bed, she told herself it was what she might have expected: it was something done to abducted girls, that's all. She thought she had read a piece about a beating. And yet when it came it surprised her. Though thinking now, listening, looking back through the dark, she realized—this despite the article she had read—something they couldn't even show in films. (126)

Margaret thus fails to feel or to know her own experience, which is drained of immediacy by her referral to what she has seen or read. At the same time, paradoxically, she realizes the enormity of what she has experienced by the fact that articles and movies are inadequate as representations.

The description of Margaret's beating is almost entirely of Thick's actions and appearance and sounds, perceived by this woman he is slowly killing. She knows her experience of the beating through the spectacle of Thick. "When he finally stopped for good she was bleeding, but not from any wound she could see" (129); like the unseen wounds, her feelings are unseeable. The beating is paradoxically both deeply, painfully felt, and also not felt, only registered, so that as Margaret is objectified by the other, becoming the means by which he acts out his sadistic fantasies, she also objectifies the self: "and no matter how much she accepted she knew it now: something they couldn't show in films. What a sight if they flashed this view of herself on the screen of the old Victoria Hall where she had seen a few pictures with Michael. What a view of shame" (129–130). Furthermore, the beating is already mediated by a retrospective perspective, so that it is very clearly something narrated. This is perhaps nothing more than typical fictional technique, but the deliberateness of this technique stands out by virtue of the fact that Hawkes does use the present tense for three scenes in the novel to portray the unsettling of the character's lives by their movement toward fantasy (30–32, 55–56, 56–61).

The narrated quality of Margaret's beating makes sense, for even in her fantasies she had wanted to be a character read by another; alone in her house, for instance, she wonders what a fortune-teller "would make of her" (64). Margaret's penchant for imagining how she would look in the eyes of others has its parallel in one of the motivating forces behind Michael's dreams. Indeed, Michael, similar to the narrators of Hawkes's subsequent novels, needs the reactions of others to effect the transfiguration of his selfhood. He is most excited at the beginning of his adventure by imagining how his actions will appear to Margaret; his disappearance will be his entrance to mystery. Looking about his flat for the last time in the guise of his boring old self, he thinks, "*She'll wonder about me. She'll wonder where her hubby's at, rightly enough*" (32; Hawkes's italics). Once he is embarked on living out the fantasy, the new object of fantasy becomes Margaret—or since the self is always the main object/subject of fantasy, about himself as he will now exist for Margaret: "*She's home now, she's thinking about her hubby now, she's asking the cat where's Michael off to, where's my Michael gone to?*" (40; Hawkes's italics). Standing in the fog ready to get Rock Castle off a barge, he relishes the wonderful sight of himself that can be wonderful only by virtue of the fact that he's apart from her, that she cannot see him: "*She ought to see her hubby now. She ought to see me now*" (47; Hawkes's italics). The experience is drained of its immediacy, instead garnering importance in the reflection of himself he imagines in the eyes of the Other.

The dynamic of looking and being looked at is introduced on the first page of the novel in Sidney Slyter's column: "So keep a look out for me. Because Sidney Slyter will be looking out for you." And he does indeed look out for and look into the sordid affairs of Michael Banks and the gang surrounding Rock Castle, feeding or engendering fantasies as much as he reports them. But a significant fantasy in the novel is the fantasy of uniqueness and freedom, including freedom from surveillance or observation. In Hencher's prologue, in his moment of most intense fantasy, when the bomber crashes in the laundry court, he "leaned against it and it was like touching your red cheek to a stranded whale's fluke when, in all your coastal graveyard, there was no witness, no one to see" (21). Banks is in the paradoxical position of depending on the imagined gaze of the other for his enjoyment, but at the same time, like Hencher, wanting to enjoy his fantasy in the freedom of privacy. More often than not, however, he finds himself the object of intent scrutiny, and therefore of control, the very thing he desires to exercise. He doesn't begin really to have fun until, dancing with Syb, he "felt that he too went unnoticed, felt that he could drink and dance and breathe unobserved at last" (120). This is, however, only an illusion, for Larry has definite plans for Banks's role in his horse race scam, and Banks is under the constant surveillance of Larry's henchmen. By the end of the novel he realizes that he cannot escape control, nor can he command the gaze of his newfound ideal Woman: "Banks saw nothing of the crowd but kept his eyes on Sybilline. Not once did she glance his way—though he was watched. He was being watched all right" (166).

Not only does the novel begin with Slyter's introducing the idea of surveillance that permeates it, Hencher's prologue thematizes the role of vision. Hencher describes a young boy of Dreary Station during the war who was devoted to a puppy: "His fingers were always feeling the black gums or the soft wormy little legs or quickly freeing and pulling open the eyes so that he, the thin boy, could stare into them. . . . the boy with the poor dog in his arms and loving his close scrutiny of the nicks in its ears, tiny channels over the dog's brain, pictures he could find on its purple tongue, pearls he could discover between the claws. Love is a long close scrutiny like that. I loved Mother in the same way" (8–9). Hencher proceeds to describe in grotesque and intimate detail his mother's face as she goes through the process of eating a piece of meat. He studies the Bankses in a similar way, with sticky attention, even as they sleep in their bed. But he knows he can see them more clearly, get closest to them, in their absence, and so encourages them to go on a picnic, thereby getting them out of the house, with the knowledge that this will add excitement to his life as well as theirs. While Michael and Margaret are gone, he prowls through the flat, draws red circles around his eyes with Margaret's lipstick, uses their bed. "But," he tells us, "red circles, giving your land-lord's bed a try, keeping his flat to yourself for a day—a man must take possession of a place if it is to be a home for the waiting out of dreams" (27). Hencher takes possession of this place, realizes his dreams, by turning what seems to be long close scrutiny on himself. The curiously suggestive act of circling his eyes with Margaret's lipstick, however, symbolically transforms his gaze, though in vague, uncertain ways. In one sense, his gaze becomes that which is desired by the "mouth" which marks him. At the same time, his vision is appropriated by this mark of the Other, so that the gaze he turns on himself speaks the Other's fascination. Such symbolically wishful merging with Margaret, and with both Michael and Margaret when he uses their bed, reveals "the waiting out of dreams" as the disappearance of love's long close scrutiny in the spectral and specular realm of fantasy.

The gaze of fantasy, not the long close scrutiny, mediates Michael's relations with Sybilline, for he uses her as a mirror in which to see himself as the exciting, virile man he dreams of being. Yet, still only in the middle of his orgiastic night, as their lovemaking comes to an end, "[a]s he turned to face his Sybilline, began on hands and knees the several awkward motions it took to reach her, he knew remorse for the empty face of himself once more. . . . No more now, he was fast returning to the old man" (143). Sybilline provides Michael with the illusion of a self, but as his time with her draws to a close and the infinity of fantasy disintegrates in his fatigue, he feels the heavy, deadening weight of his old life. Furthermore, his idea that this woman is *his* Sybilline is ironically destroyed.

After making love to the widow in whose house Larry's gang is partying, and after making love to Annie, the neighbor he has lusted after and who appears out of nowhere, as if his every dream will be fulfilled, Michael goes downstairs where the party is going on. He sees Syb on Larry's arm, and sees a "bruise, a fresh nasty bruise, beneath Syb's eye" (158). Hawkes has said that Michael "realizes, through one little bruise on Sybilline's cheek which is emblematic of a kind of power and joy, reciprocity, that Sybilline is Larry's, whether he has reasserted his ownership or not. Michael Banks is aware of that, it would seem to me, so he has to suffer both a kind of loss of love and sexuality with all these women. . . . He's being excluded because that's the state of affairs: he never was included" (Santore and Pocalyko 93). The bruise beneath Syb's eye recalls the marks Hencher makes beneath his own eyes as he imagines himself taking possession of a place. Syb's bruise represents some unseen acting out of Larry's power, and thus his possession of her, which further represents a more far-reaching ability to control the world, particularly compared to Hencher's more modest influence in the Banks's lives. While both Hencher and Larry have access to fantasies or power that assert ownership, Michael experiences the living out of fantasies that repeatedly demonstrate his powerlessness and inability to possess that which he desires. Gazing at Sybilline in bed he perceives her as continually self-renewing, able to make "her body look tight and childish as if she had never been possessed by him" (142). This quality constitutes her as a worthy object for fantasy, but also indicates the irresolvable contradictions in Michael's dream of power. Not only can he not possess the

Other, he cannot even possess himself, for he is a mere pawn in other people's games. Seeing the bruise is Michael's rare moment of sight that is insight.

The reciprocity involved in Syb's taking Larry's punches is certainly a debased joy, the reciprocity that of victim and victimizer, the victim's only power residing in the fact that she also can be a victimizer—of someone like, say, Michael Banks. For it becomes apparent that Syb's interest is not in Michael but in carrying out Larry's plan by distracting Michael. Larry hits Sybilline because she is his, and, according to Hawkes, as part of a sexual experience:

When Larry hits Sybilline, as I see it, he's merely maintaining participation in what's going on with Michael and the women. He's part of the women, too. They *love* him. He has some feeling for them. What it is I don't know, but I know that he's proud, at peace, quite serene, perfectly happy to accept a kind of adulation that strips him down to his shirt, then a bullet-proof vest, until you get to a kind of naked statue. He's simply accepting adoration. The blow on the cheek is no "You slut." He's God. (Santore, Pocalyko 93)

Larry embodies the other characters' projections of omnipotence, and so they worship him. This man who puts his mark on others is himself a sort of sign, a pillar of unassailable strength. Alan Trachtenberg describes Larry as "a steel phallus in his bullet-proof vest and gunbelt . . . a complete image of the man who can live in and control the nightmare" (7). Always erect and meticulously groomed, able to drink himself into "a stupor of civility and strength," a "state of brutal calm" (157), Larry accepts the importuning of Little Dora, the gang's mannish woman, who tears his shirt, demanding that he display his body, calling him "you full-of-grace" (157). When he gives his henchman Cowles an order, "Cowles did as he was told" (85), a line that echoes the obedience to Zizendorf's orders at the end of *The Cannibal.* He cares for Sparrow, the jockey, by shooting him up with morphine to relieve the pain of legs that had been "ground beneath the treads of an armored vehicle" during the war: "Larry, who had been the first to carry him the night he screamed. . . . Larry, who had greased his hair even in battle, was still compassionate" (85, 86). Such cruelty and compassion characterize him as an archetypal Hawkesian author figure. But the godlike, phallic authority he wields as the controller of dreams in the novel proves to be illusory, and finally he is himself defeated.

Larry is defeated by, of all people, Michael Banks. For, as weak and susceptible as Banks is, there is something in him that eludes control, just as control eludes him. Banks overturns the nightmare by achieving detachment from himself and believing, for a moment, in the clarity of his vision. Notably, the beginning of his acquiring of his dream occurs in a literal fog that reflects Michael's clouded perceptions of the violent motives and the possible ramification of realizing his fantasies: "where to discover everything he dreamed of except in a fog. And, thinking of slippery corners, skin suddenly bruised, grappling hooks going blindingly through the water: where to lose it all if not in the same white fog" (45). Firmly although ignorantly entrenched in the mysterious operations of Larry's gang, Michael is present when Larry has Cowles killed in the fog of the steam baths, a place for pleasuring the body where "activity was nothing more than a turning over or a writhing" (112). Michael, aware of Cowles's comparatively decent behavior toward him, actually questions Larry: "What did you kill him for? . . . Whatever for?" (118). He receives no answer, however, and the incident recedes from his consciousness in the further opportunities for pleasuring his body that Larry provides. Yet it is another murder—Hencher's—at the beginning of Michael's adventure that triggers his awareness of the irreversibility of the dream upon which he has embarked. Hencher is trampled under Rock Castle's hooves, and although Banks doesn't see this, when he does discover the body in Rock Castle's stall he knows that "for himself there will be no cod or beef at six, no kissing her at six, no going home—not with Hencher kicked to death by the horse" (67). This is a moment of clarity and realization of ultimacy that he is not to have again until near the end.

It takes another death after Cowles's to signal for Michael not just the mercilessness but the horror embedded in his dream, and thus to signal the dream's death. Not long after he sees the bruised Syb on Larry's arm, the murder of Monica, the young girl shot by the constable, sends Banks running into the street: "He stopped—arms flung wide—then ran at the constable. . . . Because he recognized the child—she had always been coming over a bridge for him—and because now there was smoke still circling out of the belly, smoke and a little blood, and she lay with one knee raised, with palms turned up" (161). This image of slain innocence helps propel Banks to charge into the middle of the race track later that day to stop Rock Castle and the entire crooked horse race. Running, "[h]e heard his heart—far away a child seemed to be beating it down the center of a street in the End—heard the sound of air being sucked beneath the spot where the constable had landed two heavy blows, and his feet were falling upon the same loose earth so recently struck by iron" (169). Michael's imaginative, empathetic leap suddenly grants him the clarity of vision to see the race from a detached perspective that cuts to the artifice and insanity of the Golden Bowl: "It was a park, a lovely picture of a park with a mad crowd down one edge and thirteen horses whirling round" (169).

Michael's ability to recognize the exploitation of innocence wrought by the cruel underside of the world of which he had dreamed renders him disenchanted, seemingly free of the spell cast on him by his own uncritical pursuit of his fantasies of glamour and power. As he runs to the middle of the race track, he consciously assumes the course of history, throwing himself into the world of consequences and endings: "The green, the suspended time was gone" (170). For when Michael's adventure began, as he and Hencher hauled the stolen Rock Castle off his barge, suddenly "it was not Wednesday at all, only a time slipped off its cycle with hours and darkness never to be accounted for" (49). This sense of the suspension of time stays with Michael, even when it turns sinister. Threatened with pellet bombs by three anonymous men who work numbers at the race track, Michael both hides and tries to recover, sitting on a "piece of battered lavatory equipment for an endless time" (95).

Michael's rush to stop Rock Castle in time, seen as a deliberate act of consciousness, finally grants him the power that had eluded him throughout his sought-after adventure. Standing on the track before the oncoming horses, he experiences a moment of clarity: "he had the view that a photographer might have except that there was no camera, no truck's tailgate to stand upon. Only the virgin man-made stretch of track and at one end the horses bunching in fateful heat and at the other end himself—small, yet beyond elimination, whose single presence purported a toppling of the day, a violation of that scene at Aldington, wreckage to horse and little crouching men" (170). The image of Michael Banks as a cameraless photographer violating a scene will be parodied in *Whistlejacket*, when Michael, the photographer-narrator of the novel, tells us that the artist violates ordinary ways of seeing and perceiving. Banks has indeed transgressed his own code of cowardice by flouting the will of Larry and his gang, and by doing this at the sacrifice of himself. He has had a vision, he has exerted his will and has affected the fates involved in his small world, and so his destructive act seems, in Hawkesian terms, paradoxically—and perversely—creative. Yet the work of the artist, for Hawkes, does not rest in violating ordinary ways of seeing, but rather involves the violation of conventional morality; the artist becomes "an outcast, an outsider" in order "to create something which to him is a thing of beauty, as well as knowledge and moral meaning" (LeClair 27), and it is in this light that the absurdity of Banks's reckless act can be seen.

While many critics have interpreted Banks's act as a moral triumph that redeems the violence, particularly to Margaret, that the living out of Banks's dream has caused, Marcus Klein sees it as an example, at work in all of Hawkes's novels, of "vivid, vital, instinctual" forces being finally contained by deathly stasis:

Hawkes has said that after writing the novel he saw something redemptive in the death of Banks. With arms extended Christ-like, Banks places himself before the rushing beast. But one may ask just what it is that is redeemed. By his death Banks stops a crooked horse race, and that is a triumph for honest horse-races. This horse is, however, not just a potential winner but the horse of Banks's dreams, an image of sexual prowess, money, violence, glamour and power. In his dying, Banks frustrates this rich appetancy, rather than crooked horseracing. And at the same time because the character Larry, the head of the gang of modest criminals, has planned to make his fortune from this horse and then retire to his dream of lime trees, Banks's martyrdom is doubly frustrating. That which is redeemed is merely the landscape of "Dreary Station" with which the novel begins. ("Hawkes in Love," 74)

The landscape of Dreary Station includes the limitations imposed by conventional morality; Banks's transgressive pursuit of his dream fails to become an imaginative reenvisioning of human possibilities. His moment of clarity, creative insofar as it is an empathetic, imaginative leap, still partakes largely of fear and ends only in destruction. Finally, however, his failure to transfigure the desolation of his life through the pursuit of his dream rests in the paradoxes of the dream itself, for the dream is at once marvelous and tawdry, innocent and cruel, deeply imagined and ignorantly borrowed.

Banks rejects the role of outsider that Hawkes sees as so essential for the imagination's violation of surface reality, instead aggressively adopting some abstract notion of justice that tells him "he must put a stop to it" (169), the pronoun referring loosely to all those forces, including criminals' horses, that overrun order in the world. His act of greatest self-assertion is also the erasure of his self, the fading of individuality into a type: "He was running in final stride . . . the pace so fast that it ceases to be motion, but at its peak becomes the long downhill deathless gliding of a dream until the arms are out, the head thrown back, and the runner is falling as he was falling and waving his arm at Rock Castle's onrushing silver shape, at Rock Castle who was about to run him down and fall" (171). In the language of this passage, the running Banks becomes merely simultaneous with the figure of a generic defeated runner, running against the defeated dream.

Yet individuality is problematic throughout the novel. While the desire for uniqueness is part of Banks's dream, his responses to the exciting world for which he had longed reveal his inability to escape preestablished fantasies and thus have unencumbered perceptions of his experience. Sybilline opens him to exercising his imagination, but at the same time his imagination remains dependent on that with which he is already familiar: "In his arms she was like the women he had thought of coming out of comfort rooms" (121); "her legs, friendly and white and long, were the legs he had seen bare in the undergarment ads" (145). Margaret displays a similar reliance on cliché. She answers Michael's call to come to Aldington without thinking, because she believes it her role: "A wife would always ride through the night if she were bidden. Would ride through rainstorm, villages like Wimble, through woodland all night long" (70). She responds to the unusual circumstances of her captivity by the gang and their refusal to let her see her husband like someone who has read too many bad stories and seen too many bad movies: "Do what you want with me," she exclaims, "But leave Michael alone" (85). Such responses are part of the novel's elaboration of the paradox of fantasies that are fed by, and thus tied to, the cultural constriction they are meant to exceed.

Cut loose from her life in Dreary Station, Margaret has no strength of personality on which to rely in the absence of her familiar moorings. Dressed in a hospital gown by Little Dora, she is stripped of her identity: "Thick had burned her things, identification card and all" (84). The erasure of identity, in fact, characterizes what is most promising and most sinister about the workings of the Banks's dreams. Larry sends Thick and Sparrow to the Banks's flat at Dreary Station to destroy and remove all of their possessions: "Bare walls, bare floors, four empty rooms containing no scrap of paper . . . no handwriting specimen by which the identity of the former occupants could be known" (102). Because Michael and Margaret have lead routine, unilluminated lives, the destruction of the signs of those lives can represent the shedding of their conventional encumbrances to mark the beginning of a freer, more imaginative second chance, at least for Michael. Yet the living out of their dreams and nightmares, rather than proving to be the accession to some true identity, reveals instead individuality lost to typicality. Held hostage, beaten, and tied to a bed, Margaret hears Monica awake "with her nightmares," and she takes "them to be her own bad dreams, as if in soothing the child she could soothe herself" (126). Moreover, the child's nightmares *are* Margaret's nightmares in this world in which not only the boundaries between dream and reality have collapsed, but the individual's dreams and nightmares are in strange confluence with those of others, including those of the people who will make them happen.

## III

The flowering of the desires structuring his dream of a horse proves to be Banks's entrance to plot. The "writer" in this novel, Sidney Slyter, pursues plot tenaciously in his persistent columns that preface every chapter (it is this writing that persists, while Banks's is obliterated). "[A] beautiful afternoon, a lovely crowd, a taste of bitters, and light returning to the faces of heroic stone" his first column declaims; "one day there will be amusements everywhere, good fun for our mortality, and you'll whistle and flick your cigarette into an old crater's lip and with your young woman go off to a fancy flutter at the races" (3). Slyter's last column inscribes the fulfillment of his prophecy, repeating the essentials of his first column but now placing the particulars of Michael Banks into a linguistic realization of Slyter's version of collective fantasy: "He has whistled; he has flicked his cigarette away; alone amidst women he has gone off to a fancy flutter at the races" (163). Banks's adventure is here figured as no more than the necessary eventuality of life at the race course. Slyter further conflates events into their dependence on his words; he backs up his prediction of amusements and good fun for our mortality by saying, "For Sidney Slyter was recognized last night," and the old man who recognized him exclaimed that Slyter will write about the horses again. Yet for all his self-proclaimed omniscience, his sleuthing, his guesses, his pompous "And Sidney Slyter says: my prognostications are always right" (80), Slyter must admit that he doesn't understand the circumstances of Michael Banks's involvement with Rock Castle: "Sidney Slyter doesn't know. . . . Nonetheless, Sidney Slyter will report the running of the Golden Bowl for you" (140). In his effort to report, he never gets the plot quite right, and doesn't even approach the discernment of the particular desires and machinations that generated the mystery he perceives. Slyter's obsession with plot, that element of fiction which Hawkes claims to be of least interest to him in itself, is redeemed only by the paradoxical excesses of Slyter's language: "His language is pretty good. After all, it's a version of mine," says Hawkes. "He's parodying my own language, I guess, as well as journalism, and he's endowed with a poetic voice." He does, after all, produce one of the novel's most telling and richly poetic statements near the close of the novel: "for there is no pathetic fun or mournful frolic like our desire, the consummation of the sparrow's wings. . . ." (163). "He has it both ways," Hawkes says, "But yes, some of his language reveals his despicableness" (Kuehl 176–177).

Slyter's attempt to recover the rationale of the mysterious events played out at the Golden Bowl has its parallel in the efforts of the detectives from Scotland Yard who, in the last chapter, discover Hencher's body and will attempt to "uncover the particulars of this crime" (175). According to Hawkes,

The detectives represent law and order, or the baffled and banal mind at large. Specifically, and along with Sidney Slyter, they may be seen as images of the absurd and lonely author himself. Even the author is not exempt from judgment in my fiction. But at least the detectives, in trying to learn what the reader has presumably learned already (and it's clear, I think, that these obtuse men from Scotland Yard will never solve the "crime"), are attempting to complete the cycle of mysterious experience. At least they, like ourselves, will go on hunting for clues. (Enck 155)

Michael Banks, the lynchpin of the plot, can interpret the events of which he is a part no better than Slyter or the detectives. The description of his adventure as "a time slipped off its cycle with hours and darkness never to be accounted for" (49) suggests both the freedom from having to explain one's actions and the inexplicability of events themselves. The debris of bodies with which the novel's destructive events end echoes the wreckage of war, "an iron fleet half-sunk in mud," which can be seen from the deck of the pleasure boat where Banks and Hencher meet in preparation for the arrival of Rock Castle: "All won, all lost, all over, and for half a crown they could have it now, this sea wreck and abandon and breeze of the ocean surrounding them" (44). But of course the violence, cruelty, excess, and loss signified by war cannot be had by taking in the sight of torpedo tubes and rusting hulls. And the violent events at Aldington and Dreary Station cannot be understood by taking in the evidence of dead bodies and an empty flat. Such excess and loss have their only possibility of recovery and of transformation in language, in the imagination's interplay with the text.

*The Lime Twig* parodies (as many critics have noted) the mystery thriller; it is a mystery that cannot be solved, a thriller that questions the idea of a thrill. In a mockery of plot, Slyter's plot-hungry columns often reveal the "surprise" events of the chapter that follows. Hawkes undermines the predictability and the logic of plot to create a text dependent on the associations of image and the resonance of language to explore the exigencies of fantasy and desire. He describes his aesthetic: "The constructed vision, the excitement of the undersea life of the inner man, a language appropriate to the delicate malicious knowledge of us all as poor, forked, corruptible, the feeling of pleasure and pain that comes when something pure and contemptible lodges in the imagination—I believe in the 'singular and terrible attraction' of all this" ("Notes on *The Wild Goose Chase*"). Michael Banks's dream of a horse, the image that embodies a pure and contemptible chain of fantasies, specifically signifies, for Hawkes, the supreme and talismanic quality of language. In a 1973 interview, he reads from *The Lime Twig*'s genealogy of Rock Castle:

[ "Why, it's the evolution of his bloody name, that's what it is. Just the evolution of a name—Apprentice out of Lithograph by Cobbler, Emperor's Hand by Apprentice out of Hand Maiden by Lord of the Land, Draftsman by Emperor's Hand out of Shallow Draft by Amulet, Castle Churl by Draftsman out of Likely Castle by Cold Masonry, Rock Castle by Castle Churl out of Words on Rock by Plebian—and what's this name if not the very evolution of his life?" ] Well, it's certainly taking design and heraldic stuff and writing and Britannia and putting them all together. . . . "Castle," "Cold Masonry," "Draftsman"—drafting, building, both have to do with creating; the metaphor seems to be about building, creating, writing this low life, low life in a high kingdom. "Castle Churl out of Words on Rock." I think it's the "Words on Rock" that's really important. The "Words on Rock" *are* the book. (Santore and Pocalyko 107–108)

In this figuration, the book is authored by godly authority, and words are ancient and lasting. But the idea of the lineage also grants words the capacity for endless transformation, and, perhaps most significant here, endless fascination, such that the name of the horse and the line of names from which he springs inspires desires that propel the characters, and the text, more so than any plot.

Hencher describes Rock Castle as ancient, "an ancient horse and he's bloody well run beyond memory itself" (39). Rock Castle's resurgence represents the persistence of the past as the bodying forth of incantatory names, his lineage intoned by Hencher (38) and repeated by Banks (49) and Slyter (124). Hencher is appropriate as the first pronouncer of the lineage, for he bears the weight of history in the novel. At the end of his prologue he describes his life with the Bankses, saying, "I stand whispering our history before that door" (28); Hawkes locates the responsibility for history's transmission in Hencher:

[I]t seemed to me that the drab reality of contemporary England was a direct product of the war, and that Michael and Margaret were in a sense the innocent spawn of the war. However, since Michael and Margaret were mere children during the war, incapable even of recalling the bombing of London, the problem became one of dramatizing the past, of relating wartime England to post-war England, of providing a kind of historical consciousness for characters who had none of their own. Hencher served this function. He became the carrier of Michael and Margaret's past as well as of their future; I thought of him as the seedbed of their pathetic lives. (Enck 151)

Hencher's section is itself the pre-history of the novel; the killing of Hencher a third of the way through the novel foregrounds the textual quality of the history he carries. The images and obsessions contained in his narrative leak into the rest of the text, so that the frustrated desires of the bombed-out, ruined world from which he emerges persist in the verbal web of the present.

It is the trap of words and images as much as the schemes of Larry's gang that limes the characters, for the vertigo of building the rhetoric of an underworld mystery, or the lure of a horse named Rock Castle, descended from the likes of Castle Churl and Words on Rock, and the enticements of a woman beautiful as those in advertisements and men who are strong and brutal exert a fascination potentially both deadly and redeeming. The imaginative redemption possible in fantasy reveals itself in such moments as when Banks, dancing with Sybilline, "remembered not the Baths, the Damps, poor wretched Cowles, nor the rooms in Dreary Station, but a love note he had written at the age of twelve when the city was on fire" (121). The rekindling of imaginative energy relives a creative moment of "poetry" rising out of the flames of mass destruction; *The Lime Twig*, like all of Hawkes's novels, makes creation and destruction coterminous. The form the twelve-year-old Banks gave to his feelings manifests the liberation of his imagination; his recalling it demonstrates his current awakening as well as the persistence of language, but it also suggests his inability to live in the present moment and the incarcerating prism of the past. The "form" of Rock Castle, or of any of the novel's other fantasized images, contains a similar paradox. Upon listing Rock Castle's lineage, Slyter writes: "Rigid; fixed; a prison of heritage in the victorious form; the gray shape that forever rages out round the ring of painted horses with the band music piping and clacking; indomitable" (124). Every shape, every fixed form of language or image in the novel, harbors the potential to rage out, victorious over the clacking artifice of a gray and sordid world, and harbors the potential to imprison the individual in the rigidity of cultural heritage and of the impingements of the past.

As events culminate in the Golden Bowl, the crowd is under a sun "burst all out of shape" (164), a fitting image of the excessive desires that, for Michael Banks, have broken the bounds of his control. And the attempts of the author figures to recuperate excess for the demands of their designs, whether of pulling off a fixed horse race or reconstructing a mysterious plot, have failed. Larry disappears, hurrying off into a car, and Slyter's column doesn't appear at the beginning of the last chapter. The novel devolves upon Banks's final act, an attempt to overtake control that is its own defeat, the sacrificial imagery of which leaves the reader to interpret it as symbolically redemptive. But his act brings an end to the dream, and thus brings an end to the multiple significations involved in dreams or fantasies, in symbols and representations. We are left with the world of evidence and detectives, of empirical facts and impenetrable phenomena.

And we are left with the world of the text, in which the inscribing of phenomena by imaginative language puts to the test the paradoxes of creation and representation. The reader experiences imaginative freedom and shackling as he or she witnesses the generative and destructive attempts of the characters and the text to make fantasy real. William Hencher's direct address to the reader, his question, "Have you ever let lodgings in the winter?" which begins the series of question he asks in a maneuver for our identification and inclusion in this lonely and violently conflicted world, engages the reader in the imaginative projections celebrated and critiqued throughout the novel. Sitting in the bomber miraculously crashed in a Dreary Station laundry court, Hencher settles the pilot's helmet securely on his head: " 'How's the fit, old girl?' I whispered. 'A pretty good fit, old girl?' And I turned my head as far to the right as I was able, so that she might see how I—William Hencher—looked with my bloody coronet in place at last" (23). The "old girl" is his mother and the plane's painted woman, but, of course, neither can see him. Instead, it is his own imagination seeing itself in the self-constructed mirror of his fantasy; and it is the reader seeing his or her own imagination in the designs of language that mirror our own involvement in fantasy and the construction of meaning.

# Chapter 3
# Writing the Self: *Second Skin,* the Second Sex, and the Second Take

The world washed in his imagination,
The world was a shore, whether sound or form
Or light, the relic of farewells
                        —Wallace Stevens,
                    "The Man with the Blue Guitar"

Love is, in short, the soul's *sight* for invisible things.
                    —Julia Kristeva, *Tales of Love*

The unseen vision is not to be improved upon.
                    —John Hawkes, *Travesty*

**I**

*Second Skin* (1964) is the first Hawkes novel to have a psychologically fleshed-out narrator, the obsessions of whom establish the pattern of concerns of the paternalistic and conflicted first-person narrators in Hawkes's subsequent novels. It is also, according to Hawkes, the first novel in which he lets innocence win out (Ziegler 173). The "triumph" of innocence integrally relates to the development of psychology. Whereas in the earlier novels the desire of the author figures to transcend material reality embodies all the violence and deathliness that characterize that reality, thus rendering the external landscape the perfect expression of their selves, in *Second Skin* the narrator's desire for transcendence propels a self-conscious, self-reflexive effort to overcome the victimizing violence and deathliness of the world through maintaining his vision of life-affirming, innocent love. Yet, characteristically for Hawkes, this apparent dichotomy between self and world collapses.

While Skipper, the narrator of *Second Skin,* desires and claims innocence, his assertion of his will and vision through language harbors self-
deluding, coercive, and destructive possibilities. By making Skipper the
sole speaker of the novel and by making this speaker recount, create, and
reflect upon both his past and his present, Hawkes establishes a narrative
perspective that movingly presents the artful imagination as the self's
only means of survival while at the same time encouraging the reader to
ask at what cost, and to whom.

The varieties of authorial power lodged in the narrators and author
figures of *The Lime Twig* now all find expression in the complexities of a
single voice that acknowledges itself as the writer of a narrative. Moreover, this authorial voice inscribes itself in specifically gendered terms
and manifests its primary concern as the male self's relation to the Other
that is Woman; at the same time, Skipper denies his sexual interests and
displaces his erotic energies into the figures and images of his language.
*Second Skin* recasts the displacement of sexuality into images of death and
acts of violence that characterize the earlier novels specifically through
Skipper's explicit rejection of death and affirmation of love. But the fact
that Skipper's narration reveals his repeated assertions of an ideal as being deadly and the figure of a woman as bearing the weight of his idealizations makes the inscription of the innocent and powerful imagination
in *Second Skin* a striking unfolding of the narrative processes by which
*creativity* wins out.

Skipper, a fifty-nine-year-old ex-naval lieutenant, tells his story, writes
his "naked history," in order to re-create the world that has taken away
nearly everyone he loves and that has victimized him in innumerable
ways, large and small, a world of predatory evil and death that culmi-
nated in the suicide of his daughter, Cassandra, on a dark, northern
"gentle island." His re-creation redeems this forsaken world by overlaying it with the generative, idyllic life he presently leads on his "wandering
island" where he is an artificial inseminator of cows. The benign figures
of this southern world replace the threatening ones of the northern.

This would seem to be a novel of the triumph of the imagination: Skipper overcomes death and evil by telling a story of renewal, by seeking out
a new beginning as the happy ending to his life story and strategically
juxtaposing the details of this second life of love and peace to the horrific
or unpleasant elements of his first life in order to effect a redemptive
transformation of his whole life. Before he tells his story, however, Skipper tells who he is; he is, he says, "a man of love" (1). This man who
introduces himself as a lover whose love includes his wife and child and
extends to such things as parasols and needlepoint, but is mostly for himself, in the end portrays himself as one who is loved, one whom people

"strange or familiar, young or old" (205) wait to kiss in the dark. But this, after all, is not much of a transformation: first and last, Skipper is the object of love.

Skipper indicates the inherent stasis of his position on the second page of his narrative: "Perhaps my father thought that by shooting off the top of his head he would force me to undergo some sort of transformation. But poor man, he forgot my capacity to love" (2). The constancy Skipper attributes to himself circumscribes the transformative aims of his narrative project. But the love that Skipper implies allowed him to triumph in creating an affirmative world perhaps indeed does best define him, as well as the world he creates: this narcissistic lover inscribes a history that is his "evocation through a golden glass" (49), a creation of a new world that reflects rather than opposes the old one, and a fiction that reflects the process of its own authoring. Lover of his own "harmless and sanguine self," Skipper is also a lover of the language that calls this self into existence. And more than that, he is the lover of his daughter, the woman he would have be the perfect mirror of his desire, the tantalizing image that he creates but cannot possess, the image that reflects his fears and idealizations, the erotic center who inspires the excess of his fancy. Against her image, and, more broadly, the image of Woman, he erects the artifice that reflects his longing for innocence and power. What he calls his "naked history" is his narrative of his failure to win Cassandra's love and to save her from a cruel world; the mirror image of this history, what he calls his present triumph, is his portrayal of his successful institution of love in a life of naked innocence with Catalina Kate. His love-become-text inscribes the representation of a world reversed; the dynamics of representation that constitute his relation to Woman integrally entwine with the creative aims of his narrative project.[1]

Skipper sets forth the significant factors of his story in his brief introductory chapter. After defining himself as a lover, suggesting mythical identities for himself, and, in this chapter titled "Naming Names," naming the principle actors in his story, he suggests two possibilities for the "true subject" of his narrative:

In all likelihood my true subject may prove to be simply the wind . . . simply that wind to which my heart and also my skin have always been especially sensitive. Or it may prove to be the stark elongated brutal silhouette of a ship standing suddenly on the horizon of the mind and, all at once, making me inexplicably afraid—perhaps because it is so far off that not one detail reaches the eye, nothing of name, passengers, crew, not even smoke from the stack, so that only the ugly span of pointed iron, which ought to be powerless but moves nonetheless and is charged with all the mystery and inhuman distance of the compass, exists to incite this terrible fear and longing in a man such as myself. But for now the wind trails off my fingers, the ship fades. Because I suppose that names must precede these solid worlds of my passionate time and place and action. (3–4)

The passage contains a play of the visible and invisible, the tangible and intangible; it contains the novel's key images (or non-images) of wind, skin, ship, and language. The image of the ship fades and the non-image of the wind trails off the fingers to leave the writing hand to the naming or the language that will evoke Skipper's world. The sensitive skin provides one of the major metaphors of the novel, the contrary characteristics of the changing wind demonstrate one of the major rhetorical strategies of the novel, and the ship embodies the irresolvable paradoxes encountered by the writing self.

First, the wind. Skipper's hymn to it figures it as a medium of opposites and of transformation. Later in the text he refers to the wind on his wandering island as "this bundle of invisible snakes" which

seems to heap the shoulders with an armlike weight, to coil about my naked legs and pulse and cool and caress the flesh with an unpredictable weight and consistency, tension, of its own. These snakes that fly in the wind are as large around as tree trunks but pliant as the serpents that crowd my dreams. So the wind nests itself and bundles itself across this island, buffets the body with wedges of invisible but still sensual configurations. It drives, drives even when it drops down, fades, dies, it continues its gentle rubbing against the skin. (46)

Alan Singer writes that while this description of the wind on the wandering island "seems intended to provoke an explicit contrast with the wind that lashes Miranda's perversely named 'gentle island' in the next episode of the novel," the language itself frustrates this purpose. Instead of a logic of opposition, there is a dispersal of sense:

The imagistic deployment of this passage, like the wind it apostrophizes, scatters contextual parameters and alters the relevant patterns of relatedness. While the reptilian figure weaves through the passage, restating itself as if to confirm a single contextual imperative, each circuitous restatement engenders new possibilities that do not dispose themselves along the same logical/semantic axis of the fiction. . . . Fittingly, this series of displacements climaxes with a discharge of sexual connotations that reflect the wind's own verbal genesis. (96)

The wind is the occasion for its own description; it exists and does not exist in language.

Singer's insight about the "dispersal of significations" (98) in Hawkes's prose finds related expression in Mary F. Robertson's essay "The 'Crisis in Comedy' as a Problem of the Sign: The Example of Hawkes's *Second Skin*." In light of this essay, Skipper's evocation of the wind on the wandering island can be seen as symptomatic of a style that continually yokes contrarieties in even the smallest semantic units, thereby generating undecidability; for example, Robertson points to Skipper's describing himself as the "aggressive personification of serenity," a "tiger" who walks with the "locomotion of peace itself," and who is remarked on with "admiration or maliciousness" (434). Robertson sees this pattern as illustrative of Hawkes's

ability to weave a story almost entirely out of elements which bear . . . "supplemental" relation to one another. In so doing, he inscribes not a simple inversion of the normal values in symbolic hierarchies—for example, "black and white" . . . but a permanent displacement from the opposition that alters the original question altogether by eroding the oppositional boundary even as he insists it not be abolished. . . . [The] infiltration of one term by its semantic opposite is emphatically not able to be read dialectically. (441)

Even the novel's dominant inscription of opposition, Skipper's effort to make life on the "wandering island" supersede life—and death—on the "gentle island," collapses in the vagueness and ambiguity of the labels, which lack any particular referent and, furthermore, do not suggest oppositeness.

The figure of "the stark elongated brutal silhouette of a ship standing suddenly on the horizon of the mind" which, like the wind, may also possibly be Skipper's true subject, is, in itself, an uncertain image. It makes Skipper not just "afraid," but "inexplicably" so; it is without detail and without name. The ship eludes the substance and qualities that language can grant, which is a frightening and liberating prospect for a man who creates himself by forging the narrative of his life. The vision of this dark, mysterious ship (which also earns the adjective "brutal," a word that signals the traumatic, scarring violence of Skipper's life) may indeed be his true subject, for it—like the wind—presents the challenge to language to call the world into existence. As silhouette, the ship is looming image, but also, paradoxically, invisible, lacking details, a shape on the border of shadow and solidity. While a real, working naval ship figures significantly in Skipper's story as the scene of his crew's mutiny and his rape by Tremlow, the lead mutineer, Skipper's vision of a silhouette of a ship appears only once in the body of his narrative (unlike the wind, which receives much attention). He tells us that one night on his wandering island, "I saw the few lights and long black silhouette of a ship at sea and smiled to myself since apparently our wandering island has become quite invisible. Only a mirage of shimmering water to all the ships at sea, only the thick black spice of night and the irregular whispering of an invisible shore" (109). The spice and whispering echo Skipper's description of the wind, invisible as the island is invisible, gaining substance only in language. But what is interesting here is that Skipper imagines the island's invisibility from the perspective of the ship, which is itself unknowable, beckoning and frustrating articulation. Hawkes has said he believes "that we're all islands—inaccessible, drifting apart, thirsting to be explored, magical" ("Notes on Writing a Novel," 113). Skipper's island is a projection and reflection of the self; so too is the ship. The figure of Skipper seeing the ship not "seeing" the island sets up a complex reflection of the self reflecting on the self in its shimmering imaginative constructs.

In his "Notes on Writing a Novel," Hawkes describes his vision of a ship that "becomes suddenly literal in *Second Skin*" as springing from

> a personal waking dream in which I stand alone at the edge of a straight empty shore at low tide and gaze with both fear and longing at an enormous black derelict or damaged ocean liner that looms in awful silence in knee-deep water about a mile from shore.
>
> In this waking dream I know that I am going to have to walk the entire distance from shore to listing ship. I know that I am going to climb somehow to the tilted deck of the abandoned ship. I know that I must discover its vast world, must pry open some metal door rusted half ajar and enter the ship until I discover what it contains—either its treasure, if childhood hopes prevail, or its emptiness, its floating corpses.
>
> The vision, no matter how personal, is one of potential and desolation. (115)[2]

But while the image of the dark ship embodies the desolation and potential of the self and of the world the self inhabits, "Notes on Writing a Novel" goes further to elaborate on what the emptiness or treasure might depend, intimately associating desolation with the fear and hatred of women. Hawkes examines a passage from his first novel, *Charivari*, to illuminate *Second Skin*. In this passage, Henry Van, a middle-aged man terrified of women and marriage, wanders in a stormy and decrepit world, running away from and searching for Emily, the woman to be his wife. Hawkes quotes the passage as illustrative of his ongoing fictional concerns: "the association of the 'barely remembered woman,' who is idealized for her 'faint flush of youth,' with a vast violent world of death, sexlessness, and misogyny, is in fact the thematic center of all that I've written" (117).

The anguish Skipper suffers over his love for Cassandra is the focal point of *Second Skin*'s central concern with the idea of Woman. The impossibility of realizing his incestuous desire propels Skipper into stultifying overprotectiveness, jealousy, and manifold forms of denial, as well as into the violence of making Cassandra into an icon. His feelings for Cassandra are both cause and effect of an overall deathly denial of sexuality—his own and others'. What we know of his marriage indicates that it was disastrous. His wife, Gertrude, to whom he devotes very little space in his narrative, and seemingly very little time in life, writes him letters that say, "I hope they sink you, Edward. I really do," has "motorcycle orgies" with members of Skipper's crew (130–131), and wants "to die in a cheap motel surrounded by unmarried couples" (14). He misses her burial because he is trying to attach a borrowed sword to himself. But without yet launching into an analysis of Skipper's relation to Cassandra, as well as to Miranda, Catalina Kate, and assorted other women he encounters, we can see the significance of the feminine in the space Skipper devotes in his introductory chapter (nearly four out of nine pages) to the description of his mother. Here, Skipper's tendency to deny and to reify, as well as his absorption with the invisible or the unseen, make themselves manifest.

After having listed the names, laden with literary resonances, of the principle players in his story—Cassandra, Miranda, Fernandez, Gertrude—and after having added the names of other literary and mythical figures to reflect on his history and fate, Skipper arrives at his "mother's prosaic name of Mildred" (5). This name that lacks the accretion of borrowed meanings lends his mother something of the character of a blank slate, to be written on by the son who imagines her according to the dictates of his need. Skipper sees her "with most of her features indistinct" and has "few visual memories of her" (5–6); in these few memories her face is usually hidden by a broad-brimmed hat. She was "the woman who more and more grew to resemble a gifted angel in a dreamer's cemetery" (67)—and there is no bigger dreamer than Skipper. His most vivid memory of her is not a memory of her at all, but rather a memory of a vision he had of her after she had vanished and died. In this vision, she emerges from a large white house, and "her lovely smile . . . is either innocent or blind. Then she is moving, skin and veils and featureless face—except for the smile—reflecting the peach and rose color of the filtered sun" (8). She gets into an elaborate car driven by a dramatically dressed man wearing goggles, and she rides away, "raising a soft white arm as if to wave" (9), a lovely bride whose groom is death. The veil Skipper's imagination throws over his mother hides the woman he can never know; the veil over the mother disguises death. Comparing his experience of the disappearance of his mother and the suicide of his father, Skipper says that he "knew that my father had begun my knowledge of death as a lurid truth but that my mother had extended it toward the promise of mystery" (8). The invisibility of his mother's death—and of his mother, for that matter—opens up the realm of the imagination, the transcendence of death.[3]

In his essay on *Second Skin*, Alan Singer attacks the too simplistic structuration, common to critical dissection of this novel, that uses Skipper's analysis of the death of his parents to rest in the idea that "the novel proposes an exchange of the fatalistic values of reality (character) for the redemptive values of imagination (author)" (90–91). Singer comments that "the disjunctive temporality of Skipper's narrative, along with his seeming inability to sustain a declarative statement that does not open syntactically upon a multiplicity of fresh possibilities, does not make this text conducive to a binary analysis whereby each meaning only reflects its dialectical partner" (91). The dichotomy between "truth and mystery, reality and imagination" does not hold up (90). Indeed, the failure of dichotomization reveals itself in Skipper's description of the two deaths. His relation of these deaths illustrates their failure to yield up a fruitful opposition between imagination and art on the one hand, and violent, sordid reality on the other. For while the mystery of his mother's departure allows, or even calls for imaginative replacement, the death of his father (who, as a mortician, was something of an artist of death) enacted an intertwining of art and death. Skipper plays Brahms on his cello, trying to forestall his father's carefully orchestrated suicide, but with a word his father stops Skipper, bow in midair, and shoots himself. Art, then, merely postpones or disguises or ignores the inevitable death, but, nonetheless, the scene is saturated with the music of the cello.

It is the sound of the gunshot and of this music that pervades the father's death and cannot be separated from it, in contrast to the silence that marks Skipper's mother's passing on (euphemism best describes this death, which takes place only in the imagination and language). The death of Mildred occurs while she is absent to Skipper, after having silently taken her leave of him, and it is this silence that most strongly characterized her for Skipper. After the suicide of her husband she deafened herself with candle wax to silence the echo of his gunshot, and Skipper tells us, "I have no recollection of her voice—some short time after my father's decision in the lavatory she ceased to talk, became permanently mute—and my few visual memories of her are silent and show her only at a great distance off" (5–6). Her silence allows Skipper's efforts to fill the silence with the music of his elaborate language, but the thrust of his art, of his narrative, is to "explode with a concluding flourish" and to arrive at "the still voice," the novel's last words. He will arrive at the silence that precedes his mother's death and that follows his father's. Skipper, then, uses language to absorb or appropriate what he sees as the female or maternal position of silence and invisibility at the same time that he fathers the verbal excess of this text, which so heavily focuses on his position as the father of his daughter.

## II

On the cold, dark New England island, Skipper, Cassandra, and Pixie, Cassandra's baby daughter, live in a wind-rocked house with Miranda, the young widow who owns it and whose forthright sensuality and, according to Skipper, malevolence, Skipper fears. A survivor of the suicides of his father and his wife, Skipper claims to spend his time on this island fighting to save Cassandra's life, which for him means protecting her from the attentions of the island toughs who present themselves in the figures of Captain Red and his two sons: Jomo, who has a hook in place of a hand, and Bub, an obnoxious youngster. The adventures on this island come to a close when Skipper, realizing Cassandra is in the lighthouse with Jomo, runs up the lighthouse steps to save her from sexual experience that he is convinced means death, only to find that he is too late, that she has jumped naked to her death on the rocks below. Weeks later, Miranda presents Skipper with a gift-wrapped package which she says contains, in a jar, the fetus Cassandra was carrying and that provoked her to commit suicide. Skipper writes of these disastrous events on a sunny, tropical island "unlocated in space and quite out of time" (46) where, instead of being the inadvertent clown and victim of evil plots, he is the godlike leader of amiable and admiring black natives—Big Bertha, Sister Josie, and Catalina Kate—and of Sonny, the black messboy from his navy days with whom he is reunited. As he writes, Catalina Kate is pregnant with a child by Skipper or by Sonny—or perhaps by someone else. Skipper ends his narrative with the birth of Kate's baby and his celebration with Kate, the baby, and Sonny at a candlelit graveyard on the Night of All Saints, an image that asserts his fathering of triumph over death, or at least of peaceful coexistence with it.

The novel's organization around the time in which Skipper attempts to save his daughter and the time of his impending fatherhood foregrounds the paternal—and also maternal—desires of its narrator: Skipper fathers a text, heavily pregnant with possible meanings, that takes place within the space of Catalina Kate's gestation period. The climax of Cassandra's suicide that engenders the narration will be repressed in favor of the climax of birth that will end it:

So in six months and on the Night of All Saints Catalina Kate will bear her child— our child—and I shall complete my history, my evocation through a golden glass, my hymn to the invisible changing serpents of the wind, complete this the confession of my triumph, this my diary of an artificial inseminator. At the very moment Catalina Kate comes due my crabbed handwriting shall explode into a concluding flourish, and I will be satisfied. I will be fifty-nine years old and father to innumerable bright living dreams and vanquished memories. It should be clear that I have triumphed over Cassandra too. (49–50)

The birth of the baby is the death of his writing, but at the same time, his writing is the conversion of death into the rebirth, or refiguration, of himself. He will triumph over the wayward fruit of his loins through the controlled productions of his pen which appropriate the "natural" fertility of Catalina Kate to assert the living quality of his words. On this tropical island where he flourishes, where he and Kate "finish up our little jobs together on a flourish of love" (205), where, newborn child in hand, he and his entourage will visit the cemetery and Skipper "will come to [his] flourishing end at last" (173), the growth, luxuriance, and thriving denoted by "flourishing" are transfigured into the explosive embellishments of his story, the "concluding flourish" of his writing. The paradox of love become writing, and of writing that subsumes and enacts birth and death, encompasses an explosion of other paradoxes in Skipper's text/life: his inscription of memories is the vanquishing of memories; his triumph requires confession, suggesting freedom constrained by its own articulation; and history, which purports to convey facts, is a hymn to the intangible and ineffable. His victory over the "body" of his daughter is the body of his writing, at once substantial and abstract.

The physical or bodily metaphors that intertwine with the textual metaphors of the novel meet most explicitly in the overarching image of "skin." Patrick O'Donnell writes:

One "skin" is that of the novel itself, the protective layer of language that covers the flesh of Skipper's tragic, naked history. Tony Tanner explains the image in another sense as "the vulnerable surface of our 'schizophrenic flesh,' the clothes we cover it with, the points which penetrate it. The idea of a second skin can refer to all the clothes we don according to conventions; or it can suggest the recovery of our original nakedness, and thus innocence." . . . In creating the [wandering] island, Skipper . . . sheds all the second skins of his old life for a new "skin," the exteriorized garment of fantasy and desire woven from the sloughed-off fragments of memory transmuted. (*JH* 92–94)

Tanner's reflections on the association of skin with writing further illuminate the title's appropriateness as the name of a book: "Skipper gives us his 'naked history,' sitting on a tropical island in minimal garb. Yet we should retain the paradox that to give us his 'naked history' he has to stitch together a verbal rendering of the various episodes. All art entails the fabrication of visible (or audible) surfaces, and works of art can be regarded as a form of clothing in which consciousness displays and defines itself" (219). *Second Skin* is indeed a document of Skipper's consciousness, and this consciousness constructs itself largely in response to the opaque and impenetrable surface of his daughter, the "silvery" young woman clothed in the trappings of Skipper's fantasies and whose image will be replaced by the young and yielding "rouge"-colored Kate, who wanders naked or partially clad in Skipper's pastoral kingdom. The importance of Skipper's images of these young women—and of Woman—centrally locates the erotic underpinnings of the thematic and textual significances Skipper invests in "skin." The "covering" his idealizations confer on these women determines the status of his being.

"Skin" thus works as a rich, polyvalent metaphor for psychological obsessions and narrative strategies, and it maintains an intimate connection with language as the "name" of the book. Moreover, if one thinks of a "skin" publication, what comes to mind would probably be a "skin magazine," an appellation given to a form of pornography the commonness of which would seem to place it at a far remove from the aesthetic complexity of *Second Skin*'s "high" art. Yet pornography is a repeated concern of Hawkes's, explicitly introduced early in this novel when Skipper, in Miranda's kitchen, sees "a photography magazine tossed open to a glossy full-page picture of a naked woman" (54). Skipper mentions this only seemingly to ignore it, but four pages later the image invades his fantasy. He takes a walk and has a vision of a woman on the rocks below the lighthouse: "as white as a starfish and inert, naked, caught amongst the boulders, I saw a woman lying midway between myself and the high rock. Vision from the widow's photography magazine. Woman who might have leapt from the lighthouse or rolled up only moments before on the tide" (58). As Skipper knows at the time of his writing, this vision of a naked woman on the rocks foreshadows the death of Cassandra, who leaps naked from the lighthouse onto these same rocks. Skipper, however, never looks at Cassandra's dead body, and does not describe it for us: "I felt that I had already seen her and there was no reason to look down again" (199). His dead daughter is subsumed into the image of an erotic sacrifice. She is the woman of Skipper's vision, "triangulated by the hard cold points of the day" (58), reified, made abstract, her measure taken from the distance of the grieving and relieved, attracted and repelled father and author.

Unlike the sexually obsessed narrators of "the sex triad," the three novels that follow *Second Skin*, Skipper determinedly masks his own sexual obsessions, but his language nonetheless emphatically reveals them. While the fascination with pornography shared by the subsequent narrators is so repressed as to seem absent, Skipper does emphatically share the fascination with language, its power to cloak and to reveal, to remove and to replace, leaving the dense materiality of the verbal web. Language as medium turns to language as subject, a subject with its own erotic dimensions. Alan Wilde, in *Horizons of Assent*, discusses what he calls "the new aestheticism," the emphasis in some postmodern fiction on language and style—which are, finally, self-referential—over engagement with the world: "All postmodern irony, all postmodern art in fact, proclaims itself, in its rejection of the metaphysical and psychological abysses of modernist depth, an art of surfaces" (146). He qualifies the idea of surface through reference to William Gass (whom he associates with "the new aestheticism") and Maurice Merleau-Ponty, and relates the fascination with surface to the dynamics of pornography:

Against the ultimately self-enclosed, self-referential world of words that Gass puts
forth as his ideal one needs to set a different ideal of surface—or perhaps one
ought to say, keeping in mind the reaction to modernism, an ideal of shallow
depth, "the surface of a depth," as Merleau-Ponty says, describing man caught
up in a world of shifting horizons: "What we call a visible is . . . a quality pregnant
with a texture, the surface of a depth," so that "things themselves, which are
themselves not flat beings but beings in depth, inaccessible to a subject that
would survey them from above, open to him alone that, if it be possible, would
coexist with them in the same world." Situating itself far more firmly *in* the world,
seeking in place of the unresonant flatness of the page a human, lateral, horizon-
tal depth or textured surface, this other form of suspensive irony, which Merleau-
Ponty predicts, defines the limits of Gass's aestheticism and, with it, of whatever
else, to the exclusion of the world, reduces itself to abstraction and idea. Like its
apparent opposite, pornography, the new aestheticism (masquerading as the energy of imagination, as the other does of sexuality) is finally the reflex of self-
consciousness. (146)

Skipper struggles to blow life into the images and events with which he
is obsessed by converting them into benign talismans of the life force,
writing in the persona of a reconstituted self from a new world whose
horizon includes the terrible world of his past only to substantiate the
beautiful necessity and reality of his present. The conversion of images
from negative to positive counteracts the reification Skipper himself imposes on the beings and events that constitute those images for him; for
Skipper, the imagination effects change. The extreme subjectivity and
careful structuring of Skipper's highly indeterminate narrative create a
complexly resonant texture, but at the same time suggest a self-involved
text, a highly wrought surface that is its own fascination, seeming to reveal its subjects but revealing instead the consciousness that constructs it.

The paradoxically revelatory and obfuscating qualities of Skipper's
narration find expression in his labeling his "diary of an artificial inseminator" as "the high lights of my naked history" (9), for the elaborate "second skin" of language counteracts the exposure of unadorned
facts. Skipper's assertion of his history's nakedness is, finally, an assertion
of power, of his authorial ability to create truth. But this truth is highly
contingent, a stage setting for a drama in which he will emerge as hero,
cloaked in the glow and potency of success, garnering strength from the
textual spectacle with which he surrounds himself. In the chapter in
which he reports that he is an artificial inseminator, Skipper prepares to
launch into the defeats and humiliations over which he has triumphed
by saying that his "strategy," out of both need and pride, will be to "here
reveal myself and choose to step from behind the scenes of my naked
history." He asserts, indeed must make it clear, that his "triumph is over
Miranda most of all": "So now I gather around me the evidence, the
proof, the exhilarating images of my present life. . . . But Catalina Kate,
I think, is my best evidence" (48). Recounting the present and revealing

narrative purpose and strategy constitutes stepping from behind the scenes, but this sort of "revelation" further compromises the "nakedness" of the "history." Indeed, it provides the reader with a strategy for supplementing that history with the accoutrements of the present. The elements of the past cannot exist in their original state. And the elements of the present—the people and images (much the same thing for Skipper)—are dressed in the guise of evidence, meant to provide access to the truth that will supersede the mere events of the past. Catalina Kate, in her person and in her pregnancy, becomes a reflection of Skipper. Skipper becomes a reflection of the harmonious world around him: "the green and golden contours of a country [are] reflected in the trembling and in the fullness of my own hips" (48). The narrative in its entirety is a mirror of Skipper's self; Skipper's self is a mirror of the narrative.

The degree of self-revelation remains highly problematic in this "naked" "history," a label that seems to erase, or at least to question, its own terms. After he has written two chapters of his life on the "gentle island," Skipper again self-consciously reflects on his place in his narrative: "And so I have already stepped once more from behind the scenes of my naked history and having come this far I expect that I will never really be able to conceal myself completely in all those scenes which are even now on the tip of my tongue and crowding my eye" (99). It seems an absurd contradiction that Skipper should have harbored even a hope of concealing himself, for this is his "diary," the record of his experience and perceptions in which he hugely looms. Yet Skipper would conceal, if he could, his guilt; he cannot. His narrative is, after all, "the confession of [his] triumph," a disclosure of guilt for the control he may have misused in life at the same time that it is a profession of belief in the control he exerts in writing. Significantly, confession exists only in articulation. By re-imaging his life in the textual play of history, Skipper can make restitution, attempt to reverse loss.

The dynamics of restitution function most clearly in the construction of the story of Fernandez, the Peruvian man to whom Cassandra was briefly married and who left her for a gunner's mate. On his last night of shore patrol, in New York City, before he and Cassandra and Pixie leave for the gentle island, Skipper finds Fernandez dead in his room in a flophouse—stabbed, mutilated, and strangled with a guitar string by sailors who bait homosexuals for recreation. But Skipper doesn't tell Cassandra about this until three months later, on a frigid island night after he has been humiliated at a high school dance while Cassandra has seemingly had a night of seduction. And he does not tell us what he told Cassandra until over fifty pages later, when he quotes his own words from that cold night (96–97, 148), thus calling attention to the textuality of his narrative. He tells us that he "confessed to her at long last" (148), but now, preparing to tell us about how Fernandez died, he admits that he should have told Cassandra the story the night it happened, should have let her see the body with her own eyes, instead of waiting three months, a lapse that "made all the difference." The lapse has made Skipper a passive victim of narrative constraints, for in this time, "shadings of the true tonality were lost, and certain details were kept to myself" (149); the naked and mutilated body of Fernandez lies buried beneath the cover of Skipper's words and silences. Skipper says that he can't forgive himself, but suggests that his narrative will be compensation: "But if I missed those many years ago I won't miss again. So now for everything, for what I told her as well as what I didn't tell her in the upstairs bedroom of the cold island house, everything I can think of now to restore a little of the tonality, to set to rights my passion" (150).

The "passion" Skipper refers to in this instance is ambiguous; it can refer to his feelings for Fernandez or to his feelings for Cassandra, or, more likely, to both. But, finally, Skipper's passion, inextricable from his story, exists in the nuances and figures of his language, the recurring images layered one upon another. Such tricked out passion, the substance of his "naked history," stands in contrast to Captain Red's "naked passion" (56). The opposition and intersection of these two appellations suggests the complexity and tenuousness of the order or meanings Skipper seeks to establish. The naked passion of Captain Red signifies violence and malevolence for Skipper, yet on the wandering island of his "passionate time and place and action" (4) where he has "only to drop [his] trousers . . . to awaken paradise" (46), where he walks without a shirt, and where Catalina Kate luxuriates unclothed, he has literalized the metaphor and thus transformed it: the nakedness of "passion" is the sign of its Edenic innocence. Yet it is from the naked innocence of this good island that he spins the covering of history, a word rife with the conflicted aims of representing the world and representing the consciousness of the one who constructs the representation. It is a word that encapsulates the conflict between representation and creation, and the tension between the description of a world and the revelation of the describer. Skipper couches these issues of aesthetics and reality in terms of nature and artifice. The narrator who asserts his innocence through the nakedness of his history, if not the history itself, appeals to the harmonious abundance of a natural world over which he presides as an artificial inseminator of cows, and, implicitly, a potent artificer of language, an artificer who creates the natural world in his fiction.

The beautiful, redemptive natural world is a feminized landscape for Skipper, a landscape of water and pink sand, of "flowers like painted fingernails" and "bush [that] was impenetrable" (104), and of a woman so at home in this world that she would try to have her baby in a swamp.

(Above all these female images hangs a masculine one: "the sun was an old bloody bone low in the sky.") It is Kate's adventure in the swamp, however, that gives the measure of Skipper's distance from this natural world. An iguana crawls onto Kate's back, and Skipper, summoned to help, can only make the situation worse by trying to pull the iguana off, thereby making it dig its claws in deeper. His image of himself is most important here: he is "colossus over the reptile, colossus above the shores of woman" (106). Attributing inflated importance to himself is typical of Skipper, but more significant is his likening himself to a statue, for he is both artist and his own work of art. More significant still is how he stands in relation to "woman."

The equation of woman with nature relegates woman to that which is condemned as inherently evil or that which is idealized as inherently innocent. The first possibility calls for man to triumph over woman/nature and thus work redemption; the second possibility posits man as already having triumphed through instituting his idealization. Skipper's art, designed to triumph over recalcitrant reality, invokes both possibilities, but seems to settle finally in the evocation of a benign pastoral world inhabited by woman as earth mother. The use of "shores of woman" particularly suggests the two islands of Skipper's story, for islands are defined by shores. When Skipper tells Sonny he is taking Cassandra and Pixie to "a gentle island," Sonny responds by saying that he is going to find a gentle island, too, but his gentle island is literally a woman: "Wanders around some, true enough, but she sure is gentle and she sure just about accommodates an old black castaway like me. Oh, just let Sonny crawl up on that gentle shore!" (24). Skipper has no such human embodiment in mind; instead, he identifies the island with a vague imaginative space in which he can love and protect Cassandra. Each island of Skipper's story represents his attempt at structuring his life and constructing his self, but his efforts integrally involve the construction of his relation to woman. In his last, celebratory chapter, Skipper says, "I thank God for wandering islands and invisible shores" (205). His gratefulness that he has been able to escape time and pain entwines with his metaphor of woman as shore, and of woman as invisible as his island shore, which exists for us only in his words. He can imagine and realize his benevolent, natural island world just as he can see that "Cassandra was wearing her invisible chains, invisible flowers" (25); Skipper creates it all, island and chains.

In a scene on the gentle island which corresponds to the scene in which Skipper feels himself to be a colossus over iguana and woman, Skipper, confronted with the sudden intimacy of Miranda's body in the backseat of her car, "felt like a sculptor in the presence of his nubile clay" (95). The feeling is ludicrous in terms of Skipper's relationship with Miranda, who, far from being malleable in any way, seems to subject Skipper to vigorous manipulation. Yet this marriage of the images of earth and artist again displays Skipper's desire to master the compelling as well as frightening forces of reality, converting them into his own creation. And he does in fact shape Miranda for the reader, for she, too, can exist for us only through his words. In a typical effort to control the power of her attraction, Skipper assigns a mythical, literary name to her. She is, for him, "Cleopatra," but even Skipper must admit that she cannot be bound within the confines of a mythic label: she is a "Cleopatra who could row her own barge" (64).

Skipper, nevertheless, repeatedly appeals to myth to structure his experience. In addition to littering his first chapter, "Naming Names," with allusions to literature and mythology, he later harks back to his "schoolboy's copybook" to assert the confluence of his life's journey with the words of Menelaus: "*I have soon to journey to a lonely island in a distant part of my kingdom. But I shall return before the winter storms begin. Prince Paris, I leave my wife, Helen, in your care. Guard her well. See that no harm befalls her*" (45–46; Hawkes's italics).[4] Skipper calls these words his "declaration of faith which I say aloud to myself" (45). He relates this in a short but seminal chapter titled "The Artificial Inseminator," which is perhaps his most extended reflection on his role as creator and on his writing's purposes and methods. The Trojan War is indeed imagistically significant for Skipper's story, for just as the cause of that war was attributed to the fight for a woman, Skipper attributes the necessity of his story to his fight to save Cassandra, although this fight quickly becomes the fight to save himself. Cassandra, like Helen, is consumed by rhetoric and traded for an image, which image receives all the blame and encomiums an impossible ideal entails. "Poor Prince Paris," says Skipper (50) to end the reflections of "The Artificial Inseminator," for his concern is, finally, with his triumph over adversaries—over violent men, over threatening or unresponsive women, over time, over death—more so than with the daughter whom he loves, lost to him from the beginning because she could never be his wife, lost to the hands of other men, lost to the grip of death. "Poor Prince Paris," Skipper can say, believing that he, at least, has redeemed his kingdom.

In his death-filled world, Skipper runs from sex, sublimating, denying, or ignoring his desires, attracted to and horrified by the closed and unknowable female, obsessed by his inaccessible, idealized daughter, afraid of the too accessible, demonized Miranda. On his wandering island he seems finally to have reconciled himself to the feminine, having traded the image of Cassandra for a more compliant one: "Cassandra is gone. . . . Now I have Catalina Kate instead" (46). This object of desire is younger even than Cassandra, a sixteen-year-old whose age and culture exoticize and separate her from Skipper and preclude any threat. Furthermore, the nature of their relationship is ambiguous, for Skipper may or may not be the father of her baby and it is Sonny who seems to have had relations with her during their pastoral idyll, while the sleeping Skipper certainly does not. His seeming reconciliation with the feminine is more of an assumption of domination, for while Kate's indeterminate responses to him may just as easily be read as mocking or as respectful, Skipper asserts his role as admired leader of Kate and everyone else on the island.[5] While Skipper writes of Kate as naked, sensual, and pregnant, he at the same time desexes her by assigning her the role of baby machine: " 'We can start you off on another little baby in a few weeks. Would you like that, Kate? But of course you would,' I said" (209). In Kate, daughter, lover, and mother join, stripped of threat, clothed in the colors of Skipper's imagination; she is the ultimate rosy canvas for Skipper's fantasy.[6]

Skipper appropriates Catalina Kate's fertility for himself, but he ascribes this fertility to the reproduction of his life in the "golden glass" (99) of art. This transformative, life-affirming gesture is the same impetus behind what is most destructive in him: the desire to deliver images born of flesh. This desire exerts itself most damagingly in his relation to Cassandra, whose humanity he sacrifices to the dictates of what he himself calls his "intensive fantasy" (32):

> But wasn't Cassandra still my teen-age bomb? Wasn't she? Even though she was a war bride, a mother, a young responsible woman of twenty-five? . . . I only smiled and told myself that the flesh of the cheerleader was still embedded in the flesh of Pixie's mother and so soothed myself with various new visions of this double anatomy, this schizophrenic flesh. . . . I would love them both, scrutinize them both, then at the right moment fling myself in the way of the ascendant and destructive image. (32–33)

Caught in Skipper's artificial construction, Cassandra becomes the stuff of fiction, the fetishized object around which qualities are spun by a narrator who is created by an author whose "language depends almost totally on image" (Scholes 201) and for whom "the destructive image posits the ideal" (Ziegler 178). But in the case of Skipper's vision of Cassandra, each image he assigns to her is already an ideal. It is the ascendancy of one, the conquering of paradox, that destroys, not because of any necessity in Cassandra's life, but because the ascendancy of one image would delimit the play of Skipper's fantasy.[7]

The image of Cassandra as queenly, pristine mother and as teen-age bomb (early on Skipper refers to her as "my child courtesan" [17]) demonstrates Skipper's recourse to that degradation of erotic life that divides all women into versions of the virgin or the whore. In Skipper's fantasy—

transgressive because its object is his daughter—the "whore" is both sentimentalized and disguised with the "innocence" of youth and the "virgin" is a virgin mother. His obsessive fear and denial of Cassandra's mature sexuality cause him to decide, on her wedding night, that she "would always be identified for me with the BVM" (118), the Blessed Virgin Mary represented by the small white plastic statue on the dashboard of Fernandez's car. He thinks of her as "only a silvery blue Madonna" (42) as he holds her hand while naked AWOL soldiers in the desert line up to kiss her, an occurrence she seems thoroughly to enjoy. He works to overcome Cassandra's "serious duplicity" (14)—a quality to which he attributes her leading him to be painfully tattooed—by converting human doubleness and otherness into paradox that he controls. When she jumps to her death Skipper's image of her dead body is overlaid with the image of a naked woman from a magazine, but he also replaces her with the cheap representation of the Madonna: he "thought about Cassandra and was unable to distinguish between her small white oval face—it was up there with me as well as below on the black rocks—and the small white plastic face of the BVM" (199). The image of the Virgin Mother reifies paradox into a monstrous and impossible ideal. "What a bad end for time. What a bad end for the BVM" (197), thinks Skipper as he climbs the lighthouse stairs; but the forcing of a transcendent image on Cassandra, his "museum piece" (29), had ended time for her long before.

Skipper fetishizes Cassandra's small body that combines child and woman, and fetishizes her quiet and proper voice, "the whisper of fashion, whisper of feminine cleanliness, cold love" (21). He repeatedly associates the purity of whiteness with her, and so his fixation on the "forbidden white tower" (58) of the lighthouse corresponds to his fixation on Cassandra, who is herself certainly forbidden. At the same time, the tower is an obvious phallic image, and thus an image in which the repression of his own desire and of the knowledge of its object join. Though Cassandra has the sexual experience, which Skipper so dreads, with Jomo at the top of the lighthouse, and though she jumps to her death from its height, still Skipper can say of his trip to the top of the light and back down, "The iron gut of the tower remained intact" (198); Skipper literally remains safe, and his worship of Cassandra's nonexistent virginity remains intact in the symbolically erected edifice.

Cassandra's "virginity" is the sign of her exchange value; "The virginal woman," writes Luce Irigaray, "is nothing but the possibility, the place, the sign of relations among men. In and of herself she does not exist: she is a simple envelope veiling what is really at stake in the social exchange" (186). This state of affairs comically and morbidly plays itself out on Cassandra's honeymoon with Fernandez and with Skipper, who accompanies the newlyweds on their trip, sitting between them on the car ride and staying with them at the sordid hotel where they spend their wedding night. But Fernandez will not be her "real" groom; like Mildred, Cassandra's groom is death. Her death allows for Skipper's realization of his "time of no time"; she is exchanged for Catalina Kate, and for Sonny, and, more than that, for the reign of artifice.

Miranda presents the biggest challenge to Skipper's accomplishment of his imaginative ends because she, unlike Cassandra, defies his ability to deny her sexuality. In Skipper's mind, her sexuality is animal and omnipresent. She is strong, sensual, and "Venus-like" (191), "[h]er bosom [is] an unleashed animal" (75), and her large black brassiere, "her totem" (75), appears in the bathroom of her house and on Captain Red's boat like an "albatross" and a "sign of the enemy" (52). The compelling power of her sexuality makes Miranda into Skipper's greatest adversary, for his triumph is to be over her most of all (48). In his terror of women and sex, he refuses to be seduced by her, ignoring her advances and fleeing in horror when, having invited him into her car, she removes her pants: "she had mocked me with the beauty of her naked stern, had challenged, aroused, offended me with the blank wall of nudity, and I perceived a cruel motive somewhere" (96). Miranda is her own woman, powerful and unknowable, and Skipper cannot hope to overwrite what he perceives as her blankness with the sign of his possession. His only triumph over her can be in his writing of himself, the corpus of his naked history.

In becoming an artificial inseminator of cows, Skipper transforms human sexuality into an analogous activity that is a metaphor for artistic creativity; the "muse" who inspires this creativity is Miranda, who "will never know how many slick frisky calves have been conceived in her name" (48). Skipper once actually compares Miranda to a representation of a muse, in an instance when her appearance of strength is suddenly belied by a debilitating attack of asthma: "Her lips were moist, pulled back, drawn open fiercely in the perfect silent square of the tragic muse" (65–66). This conception converts Miranda into a mask that represents the silent figure who inspires the work of representation. Such inspiration is, predictably, the role of all the female characters. His mother was "the mortician's muse" (6) who inspires Skipper's own imagination, which will allow him to redeem his father's profession (47). And Cassandra, of course, inspires the ardor of the father who will find satisfaction with the loving and fathering he can do on his island with Catalina Kate. The silence Skipper imposes on Miranda in imaging her as muse echoes the silence that defines his mother, whose image underlies his relationship with Cassandra and with Kate, both of whom he characterizes by the ambiguity or absence of their responses. Cassandra, who speaks "on the threshold of sound" (13), bears the name of one who spoke but was not believed; the words of Skipper's daughter are subsumed by the shadings of his subjectivity. He can believe only in his images, in his language. "I watch this final flourish of my own hand and muse" (210), says Skipper at the end of his narrative, and his words betray the sense of "muse" closest to his truth. The women who are his muses are projections of his own ideas; his real muse is the writing hand of the self he loves.

Skipper looks to Cassandra for the confirmation of his projections both of her and of himself. He inscribes her as cruel, as sadistic and heartless, or as innocent, "too innocent for the U-Drive-Inn," for instance, where Gertrude lives and dies (15, 14). He repeatedly proclaims his own loving innocence, and asserts the triumph of this innocence by transforming himself from "one of those little black seeds of death" (161) into a seed of life in the metaphor of his work as an artificial inseminator. This conversion to life rests on the power of the metaphor; Skipper exists at the end as the dispenser of life—for cows and Kate alike—because he inscribes himself thus. Yet Skipper also associates innocence with death. He says, for instance, "I remember most clearly our first [morning] in the widow's house, because that was the dawn of my first encounter with Miranda. Dead brown rotten world, heartless dawn. Innocence and distraction at half past five in the morning" (52–53). As is typical of Skipper's style, this passage leaves the status of innocence unclear; innocence may be inherent in a dead, rotten world, or it may exist in opposition to it. But the *possibility* of its complicity with this world has sinister ramifications in terms of Skipper's responsibility for Cassandra's suicide. He calls himself her "accomplice, father, friend, traveling companion, yes, old chaperon, but lover and destroyer too"; he victimizes her with his "destructive sympathy" (175–176), with the shackles of his idealizations. At the time of her suicide, he considers for a moment whether he is to blame: "as in the case of my poor father, was I myself the unwitting tinder that started the blaze?" (197). Skipper, however, does not want an answer to this question. "I won't ask why, Cassandra," he says. "Something must have spoken to you, something must have happened. But I don't want to know, Cassandra. So I won't ask" (199). Skipper here confounds innocence and blindness, just as he does in his vision of his mother, whose smile, her one feature visible, is "either innocent or blind" (8). In the absence of certified knowledge, the imagination can maintain its innocence, and Skipper can inscribe his own salvation.

When Cassandra directly asserts her power over her father by having him tattooed, Skipper does not know that his tattoo is the name "Fernandez" until he sees the letters, upside down and backwards, in the dirty mirror the tattooer holds in front of him: "So I looked in the mirror, the dirty fairy tale glass . . . and saw myself" (20). In this one moment, Cassandra successfully reverses the stifling authority of her father by inscribing him with the name that represents his true allegiance, for Skipper was in league with Fernandez in reducing Cassandra to a male ideal of a woman's role. But Skipper cannot bear to have his self constituted by another's inscription. The dirty fairy tale glass must give way to the transforming glass of his art: "In the very act of living I see myself, picture myself, as if memory had already done its work and flowered, subjected even myself to the golden glass" (99). In writing of his triumph the world finally reflects Skipper back to himself in the way that he desires. On his wandering island the sun has darkened his skin so that, Skippers says, "the green name tattooed on my breast has all but disappeared" (47).

Skipper's narrative, engendered by love, depends on the power of his language to construct not just a single world that reflects him, but two worlds that reflect each other in their language, images, and structure. The wandering island gains in beauty because it reverses the gentle island; the gentle island gains in desolation because it is the negative of the wandering island. Both islands gain in significance because of the way they conceal and reveal Skipper: "behind every frozen episode of that other island . . . there lies the golden wheel of my hot sun; behind every black rock a tropical rose and behind every cruel wind-driven snow-storm a filmy sheet, a transparency, of golden fleas. No matter how stark the scene, no matter how black the gale or sinister the violence of Miranda, still the light of my triumph must shine through" (48). Skipper's triumph and transfiguration reside in the insistencies of composition. He finally conquers the ravages of time and circumstance by fathering an untold future composed of the meaning produced by the juxtaposition of past and present, that is, by their existence side by side.

The image of the wandering island's golden fleas recalls Skipper's vision of his mother's wedding or funeral chariot as being "severe and tangled like a complicated golden insect" (9); he has finally instituted his romantic vision. By calling his last chapter "The Golden Fleas," he signals the completion of his quest in the attainment of a mythic transformation of ordinariness and adversity. Jason's quest for the golden fleece relies for its success on the efforts of a woman, whom he later betrays; Skipper's quest relies on the image of woman, which betrays the humanity of specific women and betrays, or reveals, the needs and practices of his narrative. The pun that produces the connection between fleece and fleas calls attention to the force of textual artifice.

Skipper ends his narrative by expressly referring to himself ending his narrative, watching the final flourish of his hand: "Because now I am fifty-nine years old and I knew I would be, and now there is the sun in the evening, the moon at dawn, the still voice. That's it. The sun in the evening. The moon at dawn. The still voice" (210). He reverses the usual association of celestial objects and hours, emphasizing luminaries on the edge of disappearance, which at the same time evokes their cyclic recurrence. And in fact recurrence takes place immediately in his sentences, upon his revelatory "That's it"; the text asserts its own truth. The repetition culminates in the paradox of the voice inscribing its own silence, the last gesture toward transcendence of a narrative that must relinquish itself to the silence that must hold the "invisible lives" (207) that are Skipper's triumphant creation.

# Chapter 4
# Dreams of Wholeness, Nightmares of Dissolution: Aspects of the Artist in the Triad

In his novels following *Second Skin,* Hawkes continues to develop the potentialities of a male character giving redeeming shape to his experience and his self through artful narration. But whereas Skipper masks his sexual interests in his rhetoric of all-encompassing, patient love, the self-consciously artistic first-person narrators of *The Blood Oranges* (1971), *Death, Sleep & the Traveler* (1974), and *Travesty* (1976) share an open obsession with sexuality as well as the imagination. The novels have thus come to be referred to, by Hawkes and by critics, as the sex triad or simply the triad. Sexuality, indeed, becomes the medium through which the imagination expresses itself; and since, of course, the imagination of these narrators finally expresses itself in language, sexuality becomes the representation of sexuality, and representation itself becomes self-reflexively erotic. For these speakers, a sentence is its own seduction. Images continue to dominate the narratives, but now in a deliberate, even analytical way as the narrators make aesthetic concerns the vital and determining interest of their sexual and narrative lives.

The heightened self-consciousness of the triad's narrators corresponds to an increased self-involvement, on the level of both character and language; the narrators turn increasingly inward to the terrain of their psyches, and the novels come to reflect increasingly upon each other. Hawkes says of these novels:

I suppose that my structuring consciousness is evident in the triad. I think of *The Blood Oranges* as the poetry of the imagination; it's the lyric version of the landscape of the imagination. I take the middle one, *Death, Sleep & the Traveler,* as the artist's descent into his unconscious, and I take *Travesty* as the final statement on the relationship between the imagination, death, and sexuality. I didn't write those three novels intentionally as a triad of fictions, but . . . discovered their relationship to each other while writing *Travesty.* (O'Donnell 119)

Hawkes refers to the narrator of *The Blood Oranges*, Cyril, as a "godlike man." In lush language, Cyril celebrates innocent sexuality; his vision of renewable virginity is meant to attest to the redemptive power of the imagination, which confers wholeness on people and forges unity between itself and its objects. In *Death, Sleep & the Traveler*, the artist's quest for wholeness disintegrates; while in *The Blood Oranges* the fragmented narration is designed to assert coherence and enact renewal, *Death, Sleep & the Traveler's* fragmented narration attests to the disintegrative world of a narrator who gropes with his dream visions without being able to achieve unity and while trying to deny murderous guilt. *Travesty*, which also utilizes a fragmented narration, most startlingly elaborates the paradoxes of the simultaneously innocent and cruel authorial imagination, revealing the assertion of power and subjugation of the other that underlies the quest of making the world conform to one's vision.

**I**

In *The Blood Oranges*, Hawkes's aesthetic interest in exploding the conventions of the novel has its thematic counterpart in the narrator's need to destroy conventional modes of perception and ways of living. Cyril wants to achieve freedom by destroying sexual conventions which he believes can only lead to limitation and pain. He insists that "the only enemy of the mature marriage is monogamy" (209) and, in a landscape he names Illyria, works to attain sexual multiplicity and harmony among four people—himself and his wife, Fiona, and another married couple, Hugh and Catherine. The archaic image of a chastity belt appears in the midst of Cyril's struggle for sexual liberation as a foreboding, sinister device. The chastity belt is, according to Hawkes, "a central image in *The Blood Oranges*. It is central to everything I've written. That is, my fiction is generally an evocation of the nightmare or terroristic universe in which sexuality is destroyed by law, by dictum, by human perversity, by contraption, and it is this destruction of human sexuality which I have attempted to portray and confront in order to be true to human fear and to human ruthlessness, but also in part to evoke its opposite, the moment of freedom from constriction, constraint, death" (Scholes 207). Cyril conceives of himself as fighting against the sexual repression as well as the oppression of women as represented by the chastity belt and embodied by Hugh, the device's advocate. When he finds that Hugh, in jealousy and possessiveness, has put the chastity belt on Catherine, Cyril breaks it off of her. He claims, "Jealousy, for me, does not exist, while anything that lies in the palm of love is good" (58), and maintains that he and all those who sing "the sex song" are innocent. Yet the novel in which Cyril portrays his idyllic world opens with the collapse of this world; picturing love as a tapestry, he asks, "Why, after more than eighteen years, does the soft medieval fabric of my tapestry now hang in shreds" (3). Hugh has accidentally hanged himself, Catherine is catatonic in a sanitarium, and Fiona has left with Hugh and Catherine's children.

The novel consists of Cyril's description of his present reduced circumstances and of his re-creation, for Catherine, of the relationships among the foursome in order to induce her recovery and return to him. And while she does return to him, instead of resuming their sexual revelry, this "godlike man" and his "last mistress" assume a "sexless matrimony." The novel ends with Cyril's listing of the relics—the flower crown, the chastity belt, and the undershorts—that hang on the wall of his monastic bedroom. In reference to these objects, Hawkes says, "The question of innocence is certainly an important one. . . . I don't know whether the three images . . . are simply dead images or whether they relate in some sense or other to the subject of innocence. I think these relics are an effort to insist on the actuality of innocence" (Emmett and Vine 169). Cyril invokes the circularity of these relics as a symbol of the continued existence of a perpetually innocent Illyria. His desire to abolish the limitations of time parallels Hawkes's desire to destroy the linearity of narrative. But the novel's concept of circularity is problematic, as is the innocence the relics are supposed to substantiate. Certainly a chastity belt summons forth a world of enforced virginity or fidelity, and force and power contradict any existing innocence. In this "timeless" world, the chastity belt is an historical artifact that collapses the boundary between the oppression of the past and the compulsions of the present, and which situates the boundary between repression and freedom at the site of the female body. Hawkes, in large measure, equates Cyril's act of breaking the chastity belt with his own act of writing fiction, fiction in which drama consists of the attempt to both inscribe (if not circumscribe) and free the Other as well as the self. Referred to as "a work of art" (245) by Hugh, the chastity belt in *The Blood Oranges* is an image that contains the contrary impulses of constriction and expansiveness, cruelty and innocence, at work both thematically and aesthetically in the novel.

A chastity belt is a device that enables the assertion of a man's power over a woman, a means by which to claim territory. In the dungeon of a ruined medieval fortress, the puritanical Hugh searches for and finds a chastity belt, the objective correlative of his dark and repressive vision. By using the chastity belt on Catherine, he demonstrates his belief that "Manhood rebels at infidelity, it's only natural" (177). Cyril's whole project aims at obliterating this sort of conventional and sexist thinking. He breaks the chastity belt around Catherine's waist, releasing her for free love, as a sort of modern-day Saint George. Yet, in a key passage of the novel, and one which has been much remarked upon, Cyril says, "Bent as I was on removing that impediment to love, was I already the accomplice of he who had forced Catherine to put it on? . . . The end of Hugh's violence was only this brief and matter-of-fact procedure smoldering, so to speak, with eroticism. . . . Yes, I was Hugh's accomplice. In all my strength and weight I was not so very different from Hugh after all" (255–256).

In his own way, Cyril is as obsessed by power as Hugh is, although he is not plagued by Hugh's guilt. Cyril refers to Illyria as a place where "a grassy wind was bound to blow away the last shreds of possessiveness," but it is also a "circumscribed country" (154). This territory Cyril has claimed is a world encircled by his vision, confined within the bounds of a liberation that collapses into prohibition and limitation. For even when Hugh finally consummates his desire with Fiona, thereby supposedly fulfilling Cyril's vision of unlimited sexual exchange, Cyril's reaction is imbued with the disappointment of exclusion. On realizing that Hugh is with Fiona in her bedroom, Cyril also realizes that Hugh "was preventing Fiona and me from enjoying our version of what he and Fiona had so recently enjoyed. But at the same time he had proven my theories, completed Love's natural structure, justified Catherine's instincts, made Fiona happy when she had given up all her hopes for happiness. What more could I ask?" (260). Cyril's unadmitted desire to be not only the creator but the primary enjoyer of the group's sexual multiplicity reveals itself long before his designs are realized. On the very first night that he and Fiona spend with Hugh and Catherine he looks at the two women "with growing possessiveness" (104), and later he refers to Catherine as "more my partner than [Hugh's]" (92). He further belies his self-proclaimed generosity by taking pleasure in his feeling of psychic, sexual, and physical superiority to Hugh. One day, for example, as the foursome stands in a line holding hands and admiring the scenery, Cyril thinks that the one-armed Hugh "could never share my privilege of standing between two opposite and yet equally desirable women. Even on our promontory of sharp wet rocks it amused me to think that, thanks to Hugh, our sacred circle would remain forever metaphysical. Nothing more" (118).

In fact, most of Cyril's concerns are, finally, metaphysical. He wants to make abstractions concrete, but ultimately ideas take on a sensuous life of their own. Joy comes not simply from sexual activity, but from actualizing an idea. On an idyllic afternoon the four adults carry out Fiona's idea of swimming naked to a small island: "in the idea as in the sea itself we snort, kick, float, swim on as if the less familiar shore will never rise to our feet" (230). At the end of the novel Cyril says, "sex-singing is hardly possible without the presence of the frail yet indestructible little two- or three-note theme of innocence . . . I have always defended the idea if not the fact of purity" (269). He goes on to say, "The suggestion is not that I myself ever experienced the slightest preference for virginal over nonvirginal girls or women. The suggestion is not that my wife or Hugh's could ever suffer significantly by comparison with the young and half-naked shepherdess chasing across the sunburnt field after her shaggy goats" (269). But the word "significantly" speaks worlds here, for there is a difference between a mythical conception of virginity and the complex realities of relationships. The destructive occurrences in these characters' lives indicate that reality in general suffers significantly by comparison with Cyril's idea of it, although his dreams themselves are less than pure.

According to Hawkes, "Cyril is pure, Hugh is a Puritan" (Scholes 199). Hugh, though convulsed with desire for a woman other than his wife, wants to prevent transgression—his own, as well as anyone else's. Cyril wants to eliminate the very idea of sexual transgression, and it is this desire that gives him the status of a ponderous rebel. Yet at the same time this desire simply transfers the idea of transgression from sex to Cyril's theorizing about sex. He works to abolish the repression responsible for the conventional attitude that marriage is sexually binding by self-consciously and continually violating ordinary ways of seeing and then by inscribing experiences, even the most ordinary, in his sexually visionary terms.

Michel Foucault, in *The History of Sexuality*, describes the aims of modern discourses on sexual repression in terms that can be applied to Cyril's apparent assumptions: "If sex is repressed, that is, condemned to prohibition, nonexistence, and silence, then the mere fact that one is speaking about it has the appearance of a deliberate transgression. A person who holds forth in such language places himself to a certain extent outside the reach of power, he upsets established law; he somehow anticipates the coming freedom" (6). Foucault's study goes on to demonstrate that this sort of language is, far from being outside the reach of power, another one of its manifestations. The proliferation of discourses about sex, rather than arising in opposition to Christian repression, were, and are, actually produced by the negative injunctions themselves: "An imperative was established: Not only will you confess to acts contravening the law, but you will seek to transform your desire, your every desire, into discourse. . . . The Christian pastoral prescribed as a fundamental duty the task of passing everything having to do with sex through the endless mill of speech" (21). Hugh's resemblance to the statue of St. Peter and to depictions of Christ emphasizes the Christian ideals that underlie his strangled sexuality and that war with the potential represented by the fact that his appearance is also Pan-like. Cyril repeatedly invokes the supposed sexual freedom of the pagan world, but his obsession with articulating the sexual content of every scene and situation, seen in the light of Foucault's analysis, is the inverse of Hugh's agonizing over spontaneous sensations escaping through a net of negation. Cyril, however, presents himself as a liberator and a visionary, a godlike man who must proclaim the truth about sex.[1]

Cyril is a visionary whose vision relies on reason; he is a methodical aesthetician (171), a sensuous rationalist (203) convinced that an idyllic world can be created if everyone will be sensible. He is an idealist, as are Fiona and Hugh. Cyril compares Fiona's idealism to Hugh's: "Fiona's idealism isn't prohibitive. It's receptive. It doesn't preclude sexual affection. It starts with it. That's the difference" (250). Cyril would say that his own idealism isn't prohibitive either, yet his vision not only tends to exclude equal competition, but also both excludes Hugh's form of eroticism and reveals itself as connected to it. The connections become apparent in the nodus of vision itself.

For Cyril, sex is an aesthetic matter and his aesthetics are heavily reliant on the visual. His appreciation of the visual includes a supreme delight in and frequent dwelling on his own appearance; he refers to himself as a "spectacular man" (24), and is, according to himself, large, strong, handsome, and golden. But he is also "spectacular" in that he revels in spectacle, which for him means eroticized natural scenes as well as "sex-tableaus" in which the foursome assume composed erotic arrangements.[2] The visual, for Cyril, makes manifest; the image or tableau is a source of revelation, meaning, fulfillment, and prophecy, and Cyril is the interpreter. At the very beginning of his narrative he sees two birds mating on his way back from the sanitarium and he calls them a sign, one which "augured well for the time I had spent with Catherine and for my own future in the electrified field of Love's art" (15). When the foursome sees a flying eagle, Cyril interprets it as a "justification of Fiona's vision and my own supportive role"; it is "a doubly significant sign" (138). While the foursome is on the beach one afternoon, a goat wanders into their midst and Cyril wonders, "Was it dream, chance, coincidence, or was my state of mind a menagerie of desire from which real animals might spring? Could it be that one of my speechless creatures of joy and sentiment had torn itself loose from the tapestry that only I could see?" (92–93) The goat is a recurring satyr figure in Cyril's descriptions of the "tapestry" of sexual love, and thus its appearance on the beach seems to confirm his vision and his verbal formulations of this vision. There is a similar conjunction of Cyril's vision and his reality after Catherine's return from the sanitarium. Cyril finally feels joined with her not so much by any internal transformation, but because they witness the natives' ritual of christening a new ship and he interprets it as a marriage. The transforming power of his vision seems to be affirmed, for Catherine speaks to him once again though she thought she never would.[3] This scene further manifests the connection between vision and language. The image and its description are both the obsession and to an extent the goal of Cyril; they are the language of sex, making the act of sex comparatively immaterial. Cyril describes himself as "the singer who spent my life quietly deciphering the crucial signs of sex" (203). The fact that he and Fiona "read" the signs of sex (259), as well as produce them, establishes them as aestheticians.

In another scene in which the four lie on the beach, Cyril "creates" by exposing Fiona's body. He removes her halter,[4] thinking that Hugh will assist in creating symmetry by removing Catherine's. But Hugh does not, and Cyril wonders, "how could any man love my wife and yet fail to appreciate simple harmonious arrangements of flesh, shadow, voice, hair, which were as much a result of Fiona's artistry as of mine. But perhaps I had been wrong. Perhaps Hugh had no eye for the sex-tableau" (43). But the sex-tableau is precisely what Hugh does have an eye for. He, too, is a reader of the signs of sex, his signs are simply different from Cyril's.

Cyril intends his physical or verbal composition of tableaux to invigorate and supplement life, and Hugh intends the same for his tableaux, the series of photographs he has been taking which he refers to as his Peasant Nudes. He is concerned with "angle, light, depth, expression" (69), or arrangements of flesh, shadow, hair, and even voice, for as Cyril says, when Hugh takes pictures he seems "to be listening to the girl's silent life rather than staring at the visible shape of it" (65–66). Yet in his photographs the composition and revelation Cyril looks for are reduced to reified sexuality and documents of male power. Wielding his cameras with excited precision, writhing on the dung-covered floor of a barn, Hugh photographs Rosella (the name Cyril gives her), the girl who later becomes Cyril's maid. He photographs her in her peasant clothing and then nude, "shoved" up against a beam, wearing a harness. Cyril views Hugh's activity with interest but also with superciliousness, dwelling on Hugh's deformity while admiring his absorption in his art and emphasizing this art's accompanying desolation. He thinks that "[a]t best a photograph could result in small satisfaction" (60), and when Hugh collapses with a chest pain Cyril first thinks he is in the throes of a climax because of the photographs he had taken, but that this climax could only be "pseudosexual" (71). Yet even before the photo session commences, Cyril "was beginning to see the afternoon through the eye of one of Hugh's cameras" (60). It is Cyril who says of Rosella "let's hunt her down" and refers to her as "our quarry" (59). He realizes "I too could become absorbed in the act of assessment, appreciation" (67), but of course assessment and appreciation are his absorption throughout the novel.

Hugh's photo session reveals the negative potential of this absorption.

As Cyril studies the nude Rosella he superimposes another image on the scene, a clear vision of the domestic tableau he and Hugh had recently left, complete with a "dog in mid-air," two waving children and one scowling child, and wives waving to them from the clothesline (68). However, "[a]t the sound of [Hugh's] choking voice the tableau of domestic multiplicity dissolved in an instant" (69). Cyril understands the crippling repression and frustration implicit in Hugh's art as the counter to the possibilities for sensual enjoyment his tableaux represent. Yet the propensities of Cyril and Hugh conjoin in the men's fascination with representation itself, even though it may be at the expense of fulfillment and involve the subtraction or domination of wills other than their own.

Hugh's aesthetic appropriation of Rosella has its counterpart in the foursome's "finding" a shepherdess tending her goats. They have watched the sunrise over what Cyril calls "our" valley, and then the goat girl appears: "It was the new day's gift to Fiona, nature's final gift to my wife" (140). They are thrilled by this added element to their pleasure, and Fiona proclaims that she must talk to the girl right away. But the girl takes the initiative herself, running up the hillside to them, then inspecting the four strangers and talking without stop. Cyril claims that her chatter is about the insignificance of her own life as compared to the magnificence of his group, "men of mystery, women of beauty" (144), and assumes that she thinks him a god. The girl may indeed think this, but she may also simply think they are nature's exotic gift to her, there for her assessment and appreciation. The goat girl's insistently self-possessed life allows the episode, which includes touching, kissing, and eating cherries, to be sensual, ebullient, and interactive. But the exchange contains an underlying assumption on the part of Cyril, and to an extent his companions, of the right and power to make people and circumstances conform to personal aesthetic needs and thereby be ripe for consumption.

The "naturalness" with which the foursome appropriates the goat girl or Hugh exploits his peasant nudes depends in part on a belief in cultural superiority. Cyril repeatedly remarks on the primitiveness of the natives of the Mediterranean region where he has made Illyria. Many of his disparaging comments are about the native language which he does not understand and considers ugly, consisting of "grunts" and "shouts" out of which he can discern only the sounds "*crespi fagag*" and "*croak peoni*" (7, 21, 124, 265). The beauty and light of the sanitarium where Catherine stays on a hill above the "primitive landscape" cause him to say, "Surely the sanctuary was conceived and built by someone who could never vocalize the harsh unimaginative language of this terrain" (5–6). The natives can be aesthetically picturesque, even if this is by way of being "aesthetically self-defeating" (as Cyril describes Rosella [7]), but

Cyril denies them their own aesthetic consciousness, which he conveys most significantly by refusing to grant them the capacity for anything more than functional language. Hugh similarly expresses a privileged position granted by his control of image and language; he captures Rosella, who may never have seen a camera before, in stereotypical peasant trappings and gloats that her "face is skintight with the beauty of illiteracy. That's what will show up in the pictures. Wait and see. The sullen face of an illiterate virgin" (64). Hugh's linking of illiteracy and virginity is consistent with Cyril's own demonstration that sexuality is a language, and the appellation "illiterate virgin" echoes Cyril's comment at the beginning of his narrative about "the ignorant virginity of Rosella's spirit" (3).

Cyril presents the foursome as superior to the natives because of their language, but he, of course, asserts his superiority over the others in his group because of his supreme verbal artistry. His power to effect his vision depends upon his ability to remake the world in his language. While this quality grants Cyril his status as the "sex singer" who is Fiona's fit cohort in the field of love, it is also a quality of which she is wryly critical, and it marks an important distinction between them. When, for instance, Fiona has led the group to the top of a hill to watch the sunrise she warns, "Don't say anything, Cyril. Don't spoil it" (135). Fiona expresses inclinations completely contrary to Cyril's in having led them to this place "where the silence had no direction" (135). Like the spreading colors in the sky, the experience, for Fiona to enjoy it, must be diffuse and glorious, and felt rather than overwritten. Cyril, however, needs to be (and for the reader, is) the writer of their reality, and after all, directionless silence is nonexistent because of the verbal existence it acquires in Cyril's sentence.

The dynamics of Cyril's need to be both interpreter and "writer" reveals itself in the image of the statue that doubles as boy and girl which Cyril, Fiona, and Hugh, and later, Cyril and Catherine, come across near the village church. The statue's suggested androgyny, which seems to point toward the male and female in us all and to the democracy of desire, is actually undercut by Cyril's commentary. The statue has a "black hole driven so unaccountably into that small portion of the stone which, realistically, should have revealed no more than sexual silence" (171). This is Cyril's way of commenting that the female genitals are not usually represented in statues, but his language goes further than that by equating female sexuality with silence. This is, after all, a novel of the "singing phallus" (191). Cyril echoes his description of the feminized statue when he describes Hugh in his emasculated state, suffering the pain of "the point of the pike in the scrotum" (247) because Cyril is sleeping with his wife: "Hugh's breathing . . . had become no more than the timeless drift of air in and out of a small orifice cut in stone" (252). Hugh is reduced to silence by Cyril's words, and doesn't find joy until he too sings Cyril's song, only to return to a final silence. Cyril is confident of his own ability to bring sexuality to its fullest voice; in his most specific description of the sexual act, he refers to "the brass voice resounding in the oracle of Catherine's sex and mine" (230). More than voice, this is, for Cyril, prophetic truth.

Cyril believes that in bringing sexuality to voice, he can bring history to light. Illyria is located in the midst of people who Cyril claims live in "historical darkness" (68). Hugh exposes this world to his own kind of light in photographing peasant nudes, a pastime he refers to as "his field trips into the old world of sex" (60), and the implication is that this world is contrary to Cyril's brave new world of free love. Yet Cyril as well as Hugh wants to achieve timelessness, and in his quest Cyril harks back to an even older world of sex, even if it is only an imaginary one. He eroticizes the landscape and the villagers by converting them to myth. The shepherd who happens upon their funeral for the dog becomes a Pan figure, a girl in the fields becomes an archetypal shepherdess, and the old man in the boat-christening ritual becomes a satyr. Cyril just as easily imagines himself as a bull in love's tapestry, various women as sheep, and Hugh as a goat or satyr or Pan figure. The two main female characters in the novel are consigned to mythic roles not only by Cyril but in Hawkes's conception of them. Hawkes says, "Catherine is the mother-version of Fiona; Fiona is the Aphrodite of Catherine. The two are probably one" (Scholes 200). Hawkes attributes a unity to the male characters as well: "Cyril is probably just as self-destructive as Hugh. Hugh in his death is at least probably as much the visionary as Cyril is. I was trying to deal with the components, the parts, the inadequate fragments of human nature" (Scholes 200). The status of the whole composed by the men, however, puts them in the position of the mythologizers, a position of power that remains unmitigated by the fact that Cyril mythologizes himself and Hugh as well as the women.

Mythologizing is consonant with Cyril's interest in obliterating the oppression of history, which he sees as encouraging repression in its "public" form and perpetuating tragedy in its "private" form. He and Fiona slough off the entanglements of their erotic lives, and, as he says, "tried to console each other for each pair of friends who, weaker or less fortunate than ourselves, went down in flames" (56). Cyril's ability to emerge unsinged from his experiences has its basis in his conception of the self, by way of sexual/spiritual virginity, as perpetually renewable; making love to Catherine for the first time he imagines himself as a "white bull" who "finally carried my now clamorous companion into a distant corner of the vast tapestry where only a little silvery spring lay waiting to restore virginity and quench thirst" (117). Cyril does not shun memory, however; memory, in fact, is an important tool for the intricate weaving of his narrative, which is a reworking of history. He contrasts himself to Fiona, who "did not share my interest in coherence and full circles. For better or worse, Fiona lived free of the shades of memory" (225). When he is trying to win Hugh over to his idea of sexual multiplicity and to get him to reconcile himself to the fact of Catherine's "infidelity," Cyril says, "if you can accept the past . . . then you won't have any reason to destroy the present" (249). But Cyril's own acceptance of the past depends on his absolute power to arrange and interpret that past, as well as his conviction that he can recover what he wants to of it.

In making his experiences conform to his theory of sexual multiplicity, Cyril juxtaposes scenes that indicate the failure of his theory with those that embody its potential success or actual realization, a narrative ordering that enacts the renewable quality of virginity. Yet at the same time he denies any need for renewal by invoking the static, immutable quality of his world: "In Illyria there are no seasons" (271). Even in the sterile present of his unreciprocated feelings for Catherine, when she will not even speak to him, he asks himself why she doesn't know that "our present relationship is already as unlimited and undeniable as our past affair? After all, there is something glorious about standing together in time as two large white graceful beasts might stand permanently together in an empty field" (121). But the beasts would stand so only if the field were the woven one of a tapestry. Cyril suggests the simultaneity of permanence and renewal when he describes the golden days of Illyria that fulfilled his tapestry, when the foursome enjoys "murmurous nonsequential midafternoons" (227); the absence of linearity allows for difference but obliterates time. Near the very end of his narrative Cyril recalls that "there was a time when all our days were only memories of hours that had not yet passed and each one of us was in some way virginal" (269). Such a conception allows Cyril to end his narrative by emphasizing the circularity of the objects on his wall, then to say "Everything coheres, moves forward" (271), which suggests linearity rather than circularity, and then to affirm the stasis of a seasonless world. His goal is to achieve a present that consumes both past and future, and his nonsequential narration is one enactment of this desire.

In order to reinstate himself as Catherine's lover when she leaves the sanitarium, Cyril takes her to the scenes and objects of their former life. The supply of landmarks and "relics" is "inexhaustible" (167–168); "what difference does it make," Cyril asks, "which kiss we recover, or which single laugh or which faint cry we hear again in silence?" (172) What is important is that they will, Cyril is confident, recover what they seek of the past. He tells us, "In an atmosphere of peaceful investigation we are traveling together from sign to sign, from empty stage to empty stage. . . . What we both know, we share. What Catherine does not know, I tell her" (168). Here again Cyril establishes his identity as a sex singer by his ability to read signs. But the signs themselves are empty, silent, until he fills them with meaning.

Cyril's experience and facility in reading the signs of sex accounts for his use of the disparaging "ignorant virginity." Yet he glorifies virginity and maintains that he and his friends are virginal, and thereby supports his idea that the sexual abundance of his world is innocent and beautiful. He grants virginity a meaning that is aesthetic and metaphoric.[5] The metaphor points to the "actuality of innocence," the very thing Hawkes says the relics Cyril lists at the end of his narrative—the flower crown, the chastity belt, the undershorts—are there to "insist on" (Scholes 169). Yet what Cyril insists on is the actuality of representation. In the last pages of his narrative he reads the frescoes on the wall of the small church where the narrative of his past in Illyria begins. Cyril says the "crude sketches" are of the "adolescence of the Virgin" (269), although he neglects the fact that this Virgin must be the Virgin Mary as he appropriates the figure for his own religion of innocent sexuality.[6] He recalls his remark to Fiona when he first saw the sketches: "Look up there, Fiona. Proof enough?" (269). But even if the sketches were clear instead of indistinct blots of color, they cannot stand as proof of anything; they can be only a testament to artistry, and the artistry here is Cyril's. "At first glance," he says, "the wordless story is simply barren, undecipherable, says nothing" (270). Cyril explicates the cipher, makes it speak the language of his changeless song, interprets hints of line and color as the substantiation of his theory of renewable virginity. He translates the images of Illyria into the marks of the painting, and, at the end of describing the painting, transfers what he sees in it to the inhabitants of Illyria: "Yellow was Fiona's favorite color. I have seen Hugh's narrow eyes downcast in the midst of his craving. Catherine's face did not betray her longing. Even at night the four of us walked in that light the color of cut wheat" (271). These aesthetic resonances are, for Cyril, his theory's only confirmation.

Cyril does not allow the fact that his present relationship with Catherine is "sexless matrimony" (97) to upset his theory of sexual multiplicity, for as important as lovemaking is to him, sex is foremost a language: "if orgasm is the pit of the fruit then lyricism is its flesh" (210).[7] Ironically, the fruit from which the title takes its name, and whose colors suffuse various scenes in the novel, is a fruit that has segments containing seeds but no pit at its center. The one "pit" in the novel is a grave pit, dug by Cyril as part of the elaborate ceremony for Hugh's dead dog. Cyril refers to himself as "the man who had dug to the center of

Hugh's fantasy and laid bare the wet and sandy pit of death" (221). The danger in all the sensual segments of Cyril's narrative is that his lyricism is just an excess of language covering over a deadly assertion of will which itself covers over a void. Hawkes describes the significance of the image of the blood orange: "The fruit is sweet, but it's streaked with the color of blood, which to me is a paradox. It means that the blood is real but also sweet; it means that no sweetness is ephemeral but on the contrary possesses all the life-drive seriousness of the rich black flow of blood itself. It suggests wound invading desire, desire 'containing' agony" (Scholes 202).[8] Hawkes uses the image as representative of his concern with the power of language to embody the ugly in beautiful form, which recalls his defining language, as well as virginity, as paradox. "Cyril's modest defiance of matrimonial conventions," Hawkes says, "is intended to lead us into realities of the imagination. He is trying to talk about paradox, or the existence of that which does not exist" (Scholes 198). In *The Blood Oranges*, paradox includes the inextricable connection between the seemingly opposite Cyril and Hugh, for as Cyril himself admits, "Hugh was also a sex-singer of sorts. But in Hugh's dry mouth our lovely song became a shriek" (58).

The loveliness—and success—of Cyril's song depends on his ability to verbalize his vision. When he removes the chastity belt from Catherine, he says, "And now what on Catherine's body had been Hugh's chastity belt alive with tension and cruelly snug, in my two hands was only a pathetic dangling contraption withered and faintly rattling" (257); one might comment that a pathetic dangling contraption is precisely what this story would be in the hands of anyone less skillful than Cyril—or Hawkes. But Cyril's narrative does have the contrivance of contraption. Cyril selects and interprets his material in accordance with his theory, and at the same time, Hawkes purposely places the scene in which Hugh accidentally hangs himself immediately after the one in which he finally makes love to Fiona in order to fool the reader into interpreting Hugh's action as a moral judgment on Cyril's attempt to institute sexual multiplicity.[9] It is Hawkes's desire to destroy fictional and social conventionality through creating worlds in which sexual repression, perversion, and death open up "the moment of freedom from constriction, constraint, death" (Scholes 207). In Cyril he creates a character whose desire it is consciously to perform this release himself.

But just as Hawkes proclaims absolute detachment, authority, and cruelty necessary to his creation, Cyril also exercises these propensities; he readily implies, and sometimes even states, his detachment and authority, but he only suggests, in veiled and mostly unconscious terms, his access to cruelty. What Cyril does insist on is the privileging of imaginative realities. When Fiona says there is an eagle in the dawn sky and Hugh can't see it, Cyril says, "Take another look. . . . He's there" (137). Cyril himself cannot in fact see an eagle, but tells us, "Between Fiona's voice and Hugh's sometimes brusque insistence on reality there was, for me, no choice" (138). Yet this same need to ally himself with imaginative realities necessitates his allying himself with Hugh: "it will take a dark mind to strip my vines, to destroy the last shreds of my tapestry, to choke off my song. It will take a lot to destroy Hugh's photographs or to gut the many bedrooms of the sleeping castle. I am a match, I hope, for the hatred of conventional enemies wherever they are" (36). At the same time that Hugh is supposedly everything Cyril is fighting against, Cyril co-opts Hugh's photographs as testaments against a conventional world. Cyril exists on a tenuous border. His various contrivances are there to enhance sexuality, as the chastity belt does for Hugh. For Hugh the excitement is in putting the belt on; for Cyril, in taking it off. The belt is—at least metaphorically—necessary for both. "Is it possible that in purging her field of Hugh's sick innocence Love purged me as well?" asks Cyril (3). But love cannot purge him, because he institutes his presence in "her" field again and again by excluding other voices.

Cyril can make a distinction between his innocence and Hugh's sick innocence, much as he makes a distinction between virginity and ignorant virginity, because his vision gains validity through opposition. Hawkes speaks of the excitement of his visionary fiction as residing in its opposition to the constraints of life,[10] and his formulations about the autonomy of his art have frequently been echoed by critics. To take an example of this in its most summary form, John Knapp's article on Hawkes in Frank Magill's multi-volume *Critical Survey of Long Fiction* refers to the metaphoric connections and directed statements held in common among Hawkes's works as constituting "self-contained fictional worlds" (1304–1305). Knapp's use of "self-contained" has, as part of its definition, the idea that the worlds of Hawkes's works are distinct from the "real world," but his meaning extends to the notion that Hawkes's works are interrelated. Clearly, then, the texts deny containment in their shifting boundaries. In *The Blood Oranges*, the closed circle of Cyril's narration, imagistically embodied by the circularity of the objects on his wall, is only a provisional containment. Not only does Hawkes comment on this text in his subsequent novels, but he also, in this text itself, implies the interpenetration of his fictional worlds and the world in which these fictions exist.

Cyril duplicates Hawkes's position of authorial detachment throughout his narration, often explicitly, as when he tells Catherine, "I can give you clarity . . . but not understanding" (116). Yet it is precisely understanding that Hawkes wants his fiction to engender in his readers: "My fiction has always been concerned with reversed sympathy, and the whole point of it has been to help the reader expand his own capacities for compassion" (O'Donnell 126). The products of such artistic detachment demand the reader's complete participation. Cyril demands that we engage ourselves, if only imaginatively, in his liberatory efforts, that we break the chastity belt with him. We must let the blood orange illumination of his prose suffuse us, too. If we do not, Cyril is simply a pompous, self-righteous egotist, verbose, self-absorbed, and insidious. At the same time, Hawkes elicits sympathy for Hugh to the extent that the reader could mistake Hugh's hanging as a moral judgment against Cyril. Neither identifying with Cyril nor remaining disapprovingly distanced can be a stable position; neither stance has the clarity of innocence. For Cyril's own position is on the shifting border of innocence and power, and his efforts to transfigure desire suffer the contradictions of invasion and containment embodied in the image of the blood orange which "suggests wound invading desire, desire 'containing' agony" (Scholes 202). Cyril wants unviolated wholeness. Yet his seeking an idyllic union between man and woman, between couples, between theory and practice, between word and world encompasses violence in its most successful moments and is threatened by violence in its most tenuous. His sex song glorifies a beautiful and permanently intact sexuality whose place is assured only in his words themselves. Outside this song lies Catherine with her "unreadable eyes" (41), the dead Hugh and the echo of his shriek, and the missing Fiona for whose footsteps Cyril listens.

## II

> At least one important theory of art has concluded that, though the world be without purpose, or justice, or meaning (as far as reason can confidently ascertain), the unified objects which art makes of these spoiling fragments renders things finally as they ought to be, for even if every actor suffered and then died during an Elizabethan tragedy (and sometimes that nearly happened), and the motives of men were mercilessly laid open like an ox that's been flayed so we might see the blood they had their baths in, the effect is not one of gloom or dismay, but of energy, wholeness, perfection, joy.
> —William Gass, *Habitations of the Word*

Hawkes describes *Death, Sleep & the Traveler* as "a reverse of the progression in *The Blood Oranges*" (O'Donnell 117). In both novels there has been a death and the narrator circles around his involvement in this death. Cyril's circling seeks to wind him back into the center of his tapestry. However fragile its fabric, Cyril's narration is an act of self-constitution; he insists on the wholeness, perfection, and joy of his fragmented, ravished, and ravishing world and self. Allert's narration in *Death, Sleep & the Traveler* is an act of self-annihilation. Hawkes says "annihilation is the twin of the imagination" (Ziegler 179), a pairing that in *The Blood Oranges* condemns Hugh to death while Cyril sings his sex song. In *Death, Sleep & the Traveler* the productive and destructive aspects of the imagination play themselves out within Allert himself, as he undergoes what Hawkes describes as "the poet's descent into the underworld or into the unconscious in search of the self" (Ziegler 178). Hawkes calls Allert "a version of the lyrical, larger-than-life singer who doesn't sing, who is beginning to act out the warmth, the fear, the lyrical stuff of sexuality in a context of its hurt, nothingness, and silence" (O'Donnell 118–119). The novel juxtaposes the ménage à trois consisting of Allert, his wife, Ursula, and his best friend, Peter, with the love triangle of Allert, Ariane, and the wireless operator, the people whom he meets and tangles with on his sea journey. In addition, the novel—or Allert, as its narrator—juxtaposes the events of Allert's life with his dreams, his nocturnal "psychic siphoning" (51). Yet these multiplicities yield no unities. The hurt, nothingness, and silence in which lyricism founders is the silence of materials that will not cohere, and of a self that remains dispersed among the events and interpretations that constitute it.

Ursula accuses Allert of dreaming his life rather than living it, and indeed, he spends much time detailing his dreams not only for us, the readers, but for Ursula, in spite of the fact that her interpretations are usually reductive and cruel. Dreams, what Freud calls the "royal road to the unconscious," are the journey underlying the actual sea journey Allert takes. He reports a dream that seems to enact a return to the womb and which allows him to "survey the desolation of my own beginning" (74). The dream, he says, is "central" to his life (75); the particulars of it are "thick with significance" (72). But it is in fact this very plenum of meaning he attributes to his dreams that allows them to elude a central position or centering function.

In discussing Freud's *Interpretation of Dreams*, Edward Said says, "in Freud wealth arises from that which is by definition unknown. For a prose text like the *Interpretation* this means that meaning cannot be imagined as residing in a finished object like the dream; nor for that matter can meaning precede its verbal description. Rather, the meaning of the unknown (unconscious) is always being produced; each segment of an analysis builds a more complex sense" (168). Allert presents his dream images and dream thoughts in verbal form, and Ursula gives her trenchant commentary which always cuts through to Allert's fear of life, fear of women, and emotional poverty. One is inclined to agree with such interpretations, but at the same time one rebels at the limitation Ursula's words impose on the rich glut of images the dreams possess. In this way the reader is ensnared as yet another third party in Allert's self-exploration, for his dreams reflect back on and enlarge the significance of the events and meditations of his life on land and at sea and inform the fragments of life related after them, thus involving the reader in the interpretation of Allert's psyche and piecing together of his identity. The dream images are diffused among the fragments of the book; the fragments of the book are distilled in the dream images. To adapt Said on Freud, the meaning of Allert's existence is always being produced; each segment of the novel builds a more complex sense. We must do what Ursula relinquishes. While she is with Allert she renders his dreams finite; as she leaves Allert she tells him, "You will find some nice young thing to hear your dreams" (179). It is we who hear his dreams, of both his sleeping and waking hours, and we who are involved in their pointing to both void and plenum, refusing any static or stable position.

A close look at Allert's dream of entering a womb, the dream he calls central, is useful in illustrating how the limitation of meaning such as Ursula imposes is inadequate. In this dream Allert carefully picks his way across a field of cow manure toward a chateau (an image associated with his boyhood), but suddenly realizes the field is not strewn with cow manure but with congealed blood.[11] The image turns from excrement to a bloody field of war and death and, in light of what follows, to menstrual blood. He enters the chateau, which is

> desolate except for one small structure standing altar-like and frightening in the center of the stone floor. I approach, I am breathing deeply. Erect and with hands at my sides I face the sacred structure which is twice my height and circular at the base and pointed on top—like some prehistoric tribal tent—and covered entirely with dry and hairless animal skins. . . . [S]lowly I descend to my knees, insert my fingers in the seam where two large bottom skins are joined, and slowly pull them apart until the darkness will accommodate my entry on all fours. (73–74)

Inside this enclosure, "in a meaningless crouch I survey the desolation of my own beginning" (74). Ursula's "only reply was that it was obviously someone else's womb, not hers, that had become so inhospitable to my regressive drives. Her own womb, she answered me, was warm and receptive always, as I surely knew" (75).

The dream does seem an obvious return to the womb, and, as Ursula suggests, reveals Allert's insecurity regarding women. But also, it certainly reveals something about Allert's relation to his mother, and beyond that, something about the meaning or lack of meaning in Allert's existence, something about the possibility of change, something about the force of history and the past, something about the force of myth, about the possibility of knowledge, about being about. Its images of excrement, of slime, of sinking, of social class, of bone, of relics, resonate throughout the novel. The dream is central in that it is significant, but it has no center itself. It points to various locations of meaning, so that focusing on only one image or set of images creates a construct which is incomplete, and so in some sense false. One cannot, finally, produce all of the dream's meanings without reproducing the dream. Furthermore, the dream acquires significance because of the fragments of Allert's life among which it exists; its "centrality" depends on the "centrality" of the events which it metaphorizes.

Ursula labels the activity of this dream, full of womb imagery, as entering the womb, but the imagery can just as easily be read as describing an anal entry. This could indicate homosexual impulses in Allert,[12] but acknowledging Allert's interest in the same sex adds little to an account of Allert as absorbed by the problem of his own sexuality in all its frustration and violence and by the problem of conceiving of his existence in relation to other people. More significant is the fact that reproduction and excretion are identified with each other. The metaphysical problem posed to men by the proximity of the sex and excretory organs has, of course, often been addressed, perhaps most pithily by Yeats's Crazy Jane; in *Death, Sleep & the Traveler* the horror of this human condition is the substance of Allert's journey. Ursula calls him an "open cesspool" (46), although Allert disagrees with her metaphor, saying that he simply is "not afraid of Psyche's slime" (75). For Allert, "Psyche's slime" is the "hurt, nothingness, and silence" of sexuality, the desolation and destruction inherent in what has the potential to be life-giving. The termination of life is itself excremental, as the indignity of Peter's death so clearly illustrates. With his hand Allert removes the excrement from Peter's body, certain that his hand "would be forever stained with the death of [his] friend" (171). But this seems the most fitting imaging of death in the midst of the "rich" sexual life Allert has so destructively experienced with Ursula and Peter—whose genitals, while he's alive, look like "some kind of excreted pile of waste" (37). In the parallel triangle of Allert, Ariane, and the wireless operator, Ariane's violent mating with this other man takes place on the floor of an excremental reptile house. In what Allert sees as a more humorous situation, Ursula is enraged when one of Allert's girlfriends sits on her handbag, "like a stupid chicken giving anal birth to my own uterine baggage" (60). Allert tells us he had also understood the "symbolic message" of the incident, but had reacted with "inward pleasure" (60). The image of anal birth is reflected in Allert's dream of uterine or anal entry. More than an obsession or perversion, Allert's confusion of reproduction or sexuality with excretion, his association of heightened life with horrible death, suffuses not only the dreams he reproduces in the telling, but also the recurring images of his exploration of his sexual self—his psychic cesspool, and his interest in the reproduced photographs that compose the sexually reified world of his pornography collection.

Allert begins relating his anal/uterine dream by describing the night in it as being "pure and dark as a blackened negative" (72). A blackened negative is one from which no clear picture can emerge. But it is precisely clear pictures that Allert longs for and it is this longing that, in part, fuels his interest in pornography. Allert's collection of pornography is extensive. Ursula explains to Peter that "[f]or Allert almost anything representing the female or female form is pornographic" (149). She goes on to say that "Allert's theory is that the ordinary man becomes an artist only in sex. In which case pornography is the true field of the ordinary man's imagination" (153). Yet although Ursula says her reasons for leaving Allert are "not at all sexual" (46), she also tells him he is emotionally dead and the least sensual person she has ever known. Furthermore, she tells him that he does not know himself. It is by taking a psychic journey that Allert attempts to redeem himself sexually and to realize his imagination. At the start of the actual journey Allert takes, the wireless operator gives him an old pornographic photograph. Allert wonders "[i]f the wireless officer was attempting to intimidate me through the photograph or tell me something about myself that I did not know" (39). Although Allert doesn't welcome the gift of the photograph, he later masturbates with its images in mind:

Though the photograph was in fact safely concealed in my jacket pocket, still the two white figures were clearly there, small and fiercely wriggling on the smooth glossy skin of the palm of my right hand, as if the pink living skin of my palm had become a little bed of photographic emulsion developed and hardened and translucent.

But when I reminded myself of the similar plight of Macbeth's poor queen, and then rubbed the offending palm against the fruit of my own genitalia, the little image of the old-fashioned naked lovers faded and fled completely away for once and for all. (70–71)

The scene associates guilt with the reified sexuality of the photograph, under which "living skin" disappears. It seems Allert's orgasm is the ablution that absolves this guilt, since it at least is a "lived" sexual moment. (The stain on his hands from Peter's defecatory death, however, will not disappear.) In a related incident, Allert, feeling excluded from Ursula and Peter's lovemaking, leaves them to copulate before a fire and then returns, seeing "[t]heir bodies . . . slick and moving and fire-lit as if in the emulsion of a photograph still hanging wet and glossy in the darkroom" (95). Allert remains the distanced viewer, as reality drains from sexuality once again. His favorite form of pornography, in fact, is black and white photographs, a preference that is consonant with a wish to emphasize the quality of the photograph as photograph, rather than as a captured moment. In a dream that Ursula says explains Allert's "collector's interest in pornography" (51), Allert dreams that he is a little boy who ejaculates sitting in a barbershop chair and looking into a mirror at a black and white photograph of a boy looking at a naked girl. Ursula comments that it would have been better if Allert had been the actual boy watching the girl, and without any photographer's intervention. The dream can be seen as referring not only to Allert's interest in pornography, but to the dynamics of experiencing love in a triad. In *Travesty* Papa speaks of seeing love "through the prism of another woman" (64), but in the case of Allert, who sees love through the prism of both the man and the woman involved in each of his triads, the men and women disappear, leaving only the prism itself—a prism reduced to black and white, with the potential for clarity but also for the obscuration of encroaching blackness.

Allert, a man whom Peter says never emerges from his "flickering cave," longs for a clarity and ideality denied by his world of dream and shadows. Transposing his fear of his own death-like state onto the ship, Allert is continually tormented by the thought that the ship has come to a standstill. When the sea is rough, he says, "I was willing to suffer any amount of motion sickness . . . for the sake of just such comprehensible turbulence under a clear sun" (31–32). Speaking of Ursula and Peter near the end of his narrative, he says, "I wish we had been only dark figures within a gilded frame" (165). But his life and the lives of those around him remain in the murky world of desire and violence and love. Finally, it is precisely this murkiness that Allert uses to his advantage in obscuring the facts of his murderous guilt. On the nudist island with Ariane and the wireless operator he is caught in the clarity he covets and sees it as the loss of self he fears. The island's sunlight "decomposed all colors to white and hence made the island landscape a brilliant unreality" (102). Comparing his large and flabby body to the wireless operator's lean and muscular one, Allert says, "the chemical horror of the gleaming sun reduced us equally to the dead white quality of the beach itself, exposed quite equally our blemishes" (102). Stripped of the feeling of protection, he has all the glaring object-ness of the photograph. Yet at the same time he experiences a degree of freedom, performing with Ariane "like two unshelled creatures risen together from the white sandy floor of the sea" (106–107).

In his interview with Patrick O'Donnell, Hawkes refers to the nudist island as

small, unrealistic, and it polarizes ordinary life against mythic life. It gets abstracted into the second island of the goats, the past. Illyria, whether it's Skipper's tropical island or Cyril's "island," becomes, in *Death, Sleep & the Traveler*, only and finally, a place where goats live eternally, without humans. It's the goats Ariane plays to, the Sedar or Pan figures who, by then, have been condensed or reduced to singleness—Pan with no humans, no love; it's an emblem. (119)

Hawkes presents here an image of life both enriched and reduced. These polarities can be seen in Allert's horror and pleasure on the nudist island, but the polarities exist not only in the opposition of the ordinary and the mythic, but within the mythic itself. While myth has the potential to grant form and beauty to reality, Angela Carter, in her book *The Sadeian Woman and the Ideology of Pornography*, points out that its application to sexual relations is deadening and dehumanizing, with pornography the clearest manifestation of this. Carter writes:

Myth deals in false universals, to dull the pain of particular circumstances. In no area is this more true than in that of relations between the sexes. . . . Since all pornography derives directly from myth, it follows that its heroes and heroines, from the most gross to the most sophisticated, are mythic abstractions, heroes and heroines of dimension and capacity. Any glimpse of a real man or a real woman is absent from these representations of the archetypal male and female. (5–6)

Allert's subjection to such archetypes is clear in his obsession with pornography, and it influences his relations with Ursula and Ariane as well. Ursula asks Allert, "Why must you always try to mythologize our sexual lives?"; Allert replies, "I am merely trying to articulate the sensual mind" (176–177). Ursula says, "I wish you'd stop poeticizing my crotch"; Allert replies, "the imagination cannot be denied" (79–80). These exchanges highlight the problem at stake for Allert and his narrative: the imagination extends the possibility of beauty and meaning, but also threatens to obliterate the individual and experience.

Allert, feeling himself developing into a lurid photograph on the nudist island, says that "In the midst of our frightening white scene [Ariane] alone was desirable and real" (102). It is Ariane's quality of realness, of enticing actuality, that strikes Allert in his first moments alone with her when they play net ball on the ship: "these circumstances could not have been more concrete, more neutral, *more devoid of meaning*, more appropriate to the surprise and simplicity of the occasion at hand, when an unknown young woman was offering me something beyond innocence, companionship, flirtation" (44; my emphasis). Such absence of circumstantial meaning is in stark contrast with the overdetermined meaning of Allert's dreams. For Allert, Ariane contains the necessary meaning within herself, and this meaning is generous and immediate sexuality. She offers him access to the real.

Yet Allert finally learns that she offers him access to the real because she offers him access to myth, and the reality embedded in myth is death. Allert's and Ariane's contrasting attitudes toward the island of goats illustrates his obliviousness to the meaning that Ariane extends to him. Ariane, enthralled by the sight of the island, says the goats are "unreal," but to Allert they seem very real (55). And in fact goats are very real animals, and in many contexts quite prosaic ones. It is only by imaginatively transforming them, by applying a myth and sexuality to them out of cultural and personal stock, that they can attain anything more than resistant animality. Ariane "owns" the island of goats (58) because she enacts just such an imaginative appropriation. When she masks her genitals in a goat's skull, the skull is a "mythical . . . garment"; in this masking which unmasks the connection between sex and death, she fuses "her own delicacy with the skull of the animal Eros" (175). Allert now understands Ariane's ownership of the goat island. After making love to this skull-clad woman, he begs her not to go to the ship's costume ball, for that will be an affair in which masks are only so many guises of an all too material and competitive world. Ariane will go dressed as a ship's officer, an incarnation of the adversary who thwarts Allert's own sexuality, and Allert will go dressed as a Dutch burgher, a dull and pragmatic accumulator. It seems Allert's motive for killing Ariane is not only jealousy of the other recipients of her generosity, but an inability to allow the slippage of the mythical expression of life into the mundane battle of affections. He can preserve the mythical only at the expense of the real.

The juxtaposition of an animal skull and Ariane's living sex imbues each with a meaning beyond their singular status, but at the same time diminishes the reality of each of them. This diminishment is presaged by Allert's reaction to the pornographic photograph the wireless officer puts on top of his suitcase: "each diminished in some small way the reality of the other, or at least altered it" (38). The fact that it is a pornographic photo that is involved in producing this compromised reality is consonant with the transformation of people and sexuality into objects or archetypes achieved in pornography itself. But the problem is not that simple; looking at the photo on the suitcase, Allert concludes "that the smallest alteration in the world of physical objects produces the severest and most frightening transformation of reality" (38). Allert's perception of the world around him is an extension of his struggle with his own being; he is unable "to believe in the reality of the human self" (90). The presence of the photo on the suitcase is "inexplicable, ringed with invisible chains of unanswerable questions" (38). But so too is his life a recalcitrant puzzle. "[S]ooner or later," Allert says, "the young child discovers that he cannot account for himself. As soon as he becomes inexplicable he becomes unreal. Immediately everything else becomes unreal as one might expect. The rest is puzzlement. Or terror" (90–91).

Allert depends on language to explain the world and to articulate an identity. The novel is his attempt to account for his existence as well as account for his innocence or guilt in regard to Ariane's murder. But Allert structures his account by juxtaposing fragments of his life in each of his separate love triangles and juxtaposing these fragments with his dreams. Each fragment to some extent diminishes the reality of the other, and so finally diminishes the reality of his guilt.

Myth is one recourse Allert has in his accounting, but ultimately myth fails him. His tortured groping for myth is in contrast to Ariane's seemingly natural evocation of it. In the early stages of their relationship, Allert sees her as a perfectly ordinary girl, yet, as Hawkes says, "She is a singer at home with the skulls of dead goats." Hawkes goes on to say that "Maybe Allert is the Minotaur that she can save people from" (O'Donnell 119). In this conception Ariane turns into Ariadne and Allert turns into a carnivorous monster; yet it is also true that Allert is a Theseus figure, led by Ariane/Ariadne into the labyrinth of himself where his own monstrous impulses are ready to devour him. But Allert is unable to use the thread of Ariane to find his way out of his self-entrapment. Instead he wanders in the tortuous cell of his psyche where his personal past and cultural myths block his reemergence into the world of the living.

When Allert disagrees with Ursula's accusation that he thinks of himself as Casanova, he says, "I am not interested in the long thread of golden hair hanging from the tower window" (84). And indeed, he is not interested in ascending to the heights where awaits love with a real woman, but rather in descending to the depths of his loveless self-absorption. The thread he follows is the auto-erotically produced thread of his own semen. In a dream of himself as a young boy dressing in a woman's undergarments and gazing at himself in a mirror, he ejaculates a "long, thin phosphorescent string" that shoots and coils "endlessly" to the ceiling (140). His predicament lies in the belief that "I myself am the only access to what I want to know" (138). Near the end of his narrative Allert laments that he, his wife, and his best friend had not known each other. Yet he images the possibility of having known Peter from the inside as the death of his own self, the result being that "[a]ll speculations, like loose phosphorescent threads shot dreamily into a cold night, would be at an end" (165). Allert's self-reproducing speculations, however, are themselves a form of self-annihilation. In composing the fragments of his life, he asserts their significance but also their resistance to the significances he would impose.

For Allert, the ship and the sea are "incomprehensible," just as he is for himself. When he feels the ship is still, it is "suddenly purposeless and hence meaningless" (7). The ship's journey achieves purpose for Allert after the murder of Ariane: "someone had at last discovered our destination. . . . Now we were on course to a destination" (171–172). The murder provides purpose and movement; the goal is Allert's trial and vindication or condemnation. Yet, although there is every reason to believe that Allert is Ariane's murderer, Allert denies his guilt, and therefore in a sense denies movement. The events he has related lead up to no conclusion. One manifestation of the absence of movement is the fragmentation of the narrative into juxtaposed achronological parts. But more than that, the stasis is within Allert's self-accounting. Peter tells Allert, "If you manage to destroy your guilt, my friend, you will destroy yourself. . . . [A]ll your generosity and even your strength depend on unfathomable guilt, which is part of your charm" (48). At the time of the novel's telling it is "eight or perhaps nine" years since Allert's acquittal, and three years since Peter's death (135). It is usually not clear whether the various scenes Allert describes between himself, Peter, and Ursula are before or after his sea journey, but Peter's words go beyond circumstance to essence. His words lend Allert's last words—"I am not guilty"— an apocalyptic quality. Allert is acquitted, but his narration indicates that he did kill Ariane. He twice reports Peter's claim that "a man remains a virgin until he commits murder" (26, 145), a formulation that presents the paradox of Allert's story. If Allert is guilty of murder, this guilt would destroy his innocence; yet, according to Peter, if he destroys his guilt he destroys himself. Allert's narration is one in which he tries to get at the reality of the self and which closes with a concise self-description—his denial of guilt. But what Allert tells us is what the self *is not*. In so doing, he both asserts and denies his self's existence; like guilt, like virginity, like paradox, like language, the self both exists and does not exist.

Allert is, for himself, the journey and the journey's end. And the end of the journey is silence. Allert concludes his narrative listing possible directions his life could take with Ursula gone, but he rejects these possibilities in favor of thinking and dreaming. The result is much the same as in Allert's dream of his own beginning, where he realizes "that I had hoped for more, had expected more, and yet in the midst of such silence and immobility I also realize that my disappointment is nothing compared with the journey I have just taken and the barren actuality I have at last discovered" (74). Allert's narrative itself returns to silence. When Ursula explains to Allert why she is leaving him she accuses him of bearing this silence within himself: "you have long since emotionally annihilated yourself, Allert, and I can no longer tolerate your silences, your silence in the throes of passion, the accounts of your dreams, the stink from the cesspool that is yourself" (46). Even in his conversations with

Ursula and Peter, Allert more often reserves comment than speaks his mind. But his silence, apparently abrogated in his narration of his inner journey, is not only within himself; finally, it is the silence of events that forever lack immediacy and do not reveal a conclusive meaning. Speaking of Ursula's leaving, Allert says, "I felt nothing, I anticipated no approaching pain, but was aware only of the perception of the event rather than the event itself. I was aware of silence. I was aware of the faded light" (112). His focus is visual and moribund (and is reminiscent of the distancing produced in pornography). In its silence the event is itself an absence. Allert tries to counteract such absence; he strives for presence and meaning by transforming circumstance through language.

Allert speaks of Ursula as a source of language, as well as myth: "Ursula was to me one woman and every woman. . . . Ursula was practical, physical, mythical, and . . . all the multiplicities of her natural power were not merely products of my own projections or even of the culture into which she was born . . . but to start with were engendered most explicitly in her name alone. Uterine, ugly, odorous, earthen, vulval, convolvulaceous, saline, mutable, seductive—the words, the qualities kept issuing without cessation from the round and beautiful sound of her name" (61). One woman and every woman, Ursula is ultimately no woman at all. The ceaseless flow of words Allert attributes to her name contrasts with the delimitation imposed by the words Ursula herself uses when interpreting his dreams or psyche. For Allert, Ursula's name breeds words upon itself, but in constructing his narration it is Allert who must give birth to words and who in fact grants Ursula's name its power.

At the conclusion of his narration he invokes the names of concrete objects: "I shall think of porridge, leeks, tobacco, white clay, and water coursing through a Roman aqueduct" (179). There seems to be no particular rationale for the content of this list; instead, the words exist as an invocation of solidity that will, however, remain only abstract. The act of concretizing is immediately undermined. The moment is reminiscent of Allert's strategy when Ariane tells him she wants to play the flute for him and he condescendingly agrees, filling his words with "whitewash and ducks and potato soup" (67). He summons the ordinary, through language, before what proves to be a very extraordinary event. Yet at the very beginning of his narration Allert demonstrates that seemingly ordinary words translate into deeper levels of meaning. Dining for the first time on board the ship, Allert says, "This consommé . . . has been siphoned from the backs of lumbering tortoises whose pathetic shells have been drilled for the tubes" (11). Allert realizes he "should not have spoken, should not have revealed in hyperbole my loneliness, my distaste for travel, my ambiguous feelings about the girl" (11). This realization suggests Allert's tendency to apply "dream work" to anything. No words are innocent of meanings.

The indirection of dreams and the indirection of metaphoric language culminate in the indirection of Allert's sea journey, a journey that acquires direction only after Allert is held guilty of murdering Ariane. But Allert denies this direction, for the destination at which it can end, beyond the event of the trial, is the finitude of the appellation "guilty." Instead, he constitutes guilt and innocence as a dialectic. As innocence and guilt are in a dialectic, so are language and silence. Allert maintains power over what he reveals and how he reveals it, but at the same time this power is transferred to the ability or failure of language to reveal. Words are not innocent of meanings, but they are innocent of a *single* meaning. At the close of his narrative Allert lists possible courses of action, including incarceration in a mental hospital, suicide, and a return to the village of his youth. But he rejects a choice among these possibilities for the open-endedness of thinking and dreaming. His claim that he is not guilty clutches at clarity, but the text shows that clarity repeatedly collapses—into a proliferation of interpretations, into the vagaries of existence, into violence. Clarity is a death. If Allert destroys his guilt, he destroys himself. His own narration discounts his claim that he is not guilty and works an inversion on the sense of innocence and guilt. Peter says a man is a virgin, or innocent, until he commits murder; Allert's narrative suggests that a text is innocent until it murders possible meanings in favor of only one. His verbal exploration of his inner self is innocent, though this self is a cesspool and this self is guilty of murder. As Ursula prepares to leave him, he thinks, "I had known her in every way yet not at all" (178). Nor, with all his self-probing, does he know himself. At the end of his journey, Allert is still innocent of knowledge.

## III

> [H]e saw her invisible, he touched her intact, in her shadowy absence, in that veiled presence which did not hide her absence, which was the presence of her infinite absence. . . . He is no less dead than she—dead, not of that tranquil worldly death which is rest, silence, and end, but of that other death which is death without end, the ordeal of the end's absence.
> —Maurice Blanchot, *The Space of Literature*

Driving "at one hundred and forty-nine kilometers per hour on a country road in the darkest quarter of the night" (*Travesty* 11), heading deliberately for a stone wall a meter thick, listening to his daughter vomit and his best friend violently wheeze, "Papa" tries to account for his existence. "Who does not fear the inexplicable fact of his existence?" he asks. "Who does not dread the unimaginable condition of not existing?" (81). But the narrator of *Travesty* rejects the suggestion of his friend and fellow traveler, Henri, that his suicidal and murderous drive is motivated by the fear of death, by the human condition of being "so consumed by what we wish to avoid that we can no longer avoid it" (83). Papa also rejects Henri's accusation that he is performing out of jealousy over the fact that Henri is the lover of both Papa's wife, Honorine, and Papa's daughter, Chantal. He instead offers the meaning of the coming explosive disintegration as an apotheosis of the imagination—for himself and Henri, as well as for the absent Honorine.

Hawkes describes *Travesty* as being "about a nameless man who sheds his guilt, turns perversity into an act of courage, and experiences what it is to be a poet" (Ziegler 181). But to call courageous and poetic an act of ultimate violence against the self and others, including, as some critics have pointed out, the reader,[13] is to call into question the ideology of such radical aestheticism. As a monologue, Papa's narrative takes to an extreme the self-enclosed form of Cyril's and Allert's narrative worlds and exposes the deadly end of such authorial control. Like Cyril, who refuses any responsibility for the cataclysmic events he relates, claiming that all those who sing the sex song are innocent, and like Allert, who refuses any responsibility for the murder of Ariane, claiming he is not guilty, Papa also proclaims that he is free of guilt, that the very idea of guilt is in fact a fiction. But instead of making such a claim a denial of responsibility, Papa makes responsibility for his imaginative act and its physical ramifications the foundation of its meaning. It is the creation of a unitary meaning, and its simultaneous destruction, that is the engine of Papa's narrative. The paradox of a creation that is a destruction finds its clearest expression in Papa's paean to "the truest paradox," the "utter harmony between design and debris" (17) that his car crash will produce: "if design inevitably surrenders to debris, debris inevitably reveals its innate design" (59). This paradox subsumes all contraries in the novel and in Hawkes's stated aesthetics, so that *Travesty*, most explicitly of the novels in the triad, enacts both authorial innocence and power and their simultaneous loss.

The aim of Papa's discourse, reflecting Hawkes's aim for his readers, is ostensibly that Henri "achieve understanding" (77) and, further, that he participate in the creation of his death. "Surely," Papa says, "I must be able to strike that one slight blow that will cause all your oppressive defenses to fall, to disappear, leaving you free indeed to share equally in the responsibility I have assumed, short-lived or not" (82). His desire for shared responsibility corresponds to his idea of the dissolution of guilt in collective passions and disabilities: "Guilt is merely a pain that disappears as soon as we recognize the worst in us all" (36). In the course of his monologue Papa will relate the worst in himself, but the details of his conflicted or sadistic relations with others—for example, his misery when Chantal is happy or his beating his mistress—only serve to meld him into common patterns of behavior. For Papa, describing the events and perceptions of his life is equivalent to "taking our national inventory" (97), and he sees himself and Henri as "two perfect examples of our national type" (99). In Papa's conception, the idea of guilt establishes values or absolutes, affirmed through transgression, and provides an excuse for isolation: "secrets and so-called guilty deeds are fictions created to enhance the sense of privacy, to feed enjoyment into our isolation, to enlarge the rhythm of what most people need, which is belief in life" (36). Papa's only belief in life is as he invents it en route to his self-directed death, and, paradoxically, this death and the narration of this death are a means of ending isolation through reconciling all difference—between design and debris, but also between Papa and Henri, between Papa and Honorine, between word and act.

Erasing differences is, for Papa, ultimately erotic. Yet early in his narrative, describing the young Chantal's forays into the parental bedroom, Papa equates "erotic lives" and "illusory lives" (13). The erotic is defined for Papa by images common to the culture: "as a child I divided my furtive time quite equally between those periodicals depicting the most brutal and uncanny destructions of human flesh . . . and those other periodicals depicting the attractions of young living women partially or totally in the nude" (21). He can decry guilt as a fiction because it masks those feelings and actions we all hold in common, but these representations of sex and death, which, particularly in pornography, give the illusion of privacy as the senses possess the image, are also explicitly held in common and are, implicitly, fictions. In his dissection of his erotic life, Papa acknowledges both its fictiveness and its association with death but links these attributes to shame rather than guilt; he is one of those "select few, for whom the most ordinary kind of daily existence partakes of the contradictory sensation we know as shame. For such people everything, everything, is eroticized" (36). Shame shuns the absolutes of guilt, allowing instead for equivocation, for desire circumscribed by knowledge of the desire, and thus allowing for Papa's pretension to being the disseminator of this knowledge.

In acknowledging the commonality of the erotic representations that fascinate him, Papa reveals his horror of being a mere product of popular culture. He describes his relationship with his mistress, Monique, whose passion is collecting pornography, as the repeated acting out of pornographic clichés, and prefaces his description of how he violently spanked her by saying, "You will agree that no one wants to find himself becoming nothing more than a familiar type created by a hasty and un-talented pornographer. We do not like to think of ourselves as imaginary, salacious and merely one of the ciphers in the bestial horde" (68). He abhors the dissolution of individual identity, yet he expresses this abhor-rence as he rides to another and final dissolution in which "human re-mains" will be "integral with the remains of rubber, glass, steel" (59). This is the projected end that has Chantal crying on the floor of the car in what Papa disapprovingly calls a "grievous tabloidal gesture" (53), yet he knows that tabloid material is precisely what his accident will be when the policemen and reporters he imagines make notes and take photo-graphs (60) of his accident to produce the very type of graphic story that obsessed him in his own lonely boyhood.

But at the same time that he incarnates this cliché Papa believes he will transcend it. He relishes the idea that the accident will be a cipher for those who witness its remains and who puzzle over its details: "it will be unique, spectacular. . . . A clear 'accident,' so to speak, in which inven-tion quite defies interpretation" (23). The resistance to interpretation cannot, however, be absolute, for while Papa wants to achieve a "private apocalypse" (47) his privacy includes the accompaniment of Chantal and Henri, from the latter of whom Papa requires understanding. (Im-plicitly, the only valid understanding or interpretation would be one that coincides with Papa's intention.) That the reader is privy to Papa's self-inventory further situates the paradox of the autonomy and contingency of Papa's act. Papa is flagrantly in the position that Maurice Blanchot describes as the paradigmatic one of the writer as he writes: "The person who is alone is not the one who experiences the impression of being alone; this monster of desolation needs the presence of another if his desolation is to have a meaning, another who, with his reason intact and his senses preserved, renders momentarily possible the distress that had until then been impotent" (*The Gaze of Orpheus* 4). Papa gains mastery over the chaos and impotence of his life by transforming it in words, which, though they resist interpretation, imply an Other as they hold out the promise of meaning.

In his definition of guilt and shame, Papa destroys one order of mean-ing to replace it with another; they are, claims Papa, "words and states [which] serve poetic but not moral functions. In the hands of the true poet they are butterflies congregating high in the heavens, but in the hands of the moralists or the metaphysicians they are gunpowder" (37). His language of accounting is not accountable—except to his aesthetic dictums. His monologue can catalogue his bitterly exultant vision of cul-tural decay that mirrors his own psychic cesspool, but his language also empowers his distress and asserts "the validity of the fiction of living" (125), thereby asserting the validity of Papa's construction of fictions—

which he hopes will be "truer" fictions than all the others surrounding him.

Like Allert, who tries to decipher his psyche by interpreting his central dream(s), Papa is himself also an interpreter, dissecting his act of self-constitution and self-annihilation by citing what is central to it. He tells Henri, "it is this idea precisely that lies at the dead center of our night together: that nothing is more important than the existence of what does not exist; that I would rather see two shadows flickering inside the head than all your flaming sunrises set end to end. . . . After all, my theory tells us that ours is the power to invent the very world we are quitting" (57). This language produces yet again the paradoxical presence and absence that Hawkes repeatedly invokes in his conceptions of the fictive process. And the cruelty Hawkes claims as part of the authorial act Henri attributes to Papa, whom he calls a murderer and accuses of wanting to punish Honorine for taking Henri as a lover. Papa admits, "what I am doing is cruel, but it is not motivated by cruelty" (124). Far from being vengeful punishment for Honorine's relationship with Henri, this act, claims Papa, will be a gift to Honorine who "will know with special certainty that just as she was the source of your poems, so too was she the source of my private apocalypse. It was all for her" (124–125). Papa's murder/suicide is for Honorine, but also *from* her. This absent woman is source and center; she is "the existence of what does not exist." She is a cipher, a symbol representing nothing and a puzzle to be broken, an absence and a plenum of meaning for Papa, whose drive is his monologue which exists to validate its own meaning and which also proclaims that this "accident" will lack meaning for those who witness its debris.

Because Papa's last act can only exist as language, his death drive is equivalent to his narrative drive, and both drives, as they move toward their climax, are equivalent to his transmogrified sex drive. His juxtaposition of scenes from his erotic life requires an understanding of his attitude toward women, or more aptly, his idea of Woman. While Papa claims his wife is the source of his ultimately poetic act, he tells his daughter that she is "the very center of my concern" (39). He describes "the undeniable world of our night driving" as "alluring, prohibitive, personal, a mystery that is in fact quite specific, since it is common to child, to lovers, to the lone man driving from one dark town to the next" (28–29). These adjectives applied to the ride also evoke the mother and beloved, the source and center, Honorine and Chantal, and are, furthermore, reminiscent of Allert's conception of Ursula, from whom words and qualities issue.

Papa makes Honorine a source of language when he labels her as Muse. But when he claims he is not a poet, Papa disclaims access to a muse. Henri is the poet, or at least the man who writes and sells volumes of poetry, whereas Papa is just "your ordinary privileged man" (100). In constituting the absent Honorine as Muse he further absents her from himself by telling Henri, "you are the kind of man who should always be accompanied by a woman who is the wife of a man as privileged as me. Only some such woman could qualify as your Muse and attest to your courage" (43). He describes himself as a man "who must get along without a Muse and for whom poetry is still no match for journalistic exhibitionism" (43). This places him in the compelling but unfulfilling world of tabloid representations, far from the experience of the alluring, personal myth that is his poetry-breeding wife.

At the beginning of his monologue Papa asserts his artistic shortcomings as well as his innocence by saying, "I am no poet. And I am no murderer" (14). Yet, despite such disclaimers, Papa's narrative exists to establish that he is indeed a poet, as he understands that word. At the end of his monologue he can admit the validity of labeling his drive suicide and murder (124) because he believes he has transfigured these words through making actual what for Henri are only ideas about poetry: "that the poet is always a betrayer, a murderer, and that the writing of poetry is like a descent into death" (80). Papa sees his ride as perfecting Henri's mildly grasped aspirations: "in our case it now appears that the poet is the thick-skinned and simple-minded beast of the ego, while contrary to popular opinion, it is your ordinary privileged man who turns out to reveal in the subtlest of ways all those faint sinister qualities of the artistic mind" (100). Because of his assumption of the role of poet Papa can reconceive his possession/non-possession of Honorine: "every more or less privileged person contains within himself the seed of a poet, so that the wife of each such individual wants nothing more than to be a poet's mistress. In this respect Honorine has been especially fortunate" (76). She is his wife *and* his mistress, as well as Henri's mistress, one woman and every woman. Honorine as Muse exists as source and object, audience and benefactress, a quantity determined by what the men in her life need her to be.

Papa's blurring the lines of Honorine's individuality, along with his desire to merge his identity with Henri's by assuming the role of poet, is typical of his desire to sacrifice all difference to his vision of coherence. But it is the very elision of difference that contributes to the pain and confusion of his relationships. Patrick O'Donnell describes these relationships as "complicated triangulations" in which

everybody involved, at one time or another, seems to occupy all the positions available within a threefold system of syllogistic relationships. In a given context, Papa is father, husband, jealous lover; Chantal is daughter, lover, and (when Papa sees her as a repetition of Honorine) wife. All the novel's triangles, if overlaid, would thus appear to be identical, revealing a structure of inescapable rivalry. At the dead center of each relation of threes, there is an absence—deceased son, sleeping wife, hidden daughter—who seems to exist as the force generating the energy by which these constructions are sustained. (*PD* 30)

Papa can master his confusedly repetitive and jealousy-inducing relationships by putting himself in the position of controlling them. He eliminates Henri as a rival by verbally overpowering and merging with him and, concurrently, disposes of Chantal. He tells Chantal, "You are no mere forgotten audience to the final ardent exchange between the two men in your mother's life, men whose faces you cannot even see" (39). Papa ignores the fact that Henri is certainly the man in Chantal's life, as well as her mother's, and that he himself would like to be the beloved man in her life. In the car she is both the audience of whom Papa is constantly aware and one of the elements that is exchanged between the two men in Papa's ardent talk.[14]

The very fact that we have a name to call this narrator only because of his third-person references to himself as Chantal's "Papa" indicates his need to emphasize his proprietary relation to her. But such things as his recounting of the intensity of his feeling for Chantal, his misery when she felt happiness that was independent of him, his delight in licking chocolate from her fingers, his commenting that the size of his mistress "mimed" that of Chantal, and his lingering over the details of Chantal's sexual initiation display a desire for her that is barely contained. "No one can rob you now of your Papa's love," he tells her (40), though clearly it is he who resents being robbed of his daughter's love by Henri. But now that they are in their hermetically sealed capsule Papa can assert his power over both Chantal and Henri and overcome jealousy by accomplishing the ultimate erotic feat of merging Henri with himself in their "ardent exchange" (39). He can ignore Chantal as he sublimates his desire for her through language. He becomes the true poet, and Henri submits to Papa's design by repeating (at least according to Papa) and thus (in Papa's interpretation) sanctioning the validity of Papa's words: "Imagined life is more exhilarating than remembered life" (127). Their bond is sealed by their privileging of the imagination, the force that rapaciously makes Honorine the Muse, the source behind the outpouring of this language, lacking language of her own, exchanged and possessed by each of the men, a shadowy presence, a shadowy absence, amenable to the creation of their poetic mythos.

At the end of his narrative, satisfied that Henri at last has become one with him, Papa says that in his pocket is "a scrap of paper on which . . . you would find in my own handwriting these two lines: *Somewhere there still must be / Her face not seen, her voice not heard*" (Hawkes's emphasis). They are lines written by Henri, but Papa asserts his confluence with Henri by saying he is "extremely fond of these two lines. I might even have written them myself" (127). The words express a longing to reach the missing woman but also an injunction that she remain absent. And in fact the actual author of almost these precise words has been suppressed: Christina Rossetti begins her poem "Somewhere or Other" with the lines, "Somewhere or other there must surely be / The face not seen, the voice not heard." [15] Her words become Poetry exchanged between Papa and Henri.

Papa adapts the description of poetic inspiration to what he sees as his redefinition of Henri's more romantic poetic attitude. He recalls when he discovered on the grounds behind a church what "according to local legend . . . was the Fountain of Clarity" (103). In a moment that echoes the myth of Narcissus gazing with love at his own reflection, Papa stares at his own face in the pool of water, "contemplating the existence of our own Honorine. Your Muse, my clarity" (104). In the mirror of the water Honorine is made in his image, an occurrence that duplicates his recasting everything, from the "clear burst of desire" (28) he imagines the crash will be to the landscape of dead passion through which they drive, into the lineaments of his need. In this drive, he says, "there is clarity but not morality. Not even ethics. You and Chantal and I are simply traveling in purity and extremity down that road the rest of the world attempts to hide from us by heaping up whole forests of the most confusing road signs, detours, barricades. What does it matter that the choice is mine and not yours?" (14). This blatant enforcement of his will excludes any idea of clarity but his, which becomes a monolithic ideal of both vision and the language that embodies vision. Papa maintains the paradox that "[t]he unseen vision is not to be improved upon" (58). He can perfect vision in language, a language he wants to be like the gauges on the dashboard: "the essential signs, the true language, always precious and treacherous at the same time" (33). His attraction to the invisible allows him to exercise his imagination, but also allows him to over-write everything and everyone in his own image. This has a most pernicious expression in his writing of the absent Honorine, for in his construction of her he credits her with the power of originating this night's destruction.

Although he so relishes the unseen vision and believes that, ideally, the accident would be invisible, "announced by violent sound" (58), Papa is fascinated by visual representations. He describes Henri's eyes as untrustworthy, "as if they have been drained of blueness in a black-and-white photograph," and says that for him, no matter how Henri dresses, his clothes are always "the garb of the unsmiling poet whose photograph is so often taken among those festive crowds at the bull ring" (41). The allusion to Hemingway reinforces Papa's envious and scornful fixation upon Henri as an icon of a poet. But his most pronounced obsession with visual representations is his boyhood fascination with pornography which carries over into his adult life. Indeed, some of the most erotically stimulating moments he spends with Monique and with Honorine center on looking at pornographic photos that become a standard for evaluating the living women. Monique "lived her very life in unwitting competition with that rare photographic study which I prepared over the years of Honorine's own erotic womanhood" (67). But Honorine herself nearly loses the competition "with the paid fashion models of the magazines" (49). What saves her from such a defeat is the tattoo of purple grapes on yellow stems on her lower abdomen. Before a man—Papa or Henri—sees her tattoo, Honorine is "the woman who appears to reveal herself completely, and no matter how attractively, in the first glance" (48). But the grapes make complete knowledge of Honorine impossible: "After seeing them, who would risk any constricting definition of our Honorine?" (51) The tattoo of the grapes is a representation different from those in pornographic magazines, which pretend to absolute disclosure, because revealing the tattoo reveals its resistance to revelation. Significantly, the tattoo marks Honorine by her choice, and is therefore some kind of self-representation, but at the same time it is a sign only of itself, a cipher that remains intact, an image that eludes the clarity of interpretation.

Papa suggests the issue of revelation when he says that when he was younger "to be recognized in any way was to be given your selfhood on a plate and to be loved, loved, which is what I most demanded" (85). This figure of speech puts the "head of the household" (20) in the position of the decapitated John the Baptist. Now, instead of love to appease his anxiety about the validity of his existence, Papa wants "not relief but purity" (85). Yet in this quest for purity Papa's voice remains stringently prophetic, dispensing the tenets of a personal mythos whose paradoxes are reminiscent of the paradoxical axioms of Christianity (for example: the last shall be first, in dying you are restored to life). Papa's apocalyptic drive is the aesthetic route to making the word flesh in which he redeems himself by proclaiming his own innocence. The allusion to John the Baptist also alludes to *The Fall*'s self-proclaimed prophet, Jean-Baptiste, whose words are one of *Travesty*'s epigraphs: "You see, a person I knew used to divide human beings into three categories: those who prefer having nothing to hide rather than being obliged to lie, those who prefer lying to having nothing to hide, and finally those who like both lying and the hidden. I'll let you choose the pigeonhole that suits me." This statement deliberately withholds revelation through its lack of clarity; the interpretation and application of the statement allow for a remarkable plurality of possibilities. Yet Papa tries to maintain a self-enclosed system that bears the mark of unity, for all opposites and all otherness can be reconciled in his vision of "total coherence" (75). In one such reconciliation he makes an accident of his younger days the forerunner of the accident he is perpetrating now. The accident was "a travesty, involving a car, an old poet, and a little girl" and it either "determined or revealed the nature of the life I would lead henceforth as well as the nature of the man I had just become" (47). The polarity here between determining or revealing is the polarity between the idea of construction and the idea of essence, or, in other words, between Papa's constructing a fiction, which would allow for the possibility of other fictions, or proclaiming the truth, which would collapse all possibility into singleness.

Papa cites that early accident as having been a moment of creativity in which he tasted "that 'cruel detachment' which was to make [Henri] famous" (47–48). The accident may or may not have been an accident, both because Papa sped up when he saw that he might hit the little girl and because he doesn't know whether he hit her or not. The triangular relationship of the participants in the event corresponds to that in the present death drive; the young girl, the "sacred child," linked to the old poet, both of whom are put to the point of death by the young Papa, suggests Papa's diminution and fetishization of his own grown daughter, and, moreover, places the old Papa in the position of both the poet and the murderer, precisely the roles he negates and assumes in his narration. Whether this event determined or revealed the course of Papa's life, he sees it as a source of his present apocalyptic drive, but the exposition of this source comes immediately after Papa's explanation of Honorine as the drive's source. In keeping with Papa's many other collapsed dualities, this duality disappears in the sameness Honorine and the first "travesty" represent to him, for they both involve an intractable otherness subsumed by the power of Papa's imagination. Naming the drive's origins at the end of the narrative is yet another manifestation of his conviction that his act of destruction will be an act of creation, because it produces a confluence of beginning and ending, a circularity that ironically undercuts the express linearity of the narrative and of the car's route. Papa describes the drive as a linearity that doubles back on itself when, after completing a particularly difficult turn in the road, he says, "again we are safely adhering to the earthly path of our trajectory— which on a white road map looks exactly like the head of a dragon outlined by the point of a pen brutally sharpened and dipped in blood" (52). A cartographical representation seems at odds with Papa's conception of the coming crash as "a clear burst of desire" (28), but is consonant with his wish for both release and control. For Papa clarity is desire's panacea. The clarity with which he can still picture the lovely face of the little girl he may have killed, and the clarity with which he can now imagine Honorine as she has been and as she will be, transfigure, for Papa, the cruelty of his acts into moments of harsh beneficence.

"The greater the incongruity the greater the truth" (20), states Papa, and under this rubric every contradictory remark he makes can only demonstrate his theory. In this theory he creates his own unassailable universe, explaining to Henri that "Like schoolboys who have studied the solar system . . . you and I know that all the elements of life coerce each other instant by instant into that perfect formation which is lofty and the only one possible" (15). But obviously it is Papa who is the agent of coercion, the enforcer of a vision that enacts exclusion through a seeming inclusion which is really a conversion to its own tenets. Papa's wish for clarity finds expression in oculocentrism and univocity, the appropriation, assimilation, or reduction of all otherness to the mastering One.[16] His suggestion that Chantal's vomiting is an attempt to escape his voice is probably at least partially accurate, but he sees this as a defect in her capacity for accepting "the truth" of what he is saying (53) rather than as a criticism. Because Papa conducts a monologue that excludes all other voices, when he does admit criticism into his narrative the criticism is already appropriated to his design through his claim on language. Furthermore, Papa not only excludes other voices, he discourages other vision, both ocular and artistic. "You would see nothing even if you looked, so don't bother. I see quite well enough for the two of us" (101), he tells Henri, not finding it necessary even to address Chantal since she is already excluded from the poetic discourse with which he is infusing his friend.

Yet Papa's insistence that Chantal is "the necessary third person" (39) indicates that concomitant with his need to be the arbiter of vision is the need to be observed. Chantal may be practically invisible, but so is the camera which Papa repeatedly imagines as recording their drive (35, 64, 80, 90). His obsession with the reification enacted in photography is a desire to possess the image with the complete knowledge granted by the clarity of form, and this desire extends to his drive to have the clarity of form imparted to him. He expresses the idea of clarity or fixity when he describes their experience in the car as "constant, virginal"; "For us the moment remains the same while the hour changes" (34–35). Just as they "have heard no variations in the music . . . from beneath the car" (34), they have heard no variation in the tone or the theme of Papa's words as he unfolds the repetitive pattern of dead passion and the design and debris that, for him, redeem it. But the crash approaches, the end is near. Papa claims that during this drive the absent Honorine has been, to him and Henri, "more 'real' . . . than she has ever been," and that the result of the explosive climax will be that he and Henri will become more real to Honorine (124). He explains,

> when she recovers, at last, she will exercise her mind in order to experience in her own way what we have known; . . . months and years beyond her recovery, Honorine will know with special certainty that just as she was the source of your poems, so too was she the source of my private apocalypse. It was all for her. And such intimate knowledge is worth whatever price the gods may demand, as she herself said. No, *cher ami*, Honorine is a person of great strength. Sooner or later she will understand. (124–125)

She will join with Henri (and the reader) in understanding, and she will join with Papa in imagining what is so extreme that it seems to defy the imagination; just as the observer wants to be observed, the imaginer wants to be imagined.

Papa thinks of Honorine's chateau, Tara, as "the very castle where the sleeping princess lies in all her pallor" (54). He knows she will sleep peacefully through the moment his car whips by the "castle," but that she will wake to a knowledge that will bear no comfort. Through the realization of his death drive he will penetrate the fortress of her consciousness. He believes that in his death he will possess her as he never could in life, for his wife has been a woman who eludes him, a woman to whom he can attach no fixed definition, a woman from whose desire he feels excluded because of its inclusiveness. In contradiction to fact, he tells Henri, "my wife is faithful" (95), as if by attributing a modified sort of virginity to Honorine he can make his possession of her all the more masterful. His act of violence will violate the wholeness he associates with Honorine and will assimilate her to the wholeness he projects for himself since she will have to enact his drive in her imagination. But the fact that Papa says she will experience the drive "in her own way" allows for an otherness that cannot be assimilated. The monovalent narrative yields to the inherent polyvalence of interpretation, of Honorine's imagination and the reader's imagination.

Although this apocalypse is supposedly all for Honorine, Papa is so busy sharing poetic truth with Henri that they pass Tara without even noting the lantern he said Honorine would have lit for them. "[T]here shall be no survivors. None" (128), yet the reason there are three and not four in the car is that Honorine must be a survivor, her post-apocalypse presence is necessary to testify to the value of Papa's achievement. There is, however, no guarantee that she will see it as anything more than an excess of the cruelty of which she accuses both her husband and Henri (124). Papa's bond with Henri may be sealed, but his paradoxical efforts to possess and to be possessed by the Other that is Honorine lack both certainty and clarity. But, of course, this maker of a supreme fiction thrives on impossibility, calling the carefully planned and intentionally uninterpretable outcome of his drive a "clear 'accident' " (23), deliberately drawing attention to the fictiveness of his language. In aspiring to poetic heights he constructs a personal universe as spectacular and fragile as "butterflies congregating in the heavens," an image of beauty but also of distance and thereby appropriate to this narrator who strains to negotiate the distance between turning the key in the ignition and crashing into the stone wall, between self and other, between word and world, between desire and death.

*Travesty* is Hawkes's most explicit parody of the authorial act, an idea O'Donnell succinctly summarizes: "*Travesty* appears to travesty Papa's self-authorized vision, the aesthetics of the 'real' author who wrote it, the progression of novels which it concludes, and the encompassing act of writing, and reading, fictions" (*PD* 38). Papa combines Cyril's dream of wholeness and Allert's nightmare of dissolution in a maniacal assertion of control that celebrates a transgressive "cruel detachment" aiming at innocent transcendence. Driving his death car, "a rocket firing in the caves and catacombs of history" (78), Papa speaks to get beyond the wounds of the past and the obligation to the future; he seeks to get beyond resistant surfaces and disembodied words to some kind of absolute real in a lethal act that he proclaims absolute poetry. In all the many congruencies his imagination forges, Papa takes to a radical extreme the dark potential embedded in Cyril's and Allert's narratives by creating a web of coherent meaning and identity that harbors its own literal destruction.

In line with Ursula's disgust with Allert's solipsistic need to create meaning from his dreams and with Fiona's impatience with Cyril's "interest in coherence and full circles" (225), Honorine criticizes Papa: "According to Honorine," says Papa, "this is my other greatest failing or most dangerous quality, this propensity of mine toward total coherence. . . . In this sense there is nowhere I have not been, nothing I have not already done, no person I have not known before" (75). But the corollary to this, says Papa, is that "everything known to me remains unknown, so that my own footfalls sound like those of a stranger, while the corridor to the lavatory off my bedroom suddenly becomes the labyrinthine way to a dungeon" (75). Ensconced in the closed circle of narrative control is the endless maze of the unknowable self; outside the containment of narrative lies the unknown Other. Cyril listens for the footsteps of distant Catherine or of absent Fiona returning to his vision of paradise; Allert thinks obsessively of Ursula leaving him, and says he "shall dream of she who guided me to the end of the journey, whoever she is" (179); Papa imagines the sleeping Honorine, "the lady of the dark chateau" (122), who will wake to imagine him. These women, representative of other voices, other imaginations, endure their existence and their lack of existence in the inscription of authorial power, but it is they who mark this inscription as power and thereby offer its critique.

# Chapter 5
# The Artist in the World of Women: The Imagination and Beyond in *The Passion Artist*

> I've decided that the three most important subjects are conscious-
> ness, the imagination, and the nature of woman.
> —John Hawkes (LeClair 29)

**I**

In *Second Skin, The Blood Oranges, Death, Sleep & the Traveler,* and *Travesty,*
Hawkes explores a range of perspectives on the imagination as it expresses itself in the creative and destructive possibilities of male narrators
self-consciously rendering their lives in language. *Travesty* represents
something of an endpoint; Hawkes refers to the novel as "the closest I've
come to creating the character of an artist or man whose entire being is
committed to the imagination" (O'Donnell 116). This commitment to
the imagination depends upon Papa's self-consciousness and absolute
control of the fictional world. But the potential critique of this absolute control constituted by Honorine, itself continuous with the possibility of a differing female perspective latent within the triad, points in the
direction of reenvisioning the artistic imagination as developed by the
domination of a personified male narrative voice. *The Passion Artist*
(1979), following upon *Travesty,* presents a male character who desires
absolute control but is afraid of consciousness and who, in spite of his
many claims to knowledge, doesn't understand the imagination. And it
presents this character from a third-person perspective, so that the male
character now becomes the object of the text rather than its subject, and
becomes, in addition, subject to the actions and words of female characters from whom he will learn what it is to be an artist.

Hawkes returns, in *The Passion Artist*, to the barren, desolate landscape of his earliest work as well as to the use of third-person narration; at the same time, he pursues the concerns he developed with the first-person narrators from *Second Skin* through *Travesty*. The protagonist of *The Passion Artist*, Konrad Vost, exists in a death-ridden, incarcerating, misogynistic world in which he attempts to exercise rigid control over himself and others and to articulate the relation of his desires, both conscious and unconscious, to external reality. Yet because he is not the teller of his story, Vost does not act as the artist/narrator linguistically determining the substance of his existence and the texture of the "real." Instead, he is the interpreter of his experience, subject in turn to the interpretation provided by the distance of third-person narration. This distance enacts the "extreme detachment" that Hawkes deems necessary for the creation of fiction that aims at finding "all the fluid, germinal, pestilential 'stuff' of life itself as it exists in the unconscious" (O'Donnell 126, 125).

The authorial detachment exercised by Hawkes, however, has, from *Second Skin* through *Travesty*, produced characters/narrators who seek to abolish distance by actualizing a vision that forges unity between the imagination and its objects. In their quests, these male narrators subsume to their designs a recalcitrant reality figured as Other, including, most significantly, the Other that is Woman. *The Passion Artist* makes "woman" the central locus for the conditions of art in a more explicit manner than in any of Hawkes's previous novels. Because the women characters' interpretations of Vost in particular and of the male condition and the female condition in general rank along with the interpretations offered by Vost and by the narrative voice, the women characters provide a trenchant critique of the oppression exercised by a violent, repressed, and exclusionary masculine psyche. In this novel, the longing for the transfiguration of self and world evinced by previous narrators and pursued through language is accomplished through the actions and words, the "flesh and light" (122), of imprisoned women who rebel, and most especially through the erotic wisdom of Vost's mother, Eva Laubenstein, and of Hania, a woman whom he first encounters when she bears a "transfiguring hatchet" (121).

Vost attains the status of artist through the bridging of distance in "the willed erotic union" (181); the will that formerly (in this novel and in previous ones) acts as the deadly imposition of self, and of form, on the world becomes the means for creative action. His realization at the moment of union "that the exterior [of the woman's body] could no longer be distinguished from its interior" (180) figures the possibility of a more general correspondence between the self, the Other, the imagination, and the world. But in this novel riddled with paradox, the willed erotic union, which makes it possible for Vost, who has thought "that the interior life of the man is a bed of stars, that the interior life of the man is a pit of putrescence" (31), "to lie flat on his bed of stars . . . to lie magically on his bed of hot coals" (181), also becomes the site of rupture. The erotic union is the dissolution of the boundaries of separate identities in the merging of wills, and it is Vost's realization of his own identity as artist and man; it is the redemption of the self through the triumph of the imagination, and it prepares for the eradication of self in the death that is beyond imagining.

Paradox, indeed, becomes the mode that embodies the plural and digressive truths of experience and that constitutes art and sexuality. Vost is able to achieve the erotic union that engenders self-definition and self-dissolution largely by virtue of the words of Hania and of his mother, whose concern is defining man and woman. She approves the opinion of the prison doctor who claimed that "the man and woman are . . . the same" and that "the man and woman are the same and opposite" (160). Union and disunion are linguistically constituted in this paradox, a trope that is, for Hawkes, the condition of all language and that is also the condition of Konrad Vost at the end of the novel, when his dying words, "I am who I am," presage his discovery of "what it was to be nothing" (184). Vost approaches a state beyond representation, beyond the bounds of the imagination, a state of transcendence that exceeds definition but which has been made possible by definition. His self enters a condition of otherness which he has attributed to women, so that he ends as the distanced object which the text works upon in a necessarily doomed attempt at liberation at the same time that it proposes the liberation of women.

## II

Vost lives in a dismal, ugly, provincial, unenlightened European city that exists because of the prison for women, La Violaine, in its midst. His mother is an inmate of this prison, incarcerated in the distant past for having killed her husband, Vost's father, by setting him on fire. Her presence in the prison, and thus her absence in the world, is what keeps Vost in the nameless city. His wife, Claire, has been dead for five years, and Vost still grieves obsessively for her; for the last six years of her life she had a lover, a situation that does nothing to sway Vost's opinion that her nature was guiltless. He refuses to acknowledge the maturity of his teenage daughter, Mirabelle, and treats her like a helpless child; she is, in fact, "a female genie who had already discovered how to escape at will from her bottle" (3). In his desexualized conception of Mirabelle as a child, Vost escapes confronting his horror of female sexuality and of his own sexuality. But the security of his denial collapses when "one day he was confronted, quite by accident, with his daughter's appalling womanhood" (3). This confrontation, however, occurs in Mirabelle's absence, by way of substitution and projection. Vost goes to pick up Mirabelle after school, finds that she has already gone, sees instead another girl, very much like Mirabelle, who turns out to be a prostitute, reveals Mirabelle also is a prostitute, and ends up performing fellatio on him in her mother's apartment. Vost responds to the experience with the guilt and confusion of a child, with joy and mortification, and with the final hypocrisy of reporting Mirabelle to the police for prostitution. It is this experience that sets the stage for the disruption of Vost's life, which up to now has consisted of working at a pharmacy and spending his free time visiting Claire's grave or sitting in the café named La Violaine, located across the street from the prison La Violaine. The café is frequented by men who, like Vost, long ago lost a woman behind the prison walls.

When the inmates of La Violaine rebel, Vost answers the call for volunteers to quell them; he enjoys an orgy of violence, joining eighty or ninety other men in the elation of beating women. But the women prevail, and Vost loses consciousness, only to wake in a hospital ward among other wounded men and with his right hand encased in a black glove. He leaves the hospital, and thus begins his journey through the marsh on the outskirts of the city, the landscape that provides the physical medium for what is the journey of this "stationary traveler" into his own consciousness. Vost himself formulates this oxymoronic description of himself as journeyer: "He had the precise phrase clearly in mind—the stationary traveler—and he was pleased that he, an ordinary widower, had become so remarkably self-defined" (14). Vost's self-definition is a self-reification, mimicking the rigidity he places on the women in his life—the mother who must stay imprisoned in La Violaine and in his need, the wife who must stay imprisoned in purity and maternity, the daughter who must stay imprisoned in asexual childhood. His oxymoronic self-definition embodies a paradox meant to indicate that his journey is through the labyrinth of his psyche; the paradox extends further, however, for the rigidity and exclusion, as well as knowledge, involved in self-definition will give way to the occasion for definition by others, specifically by the women of La Violaine, who will both formulate and destroy definitions of the male and the female, and with whom he will experience the abrogation of boundaries, thereby achieving the realization and the loss of self. While he begins his journey as a man who "had come to prize his superiority, his irony, his self-condemnation, his intractable belief in his identity as Konrad Vost" (20), he ends by experiencing the dissolution of his individual identity.

After he leaves the hospital, he first walks the gloomy streets of the city and finds himself surrounded by maimed and disfigured people. He has to work to assure himself that he is different from them: "He listened to the dead weight thumping against his thigh, and its message was clear: nowhere in all these streets or alleyways, in all the labyrinths, was there another Konrad Vost" (75). The weight that thumps against his thigh is what he has determined is a silver hand, "[t]he secret concealed inside the glove" (71). But the "revelation" of this secret yields an image that can acquire significance only through metaphors plumbed from the past: as a child, Vost was an "innocent trumpeter" (21), "the little trumpeter of the silver hand" (112). He remembers "holding on his lap his silent horn" as he looked at the stove, the territory of his mother. These images entwine the innocence and beauty of art—in this case, music—with the innocent sexual impulses of the child through the displacement of metaphor that makes a trumpet stand for the phallus. "His fingers on the valves of his trumpet were like mice in a forest filled with snow" (78), for his first expression of sexual curiosity, in which he explored the hindquarters of a horse, exacted punishment from his caretaker, Anna Kossowski, as he listened to mice running in the walls of the barn. The skill of the silver hand, with its connotations of beauty and swiftness, that made music with his trumpet/phallus becomes the rigidified, reified appendage with no feeling, a secret adornment hidden from even his own view. This thumping hand, the over-determined, meaningful, simultaneously clear and concealed sign, confers Vost's identity. It holds his history. Vost conceives of memory as a storehouse in which everything is retained: "Every image, every sensation, concept, has its own invisible track" (43). The seen, the felt, the known disappear into the invisible realm of the psyche to be reborn as manifestations of the artful unfolding of Vost's and the narrator's analysis. Memory itself will be refigured in the track of narrative. The example of the "silver hand" concealed beneath the glove demonstrates how Vost does not *uncover* meaning— the hand remains concealed—but instead constructs it through a network of metaphoric and metonymic substitutions.

The images, concepts, and sensations of all Vost has experienced and known refigure themselves in the marsh where "[t]he inner landscape had become externalized" (84). (This formulation of the externalization of inner life makes self-conscious the creative method of Hawkes's early novels.) But here Vost's penchant for self-definition confronts the abyss of non-meaning: "Konrad Vost was alone and unable to move in a landscape without shape or meaning, belonging to neither city nor countryside. . . . For him there was only sun, emptiness, the smell of salt and putrefaction" (83). Vost must bring the apparent emptiness of the world and the void in himself to some kind of meaningful order. This will involve bringing emptiness to fullness through language. Vost is confronted with a problem similar to Allert's in *Death, Sleep and the Traveler* and Papa's in *Travesty*: he must try to account for his existence, relying on the power of language to explain the world and to create a self. The success of this project depends on the imagination's articulation of images, the dynamics of which become apparent in the desolation of the marsh, where Vost sees a rusted, severed train track and suddenly understands "what previously he had merely feared: The unaccountable is the only key to inner life, past life, future life. From the silence of the purple distance came the rattle of couplings, the sound of gunfire, the chugging of a locomotive that did not exist" (83). The unaccountable existence of the tracks reflects the unaccountable existence of the self; the language that establishes the nonexistent locomotive renders substantial the elusive elements of identity and experience. The passage recalls, again, Hawkes's citing of Breton's image of a rusting locomotive abandoned in a jungle as significant to the aesthetic premises of his work: "I realized that throughout my writing life I too had been taking the ruined object, the dead object, as much more revealing of the thing itself than the live, functioning object" (LeClair 28). Incongruity arrested in the fixity of form allows for the possession of the object by the workings of the mind and senses, and yields to clarification in the form of language.

The revelation ascribed to objects intrudes itself on Vost's consciousness at the time of Claire's funeral. After her burial, he returns to the empty church and comes upon "the two small metal stands that had borne the immense and even intolerable weight of the casket" (10). Their object-ness, now that they no longer have a function, now that they are only "two incongruous reminders of what had already occurred," overwhelms him. He can control this feeling, however, by deciding that they are "[t]he obverse of the tomb of Christ. . . . The obverse" (10). The presence of the metal stands implies the absence of Claire, as well as the conversion of the past to totems of what no longer exists. In contrast, the tomb of Christ encompasses an absence that implies the presence of Christ in the world, and the abolishment of death in an endless future. The comparison, however, does not stand as an invocation of the redemptive possibilities of religion; instead, it points to the paradoxical presence and absence achieved in narrative, in which the play of images and the form of language embody the persistence of the past as well as its eradication, and engage the elements of being and the process of becoming.

In the course of the narrative, Vost will encounter the ways in which his past impinges on his present, and he will move toward the future by undergoing a resurrection: "exactly three days following . . . the rebellion in the prison" (121), when he is dragged as a captive to La Violaine and he is alone in his cell, "all his sensations were the opposite of deadness: he had already been hanged, cut down, revived" (124). (This language suggests Vost as the puritanical Hugh of *The Blood Oranges*, resurrected by Hawkes from his hanging and allowed the opportunity of change.) His cell has only a small wooden table, a stained mattress, an iron sink, a porcelain toilet, a single bench, "plaster walls covered with the handwriting of innumerable women," and "a profusion of scattered articles of clothing worn only by women" (125), but these things constitute an apotheosis of paradox: "here at last was the splendor of deprivation, the pleasure that had been taken in the disordering of the familiar world, the excitation inherent in everything discarded, the joy of completion doubly evident in the ruin. . . . Never before had he so known the power of the physical object. Never before had he recognized the joyful indecency of wreckage. The broken vase, the bar of music already sung, what was there more?" (125). These last words recall the words of Braque which Hawkes has said "really should have been the epigraph for *Travesty*": "The vase gives shape to space, music to silence" (Emmett and Vine 167). The objects in the room imply form conferred and denied. Vost's appreciation of these signs of life not only reveals his joy in ruin, but also suggests the potential for revelation by the elements of a world which, though it seems to confirm him, will also transform him.

Inner life, past life, future life achieve coherence in the process of narrative. Until the disruption caused by his knowledge of Mirabelle and his experience of the women's rebellion, Konrad Vost's life of emotional constriction in the confines of La Violaine, the café, consists of the stasis of repetition, down to the smallest details of "the sounds of glass and china," the behavior of the café dog, and the scraping of chairs: "in all this was implicit the boredom and security of time passing as it was expected to pass, indifferently, *without meaning*, without the threat of impending unwanted change or even disaster" (5; my emphasis); Vost "passed his days in time uninformed by chronology" (20). This condition mimics timelessness, the very state sought by the narrators from *Second Skin* through *Travesty* as the alleviation of life's painful and uncontrollable vicissitudes. Yet at the same time, these narrators envision a plenitude of meaning in the absence of time, whereas *The Passion Artist* presents a world impoverished of meaning by virtue of its fixity. Events beyond Vost's control, however, intrude upon his unchanging hours to effect the generation of significance:

Only in the midst of the disordering of his small world did he come to learn that without chronology, without unexpected events suddenly manifesting themselves in series like the links of a chain, a person could never uncover the sum of his own secrets or profit truly from the lessons of devastation. When the time arrived, and disorder surrounded him with the force of shattered morality, he was stunned to discover how rigorously he clung to this former self and how bestial he had in fact become. (20–21)

The series of events suggests the linearity of narrative, and the comparison of Vost's former self to his present self indicates the importance of chronology's determination of existence. The narrative process enables Vost's return to his origins and progress into his future; it also entails the release from the confines of the self into the world of others. As he sits alone in his dark apartment listening to a radio announcer giving news of the revolt, "[e]ven then, in the drabbest and cruelest of those night hours, he had only the first and faintest intimations that his life had collapsed into chronology, that private axis had coincided with public axis, and that the disordering of his small world had in fact begun" (42). Vost's own assertion of control and need for order give way to disorder that is reordered in narrative.

The coincidence of private axis and public axis occurs as the hatred, fear, and resentment of women that determine Vost's personal world manifest themselves as the determining factors of the dark world in which he lives; the most sinister political structures have always informed Vost's life. "How could the hands so suited to gripping the truncheon be comfortably exercised in the preparation of his daughter's meals or making her bed," Vost sometimes wonders. The answer is that "for Konrad Vost even domesticity was a form of tyranny" (4). His encounter in the marsh with an old woman who has clearly escaped from La Violaine demonstrates the cruelty latent in even his smallest gesture and seemingly insignificant action. He comes upon the woman standing alone and laughing to herself, and is "infuriated that someone so old was still a woman" (89). He raises his gloved hand with the intention of frightening the woman, not striking her, but his movement is unexpectedly powerful and violent, and he sees "the uplifted hand as did the old woman"—and much as Il Gufo sees his own hand in *The Owl*—"black, clawlike, murderous, some interminably heavy and destructive weapon" (90). The woman dies of fright, and Vost runs: "For Konrad Vost, he told himself, the world was now in a constant state of metamorphosis, duplication, multiplication; figures deserving existence only within the limits of the dream now sprang alive; the object of least significance was inspired with its secret animation; no longer was there such a thing as personal safety; in every direction there rose the bars of the cage" (90–91).

Metamorphosis, duplication, and multiplication, part of the collapse into chronology, also attend the interpenetration of desire and reality and the movement toward metaphor and meaning. The "bars of the cage" Vost perceives in his marsh experience become concrete when he is led back to La Violaine as a prisoner, now fully aware "of the crossing of public axis and private axis" (121), and, in addition, "disordered, demoralized, dislocated" (122). This last series of negations itself metamorphoses; that is, the paradoxical nature of being disordered, demoralized, and dislocated becomes apparent in the relation of experience to narrative. Not only is the disordering of Vost's world precipitate to its reordering in narrative, but his demoralization signals his coming alleviation from the bonds of conventional morality, which Hawkes sees as a major intention of his fiction.[1] And Vost's sense of personal dislocation reflects the structural importance of the narrative dislocations that juxtapose past and present, dream and reality, in order to effect meaning and understanding.

Vost's initial violent foray into the prison yard commits him to the quest for meaning and understanding as the journey to the sources of his violence. His loss of consciousness produces the need for its recuperation, figured in the interplay of metaphors of illumination and reflection with Vost as the spectator of his own psyche. In the interior world,

the spectator is never allowed to forget that the illumination occasionally and slowly gathering . . . is not in fact the light of day or the light of dawn, but is only *a reflection of that light-in-time by which a certain day once existed, or will in the future exist, or now exists but as imaginary without genesis in either the past or the future. . . .* Now he himself is only a figment of his own psychological function within the only domain that is eternally dark, even when "lighted," and eternally insubstantial despite the sights and sounds with which it is either suddenly filled or emptied. (58; my emphasis)

This long passage sets forth the imaginative demands conditioned by the labyrinth of consciousness, which defies the imagination; the sense of the passage returns us once again to Hawkes's distinction between representation, which he says he is not interested in producing, and creation, the goal of his fiction. Having experienced his consciousness on the verge of disappearance, Vost encounters the possibility of pure imagination, cut loose from the anchoring of time and event, and the possibility of reflection, in which past and future, events and objects, are related to consciousness through endless mirroring.

In Vost's dream vision, before he wakes in the hospital, he travels by train through a marsh; the landscape and every object he sees are "all the same, each was a version of the other, together they composed the darkness that was himself" (60). When he actually does stalk through the marsh, adrift in its emptiness and decay, he feels that "[t]he inner landscape had become externalized" (84); "it was all an agglomeration of flashing mirrors" (85). Thrusting himself into a world that so mirrors him, Vost acknowledges what can no longer be denied: he has embodied the most death-ridden elements of life; and the destructive and violent elements in himself, and in those who share his obsessions, have reproduced themselves in the desolation of the world. This circular structure allows for an incarcerating structure: "[T]the degradation concealed within La Violaine was no different from that implicit in the city in which the prison thrived" (24). After Vost arrives inside the prison as a captive, as he first encounters his mother with Hania, he stands rigidly, frozen in his self-incarceration, his upper teeth tightly clamped on his lower lip, as if he is trying "to bite in half the hated smile," that token of his innocence, and "[h]e felt that nothing could pry apart his jaws, that no man before him had ever become, as he had now become, his own ridiculous effigy" (127). At this pinnacle of alienation, he has become a representation of his hated self. His innocence, consisting of denial and lack of knowledge, has engendered the reification that blocks imaginative creation: "Innocence leads inevitably to ice and iron: to bones that become iron, to skin that freezes gradually into a blue and glittering transparency, and then cracks and refreezes until the entire surface of the body is encased and encrusted in scales and broken mirrors of ice, frozen in place" (145).[2] The self formed of mirrors produces a dead world that can only reflect the self's denied humanity.

## III

While the landscape of the marsh "mirrored light without meaning" (12), the advent of Vost's mother on the scene of his captivity brings light that reveals clarified meaning and opens the way for his accession to artist. Vost has let the course of his life be determined by his mother's setting fire with kerosene and an oil lamp to "Konrad Vost the Father." The reasons for her action remain unclear, since the incident is related from the perspective of Konrad Vost the child, but they could well have included self-defense, since the Father approaches her with something shiny in his hand (118). But the reasons matter little to Vost; throughout his adult life, he grieves for his mother, who "constantly reminded him of the maternal love that he, as a child, had never had and who also made him constantly aware of the stigma that illuminated both his correctness and his precision in the most brutally ironic light" (2). The real irony, however, consists in Eva's illumination of his correctness and precision not as undercut by her past action, but as defunct in themselves. Vost's punishing constriction of his own and other people's impulses, and of the phenomena of his world, so that they conform to the confines of his self-righteous and negative conceptions of the ideal, has made for an impoverished existence; his rigorous adherence to his conception of manhood, the cover for violence and denial, turns out to be the needy grasping of a child. When he enters La Violaine as a prisoner, he realizes that "the closing of the darkest gate is like a burst of light" (120), but he first experiences this "light" in his cell as "[t]he rich light of expiation" (125). The revelation in store for him in the prison, however, abolishes the need for expiation as it abolishes guilt, replacing them instead with a creative act of the will; the confirmation of self he has sought in an endlessly mirrored existence collapses in the clarity of understanding himself in relation to women, who, he must realize, have their being apart from him. When his mother and Hania first come up to his cell, he thinks there is a third figure with them, "numinous, transparent, composed entirely of the fiercest light" (126); this figure turns out to be an oil-burning lamp held high by Eva Laubenstein. The lamp she held in the distant past caused the death of Konrad Vost the Father in "the light he had at last become" (119); the lamp she holds now figures the possibility of transfiguration. With Eva and Hania, Vost has the chance to get beyond the closed circuit of thwarted desire: they are "women who promised him not sentimentality but flesh and light" (122).

Vost's misogyny involves the sentimental idealization of women. Soon after he causes the death of the old woman in the marsh, he comes upon a beautiful young woman standing and splashing herself in a pool of water in front of a dilapidated mill. He recognizes her as "the selfsame person whom he and Spapa [a fellow habitué of the café La Violaine] had beaten into unconsciousness in La Violaine" (93) by the bruises, "the livid signs of his own righteousness" (94), all over her body, and by her great beauty. Because of this beauty, "the sight of [the bruises] so offended, suddenly, his proud and sentimental eye" (94). The violent rage toward women he so recently exhibited coexists with the idealization of undefiled womanhood. Gazing at her in secret, Vost appropriates her for his dream of innocence; in her solitary ablutions, bathed in water and light, "it was she who imparted to the sinister ruins behind her back a lifelike pastoral completion" (95). Her purity redeems the decay of the marsh, which is, of course, also the putrefaction of Vost. But her pristine, beauteous image changes for Vost when "[t]he sight of her body bent down from the waist in precocious but unconscious self-display destroyed in an instant his tranquillity" (95). His tranquillity turns to loathing because his perception of beauty has turned to his perception of eroticism. Vost turns away because he is aroused; he needs to erase the erotic image so that he can "preserve in his mind the vision of the bather" (5), washed in all the sentimentality engendered by his denial of human desire.

The woman is "close enough so that he could study as if in the magnification of a large and rapturous lens" every detail of her body. He spies on her from behind a screen of trees with the thrill of voyeuristic

possession: "surely he who had beaten her on head and body could now
be allowed to spy on her innocent nudity; after the first violation peering
at her through green trees was nothing" (94). The assertion of physical
power translates to the assertion of aesthetic power. Proud of himself for
not having harmed the woman a second time, as he walks away "he had
eyes only for the nudity of her whom he had spared" (96). By denying
himself the pleasures of violence, he rewards himself with the contemplation of her image; either way, she is, in his mind, subject to him. The
scene provides another figuration of the conflict between men and
women played out in the rebellion at the prison. The men who volunteer
to put down the rebellion "were confident in their purpose, in their mas-
culinity, in the power of the sticks that they held aloft and shook as they
charged. Workers, shop owners, professional men, together they were
sweeping forward into the violation that had been sanctioned and the
conflict they could not lose" (53). Vost is surprised that the women
"were flinging themselves into conflict without protection, unadorned,
wearing no individualizing rings or lockets, carrying no papers of identification, risking their persons in utter nakedness, except for the gray
dresses and the stolen kepis" (53). The absence of those signs with which
society would typically mark them according to status and the men to
whom they belong renders the women, in Vost's perspective, exposed for
the taking. The men's violation of the women works by the assumption
of right and power to which Vost still clings in the marsh. While the "un-
protected" women overpower the men in the prison yard, Vost brings
about the death of the young bather by informing the police officer who
comes upon him of the escaped prisoner's whereabouts. He sacrifices his
"innocent" vision not to eroticism but to a gun.

The violation constituted by Vost's gaze has a parallel in the photographic experiment of Slovotkin, the prison doctor of whom Eva says
Vost is "the image" (157). (Vost clearly is the image of Slovotkin in the
kind of man he is. Their appearances are dissimilar: Vost is tall and clean
shaven, Slovotkin has a "short stature and bushy beard" [158].) Slovotkin, "vile and unscrupulous in every way," says Eva, "was nonetheless
obsessed by a single question: the difference, if any, between the man
and woman" (157). In seeking an answer, he chose fifty women prisoners
and fifty men from the ranks of the Prefecture of Police:

He ordered the shaving of the hundred heads; he ordered that the hundred
naked heads be photographed on their naked necks; he ordered that the photographs be arranged in fifty sets, each containing the head of a man and the
head of a woman paired according to similarity in size. . . . [H]e ordered that a
mixed and randomly chosen group of more than five hundred men and women
be exposed to the fifty pairs of photographs and required to indicate which were
the images of men and which of women, and to offer brief descriptions of each.

The results? Conclusive beyond a doubt: fifty men identified as such, the same with the women. As for the descriptions, they too were conclusive. The dominant opinion was that the men were not sane but that the women were not human. . . . How proud he was to have discovered as fact that in the souls of their bones man and woman are opposites. (158)

Slovotkin's experiment parodies the pornographic impulse that is so prevalent among Hawkesian characters. He seeks the "truth" about man and woman in the artifice of photographs and the construction of viewing that pretend to the revelation of essence and the naturalness of perception. The appropriation of individuals for his photographic project and production of truth about man and woman does violence to the men, and particularly the women, the pictures and facts are supposed to represent.

Yet the idea that man and woman are opposites began as only the second of Slovotkin's theories about men and women. He also proposes "first, that the person is essentially a barren island and that for each of us life's only pleasure is the exploration of other barren islands: in this way to be a man or a woman merely enhances the interesting differences of people who are in fact the same" (157).[3] His third proposal is "that the man and woman are both the same and opposite" (157). And the first and third theories are the ones Slovotkin decides are valid. Although Eva describes Slovotkin as "an injurious brute" (158), she says,

Even this man whose dedication to his single question was no more than a ruse to feed his insatiable craving for the bodies of women, even this terrible Slovotkin revealed in all his debasement a certain truth, a certain respect. Mere hours before his death he insisted . . . that reproduction aside, the man and woman were in all their capabilities the same. . . . He claimed that his third theory was also true: the man and woman are the same and opposite. You cannot be the one without knowing what it is to be the other, reproduction aside. Of course he was right. (159–160)

The monolithic truth extracted from the photographic experiment collapses in the plurality of paradox arrived at by way of experience. The paradox, however, encompasses not only the validity of contradictory theories, but the paradox of theory itself in its capacity for both constriction and liberation.

Vost has lived his life not only acting as though man and woman are opposites, but never knowing what it is to be a woman, and thus not fully being a man. Knowing what it is to be a woman would require experience of women and, most important, imagination. Vost's limited experience of women has been further limited by his inability to view women as anything more than a reflection of his need and his guilt. His limitations coexist with his propensity for summing up the world in innumerable theories; "He had his theory of memory, his theory of clear sight, his theory of travel," his theory of everything (20). Such incessant theorizing recalls Papa's approach to life—and narrative—in *Travesty*. Papa's elaboration of his theories as he prosecutes his murderous and suicidal journey in his sportscar actualizes what in *The Passion Artist* is the metaphor of the stationary traveler who explores the incongruous and the lethal within himself. Like Papa, Vost enjoys and suffers the sexual dynamics of paternal power which corresponds to his attempts to be the author of his experience. And like Papa, Vost desires a correspondence or a union between his verbal formulations and the world in which he finds himself.[4]

The world and the words that describe it seem to coincide for Vost with the unsettling of his regular life that begins with his encounter with the teenage prostitute and his fighting against La Violaine's inmates. He exults when his theory that "the imitation of a hand in a black glove . . . adds splendor to the body presumed to be merely maimed" (20) becomes, in his viewpoint, embodied in him when he wakes up in the hospital the day after the rebellion: "He was thinking that only the hero is awarded the magnificence of the silver hand, and that he himself had become living proof of his theory about missing and artificial limbs" (73). But the artifice that substantiates his theory both exalts and reifies: "He was both maimed and adorned. His character was now externalized in the gloved hand. Inner life and outer life were assuming a single shape, as if to conform with one of his theories. He was crippled, he was heraldic, soon the rest of him would follow the way of the hand until he could be mounted upright on a block of stone" (72). He conceives of himself as a monument to his own control (of himself and the world), at once enacting and negating transformation.

The union of interior and exterior, and of theory and world, extends to Vost's conception and perception of woman. He is, after all, "a man who spent his life among women, or whose every move and thought occurred only in a context of women" (1). But these women, in the case of his incarcerated mother and his dead wife, are absent, or in the case of his daughter, as good as absent, since the child he thinks her to be no longer exists. Women are constituted by the workings of his imagination, and so when his self-incarceration finds release in violence against the rebelling women of La Violaine, and when the rebelling women have been victorious, Vost finds himself confronting fears and desires, unleashed and as dangerous as he has dreamed them to be. When he sees a woman, a prison escapee, hiding behind a gravestone in the cemetery where Claire lies buried, "the sight of her filled him with anger: the prison had exploded, so to speak; interior and exterior life were assuming a single shape; rebellious women appeared to be arising even from the graves of the dead" (74). This joining of Vost's consciousness and unconscious with manifestations of a magical and frightening world reflects his most essential and paradoxical idea: "The poles of his most general theory of the psychological function were these: that the interior life of the man is a bed of stars, that the interior life of the man is a pit of putrescence" (31). Yet the confirmation of his self and his theories that Vost finds even in the upheaval of his existence collapses when he loses control of his person, becoming the prisoner of two women from La Violaine who lead him back to the prison by a rope tied around his neck. Paraded across the prison yard to the hoots and whistles of groups of women, Vost wonders, "did his theories of the psychological function apply to women? Could such a person as himself be brought to even rudimentary knowledge of submission, domination, the question of woman?" (121). He faces the possibility that the ordering of existence in his theories rests in contingency and exclusion.

The first woman whose theories about consciousness counter Vost's is Claire, though Vost does not even consider, during Claire's lifetime, what her theories might suggest about women. "Poor Konrad," Claire used to say, "you cannot understand how you achieved consciousness, and you are always detesting the enigma, refusing to believe it. . . . Human consciousness is only the odd flower in the unbounded field. It exists in the natural world and as such is natural, whether it is enigmatical or not" (42).[5] Women torment Vost for the same reason his consciousness torments him: they are both, for him, shrouded in mystery. Speaking about *The Passion Artist* in his interview with Heide Ziegler, Hawkes points to Vost's inability to see particular women as unique and individual; instead, each woman he encounters throughout his life merely substitutes for the woman of some primary relationship: mother, daughter. Individual women are lost to the conception of the mythological female. "It is essential to demystify woman and at the same time to overcome ignorance," Hawkes says. "We must have knowledge of both the male and female and destroy their mythological roles in order to experience what is in fact their mystery" (186–187).

Konrad Vost's ignorance of himself and of women is such that he never understands, while Claire is alive, why she has a "boyfriend" to be her lover, and he never understands himself or his wife any better even when she tries to explain his relationship with her: "The weaker the child, Claire used to say, the more fanatical the man. And my dearest, where is the woman who does not love a fanatical man. . . . But never once while she was alive did he understand that he was the subject of this the rarest of Claire's aphorisms" (31). It is not until he encounters his mother for the first time since he was a child that he receives the knowledge of how his fear and need had corrupted his marriage: "the first dictum of his notorious mother . . . was that marriage must never in any way become maternal. The truth of the pronouncement was like the removal of the hood from a man about to be hanged, and thus completed in the prison that annihilation of Claire which had commenced with her death" (121). Eva's illumination of his existence also illuminates the realm of the prison of self-liberated women as the realm of words with the power to transform.

Vost's consciousness, "that interior world into which no light can shine," has its "nomenclature . . . only in the formulations of the psychological function" (58); it is in this nomenclature that Vost has sought his psyche's illumination. His consciousness exists only insofar as he can articulate it, but his articulations are only one type of fictive construction naming a fictive self, the "figment of his own psychological function" (58). Vost's incarceration in the prison liberates him from the confines of his own formulations into the world of other voices, other "languages," and also into a world beyond language.

The limitations of Vost's hold on a verbal world are comically apparent at the beginning of the novel when he meets the teenage prostitute whose shirt bears in block letters across the front "the message WE AIM TO PLEASE." Vost "noted the boldness of the letters but did not understand the pathos of the double meaning, since the message on the shirt was couched in that language he had never learned to read" (34). The language of sex, that forte of Cyril in *The Blood Oranges*, eludes him. But a dream he has after he loses consciousness during the revolt refigures him as a man who poeticizes women, much as Cyril does, but who, by virtue of this very predilection for displaying desire in words, ignores the "language" of the flesh. In this dream, Vost is a penitent, bound and hooded with sackcloth that covers head and body, "as if the others in the room could not bear the sight of any part of him," and faced by a featureless judge and a beautiful female accuser. This accuser states that Vost is "a man who does not know the woman" (64). She is outraged because, she says, "This man did not even use his lips for kissing. He told me my mouth was a little golden wasp, but he felt no responsibility for kissing. Such language! With words like that a person can only drink her wine and sulk to herself" (66). The replacement of action by language here impoverishes experience. In converting desire into language, Vost stands accused of ignoring the desires and reality of the woman, converting her into a category of his knowledge: "He commented on my size! My small size! . . . He said that the smaller the woman, the greater the capacity of her organs of love. . . . He used those words, he spoke to me in just that way! He dared to admire me for my small body but could not lay a hand on me. What could he know?" (65). The accuser illuminates the hubris and fictiveness of Vost's formulations, and both mocks and laments the disappearance of any real communication between the man and the woman.

At the end of his life, as he and Hania make love in a cell of La Violaine, Vost hears "[a] female voice . . . singing in a language he had never learned" (178). The description is both straightforward and metaphoric, for even after having experienced the transfiguration of the erotic union, Vost has only glimpsed a world outside of himself. The voice comes from a record playing again and again on a phonograph in the prison courtyard: "But the voice of the woman was only a mechanical rendition of silence; the music itself was only the shape, in sound, of a dark space that had once been a cabaret in the past that was gone" (181). In giving shape to absence and so embodying the past, this voice and music perform the significatory function that Vost had formerly attributed to objects and to his verbal formulations, his endless theories. His theory of the psychological function has as its first premise the idea "that in the storehouse of memory everything is retained" (43), and his memory acquires substance in images and narrative, but his experience in the prison reveals that the past can be given shape by consciousnesses other than his own. And these consciousnesses express themselves in the words, both spoken and written, of women who have spent their lives in prison.

The first time Eva Laubenstein and Hania come to his cell, Vost expects he would now "hear his own name on the wings of [his mother's] voice" (131). But Eva does not speak his name; instead, as Hania kisses his face and body, she tells the story of her terrible, painful pregnancy, nearly thwarted by the viciousness of a doctor who falsely told her the baby she was carrying was dead and that she must expel it. Born nearly dead, Vost now is reborn in the memories related by his mother. When Eva and Hania leave the room, Vost remembers events from his orphaned childhood during which his innocence withered and his curiosity warped under the sexual cruelty of his surrogate mother, Anna Kossowski, on a farm for "disordered children." He sleeps, and wakes to a transforming sight: "a woman had had the presence of mind to write her name on the wall: *Innocenta*. At that moment he again knew who and where he was, exactly. . . . It was dawn of his first full day in La Violaine. If he had had a stub of pencil he would have written his name beside the woman's: *Konrad Vost. Prisoner*" (153). He is a man who is finally "exactly where he had always wished to be without knowing it: in the world of women and in the world of the prison" (120). The name tag that had been tied to his wrist in the hospital is gone; his mother does not give him his name; but now Konrad Vost wishes to reinscribe his name himself, identifying the metaphorical condition imposed by his past and the literal condition endured in his present, and at the same time listing himself among the ranks of women. Yet although "Innocenta" inspires him, the women's names on the wall are mostly an affront: "In icy consciousness each name, to which he allowed no personal significance, was a crime that denied his own courage, a woman he could not have known" (155). The independent and unknowable identities of these women compromise his own claim to correctness and understanding. The "storehouse of memory" retains "[a]ll perception, all psychic life, everything remembered, everything dreamt, everything thought, all the products and all the residue whatsoever of the psychological system . . . down to the last drop, the last invisible hair" (43), but it cannot encompass the experience outside the bounds of his own personal existence. The names attest to a past not included in the storehouse of Vost's memory.[6]

The oppressive omnipresence of the past to which Vost so tenaciously clings slips away under the pressure of other ordering consciousnesses: "Indifferently he watched a few last scraps from the memory he could not recover, a few ragged edges of the story that had been his own" (154). The "story" of the novel has progressed through the elaboration of meaning refracted through Vost's psychological function; but in the confines of the prison, the narration expands to include the ideas, reactions, and directions of women. A man obsessed with messages, Vost now reads the messages scrawled by anonymous women on the prison walls. The writings of the women are "humorous or violent," and express "vulgar cravings [that] were the equal of the vulgar cravings of any man" (155). He is impressed by two inscriptions because of "their simplicity and shocking contrast to the others":

*In memory of a Sunday in summer.* Was it possible that a woman, especially in this place, had been capable of such generosity? After all, the nostalgia and resignation captured in the expression were as shockingly appropriate to the mind of a man as were the obscenities that made him flush with embarrassment. The second inscription was similar: *Love is not an honest feeling.* Again, who but a man could have written these words? . . . Yet the authors of these sayings had in fact been women. (155)[7]

While these two messages, wise and illuminating but still comfortable because they include sentimentality and address guilt, reveal for Vost a startling similarity between men and women, the message written between them transfixes him in "rigid contemplation" because of its revelation of difference: "*Between my legs I do not have a bunch of violets.* It was a statement that excluded him forever; it was the clue to the object of his desperate quest; it could not have been written by a man" (156). (One irony, of course, is that these words that could have been written only by a woman were written by John Hawkes.) The statement attacks the erasure of a woman's reality by a logic of sentimental and aesthetic replacement. It establishes the existence of a female body and subjectivity that crack the illusory mirror of Vost's desire. It holds the possibility of there being "the thing itself," and thus of Vost's liberation from the bonds of memory, fear, and need that compose his consciousness and that have determined his world.

Vost's absorption with the terms of the psychological function harbors the question of what women want and of what women are. One answer that Eva presents to the latter defines what women are *not*. She quotes a proverb from her childhood: "*Devils and angels do the same things; but you always know which one has been at your door.* You, dear Hania, will recognize these words as the words of an old woman. Never could they have been spoken by an old man, though in a sense they bear out Slovotkin. But more important, Hania, these same words gave rise long ago to a truth of my own: *The woman is not naturally a martyr; the man is not naturally a beast*" (160). The proverb from Eva's childhood proposes that devils and angels—or, in Slovotkin's formula, women and men—are both the same and different; Eva's own aphorism proposes that the identity attributed to women and men is culturally constructed. The two axioms together pose the problem of perception, the possibility of essence, and the determining role of language in constituting individuals who fit their labels. From his experience in "the grove of laughter," that place in the marsh where he finds and causes the death of the old woman, Vost learns "that whatever his own previous misconceptions, nonetheless age never obliterates entirely the streaks and smears of masculine and feminine definition. Never" (91). The novel's concern is with how these streaks and smears acquire significance through the individual and cultural imagination.

Eva, an old woman now herself, addresses all her words to Hania, rather than Vost, and "[t]he words of his mother . . . come to him on the tongue of this woman" (133). Seen by Vost as the origin of himself and his story, Eva tells something of her own story, clarifies Vost's past and present, and allows him to live in this present as well as approach the future. The last visit made to Vost in his cell is by Hania alone, for by asserting her own status as a strong and complex individual, Eva has dissolved the bonds of her son's childish need. She has prepared the way for Hania, who, in Hawkes's words, "is beyond the mother, and the simple way we know that is that the mother disappears and leaves Hania behind. Not as a substitute any longer, but as a unique woman" (Ziegler 186). Hania, who has said little up to this point, now conveys some dictums of her own. As she begins to make love to Vost, she says, "watch me, look at me. You must see what I am doing in order to feel it. Passionate sensation depends on sight" (179). Her statement follows Eva's earlier comment that "[f]or the child the first mystery is what cannot be seen" (160). This mystery corresponds to the "mystery" of "woman," whose "absence" of a phallus translates to sexuality that cannot be seen; and the mystery corresponds to Vost's Oedipal anxiety over his mother: "He had hardly dared look at her as a child, yet even now he loved the sight of her, though he averted his eyes" (127). But he does look at Hania, who gives "him the gift of the majestic consciousness that shone in her eyes" (131). The ability of this consciousness to formulate the workings of the psychological function opens Vost to the experience of otherness in which sight does not constitute a means of receiving self-reflection, but instead enables a more insightful vision. "You are now aware," Hania tells him, "of your own respect and mine" (180).

The distancing resulting from the projections of his fear and self-loathing onto the mysterious, impenetrable surface of Woman collapses when Vost discovers "that the woman's dilation was such that the exterior of her body could no longer be distinguished from its interior" (180). The abolition of boundaries counteracts the physical and psychical walls that abound in Vost's world; it also counteracts the mirroring correspondences Vost has elaborated between his inner world and his outer environment. Correspondence gives way to creative union. Experiencing the communication of Hania's body and his own, he thinks of his encounter with the young prostitute that began his journey, and realizes that "the distinction between the girl and the woman who is more than mature lies only in the instinct of the one and the depth of consciousness of the other" (181). The imaginative leap involved in Vost's perception of a consciousness other than his own goes along with the imaginative demands of experiencing eroticism: "Konrad Vost knew at last the transports of that singular experience which makes every man an artist: the experience, that is, of the willed erotic union" (181). (One must wonder if the experience makes every woman an artist, too.) The will is that of both parties; the artistic/erotic moment abrogates the conflicts of power and the distancing of aestheticism that have plagued the designs of Hawkes's past narrators.

In finally better understanding what it is to be a woman, Vost better understands what it is to be a man. The realization of identity as man and artist in the erotic moment, however, not only coexists with the dissolution of separate identities in the union with the other, but also precedes the moment of annihilation. After making love with Hania and dancing through the night with her and with the other women of La Violaine, Vost suddenly finds himself alone and starts through the open gates of La Violaine to the café La Violaine. His friend and fellow habitué of the café, Gagnon, is waiting for him against the wall of the prison; "It is you who will die!" Gagnon cries. (It seems likely that the beautiful young woman whose death Vost caused in the marsh was Gagnon's daughter.)

Gagnon shoots Vost and Vost says, "Poor Gagnon. . . . They may destroy me, they may devour me. But I am who I am. . . . With this remark Konrad Vost achieved his final irony, for as he spoke he was already smiling and rolling over to discover for himself what it was to be nothing" (184). The irony inheres not only in the paradox of proclaiming his existence as he is on the verge of nonexistence, but in his tautologous final remark itself. The repetition within the sentence suggests both the inadequacy of words to name the reality of the self and the idea that there is nothing, including a self, beyond words.[8] The tautology further suggests the formula that encapsulates the action of the novel: "*La Violaine to La Violaine.*" This, "to the special habitués" of the café La Violaine "had become an aphorism" because whenever there was an infrequent release of a woman from the prison, without fail she would come across the street to the café bearing the same name (7). Late in the novel Vost thinks to himself, "*La Violaine to La Violaine.* . . . For him the aphorism was now actuality. What was there more?" (125). But the referents of the aphorism have been reversed; now, instead of referring to a woman going from the prison for women to the café for the men who love and hate them, the aphorism refers to a man going from the locale of his self-incarceration to the liberation of the women's prison. More than that, however, Vost's satisfaction with the actualization of the aphorism reveals the importance granted in the novel to the linguistic determination of the world.

Eva Laubenstein, however, at one point casts the relation of language to the world in a different light. "We who spend our lives in prison," she says, "know three things: that the family is the first prison; that among prisons the actual is preferable to the metaphorical; and that the woman is not a mother until she leaves her child" (129). This last dictum is consistent with the emphasis throughout Hawkes's novels on the importance of absence to the imagination's engendering power. The first of the dictums reveals Eva's experience as consistent with Vost's own bondage in the web of familial desires and demands. Her claim "that among prisons the actual is preferable to the metaphorical" indicates the extent to which the family dynamic constrains and suffocates. But this claim by a woman who attempts, through language, to transform her son also posits the desirable existence of a realm beyond that constituted by the endless substitutions of language.

It is a "beyond" that Vost desires. He has gone through life relishing the idea that he exceeds the bounds of others' imaginations, that in his pleasure in desolation "he himself could not have been imagined by even the most morbid of the ancient poets" (13). And he takes pleasure in the idea that "[t]he irony of order existing only in desolation and discomfort was a satisfaction beyond imagining" (12). He imagines the "beyond" as his lived reality. In contrast, as a child on Anna Kossowski's farm he spent his days in the barn "beneath the massive legs of his favorite horse" where "he was safe . . . he was the happy insect among the monsters he could not imagine" (135). In his innocence he cannot imagine the sort of monster of repression and cruelty that this very innocence allows him to become. And it is this very monstrousness that prevents him, even in the midst of his excessive desolation, from getting beyond the confines of his self and the dynamics of mirroring and repetition; it prevents him from getting beyond the wall presented to him by the idea of Woman.

Vost's experience in La Violaine occasions, finally, the approach beyond the strictures of mystification and repression in a creative act of imagination, which holds the potential to destroy the boundary between man and woman. But he ends by coming upon another boundary, proclaiming "I am who I am," asserting his existence as inextricable from language as he approaches the death that will actualize the paradox of language's, and the self's, existence and nonexistence. Instead of Vost's transcendence, however, this is only Vost's eradication. The novel ends with a paragraph, italicized so that its textual quality is emphasized, that inscribes a world beyond the structuring of Vost's consciousness:

*For some months following the death of the fanatical but chastened Konrad Vost, rumors persisted that from the east there had been dispatched a military convoy intended to subdue once and for all the inmates of La Violaine. But gradually these rumors faded and then disappeared altogether. In the words of the noble person who led the revolt and attempted to attain the liberation of her only son, La Violaine is no longer a prison, and yet remains, as it should, under the sway of women.*

The rumors go the way of Vost, and we are left with the women who have destroyed "prison" and transformed a structure of oppression and incarceration into one of liberation. But the particulars of the actual rather than metaphorical liberation exist beyond the bounds of textual representation, beyond imagining.

# Chapter 6

# The Labyrinth, the Wilderness, the Female Voice: *Virginie: Her Two Lives* and *Adventures in the Alaskan Skin Trade*

**I**

Konrad Vost experiences a transformation of his inner and outer world by reading women's writing on a prison wall "as if on the blank page of an intimate journal for all the world to see" (156). *Virginie: Her Two Lives* (1981) is a novel in the form of just such a journal; the novel thus returns to first-person narration, but narration that now explicitly asserts its form as writing (to an even greater degree than that of *Second Skin*), and that now is from a female perspective. Virginie is an eleven-year-old girl who lives and writes her journal in 1740 and 1945 France, the first date significant for being the year of the Marquis de Sade's birth, the second for marking the end of World War II. In 1740 Virginie is the companion of Seigneur, an imperious man who runs a school to prepare women to be mistresses to aristocratic men; in 1945 Virginie is the companion of her brother, Bocage, a Parisian taxi driver who gathers together a group of women and a few men for the purpose of engaging in "charades of love." These eighteenth-century and twentieth-century "artists" provide historically inflected figurations of the male artists and narrators who dominate Hawkes's preceding novels. Virginie, "the insubstantial voice of the page that burns" (11), is both the innocent virgin girl and the innocent text, neither of which partake in experience but instead inscribe it; as such, this narrator and narration provide a new vantage from which to view the male author figures and to reenvision the possible attainment of authorial innocence through the beauty of language.

The novel consists of a repetitive rendering of erotic tableaux viewed by Seigneur or Bocage, their orchestrator, and Virginie, their recorder. Intended as a parody of a pornographic novel, *Virginie* thus plays on the paradox of male vision (Hawkes's, Seigneur's, Bocage's) rendered in female voice. This is simply one of many paradoxes, for the text is not only rife with paradox but is structured by its very principle, an idea suggested even in the novel's epigraphs: "Birth was the death of her" (Samuel Beckett) and "beauty is paradox" (Heide Ziegler). Virginie's virginity, a state Hawkes calls "the negative existence of sexual experience" (Emmett and Vine 169), embodies the simultaneous presence and absence that Hawkes attributes both to paradox itself and to language. Through the narration of Virginie, Hawkes exploits paradox on several levels. In the erotic landscapes of Seigneur and Bocage, imprisonment means freedom, pleasure requires pain, death inspires life, and innocence is gained through sexual experience. More significant, Virginie, who begins the novel "Mine is an impossible story," inscribes the paradox of authorial transgression cast in narrative innocence and of the death of the author insuring the life of the text. Hawkes thus prolematizes innocence and power, the poles of the authorial self, played out between the sexes and on the page.

Parody is one technique Hawkes uses to elaborate paradoxes. In a prefatory note, Hawkes writes: "My subject was, from the start, that wisp of shell-pink space shared equally, I am convinced, by the pornographic narrative (in color photographs) and the love lyric, from the troubadours, say, to the present. Thus parody, archaic tones, and an overall comic flavor were inevitable, as were sources and influences." Among these sources and influences are Sade and Bataille, as well as Charlotte Brontë. John Kuehl, in his essay "*Virginie* as Metaphor," comments that this parody includes "the comic treatment of those virginal narrators exemplified by Pamela Andrews, Clarissa Harlowe, and Jane Eyre, who are erotically but covertly attracted to virile masters" (149). Donald Greiner points out that the novel parodies "the various forms of the narrative as journal, history, and fiction" and adds that "for Hawkes, first-person narration invites parody of the novelist's role" (*Understanding John Hawkes* 153). *A Dictionary of Modern Critical Terms* defines parody as "one of the most calculated and analytic literary techniques: it searches out, by means of subversive mimicry, any weakness, pretension or lack of self-awareness in its original," and goes on to say that "parody is a mirror of a mirror, a critique of a view of life already articulated in art" (172–173). Parody is both tribute and criticism, an interpretation of historically constituted articulations and an acknowledgment of its own status as discourse. The historicity implicit in parody is furthered by Hawkes's juxtaposition of Virginie's 1945 and 1740 journal entries which record the differences between a world left random and disintegrative in the aftermath of war and a world of apparent beauty, symmetry, and order. This juxtaposition itself parodies the chaotic, disjunctive worlds of

Hawkes's early novels and the aesthetically ordered worlds summoned by the narrators of the later novels.

The self-consciousness implicit in parody in itself would seem to abrogate authorial or textual innocence, yet Virginie exists as the author/text—as well as character—in both time periods of the novel, and her existence is insistently called innocent. Roland Barthes's statement that "[l]inguistically, the author is never more than the instance writing" (145) precisely applies to Virginie's existence as character and text. In "The Death of the Author," Barthes goes on to say:

The Author, when believed in, is always conceived of as the past of his own book: book and author stand automatically on a single line divided into a *before* and an *after*. The Author is thought to *nourish* the book, which is to say that he exists before it, thinks, suffers, lives for it, is in the same relation of antecedence to his work as a father to his child. In complete contrast, the modern scriptor is born simultaneously with the text, is in no way equipped with a being preceding or exceeding the writing, is not the subject with the book as predicate; there is no other time than that of the enunciation and every text is eternally written *here and now*. (*Image/Music/Text* 145; Barthes's emphasis)

Virginie's existence as author/text complicates Hawkes's critique of authoring embodied in Seigneur, who represents the omniscient eighteenth-century author, and Bocage, who represents the twentieth-century author, and both of whom stand in a paternal relation to Virginie.

Seigneur and Bocage both live for (and ultimately through) Virginie, who is daughter, sister, soul. The purpose of Seigneur's school is to mold women into the form of innocence that Virginie naturally possesses. Seigneur, who wears a "plain gray shirt . . . like some sort of punitive undergarment" (21), must overcome the guilt of incest, the transgression of law that begot Virginie. After a scene in which he hides his covoyeur in what he refers to as "Virginie's confessional" so that they can watch a woman ravish a pig, Seigneur tells Virginie that "the first principle of love is secrecy" and that she is his secret (113). In another scene he tells her of a day when he doubted the value of his work: "*How* work for men who insisted that my women were women and not works of art!" (Hawkes's emphasis). He arrived at the answer by thinking of Virginie and concluded "the created woman is reason enough for her creation" (137). This dictum casts his original transgression in the light of creative good and explains his current activity as a sublimation of what is violent and chaotic. When Seigneur's mother, La Comptesse, wants to repeat their incest, Seigneur refuses, saying that Virginie "has no right to life . . . should not exist . . . to risk a repetition is but to mock the sacred irregularity that she is" (170). But it is precisely repetition that Seigneur enacts in his art. His "cloister" consists of a series of five women at a time, each woman renamed for one of the five qualities of "true womanhood" which Seigneur has decided upon and each woman instructed in the same curriculum. Virginie realizes that it is she who enables this repetition: "without my passive presence . . . he would not have been able to repeat himself with such perfection, while I awaited every word and flow of form, or to create still more ingenious ways of bringing into life the women he but had in mind" (182). The innocence of Virginie's eyes, which witness without judging, renders all experience, no matter how perverse, a form of beauty. Furthermore, although Virginie is the model of innocence, Seigneur also wants innocence inculcated in her; in her he expiates his past and obviates her future by projecting any experience she could have as a woman through the eyes of a child.

Donald Greiner notes that in "[a]ttempting to maintain a tenuous hold on his own innocence by never touching Virginie, Seigneur finally personifies the male passion for order" (*Understanding John Hawkes* 159). Orchestrator of Dionysian experiences, he is an Apollonian artist. He denies not only the humanity of the women he forms, but also his own, all in quest of an apotheosis through art. He has the cold detachment that Hawkes maintains is necessary for himself as artist. Bocage also is detached, but orchestrates only in that he brings together a group of people and costumes the women in brightly colored undergarments (the twentieth-century variation on Seigneur's use of brightly colored gowns). Mostly he sits back and observes, occasionally shouting approval, throwing out a direction, or discoursing on the purpose of his Sex Arcade. But Bocage loses his detachment when he consummates his love with his sister, Virginie, and in the consummation that is their lovemaking and the fire that kills them Virginie realizes that it was she for whom the Sex Arcade existed: "So was our life then all for me? . . . For me that he invented Bocage's Sex Arcade, as he came to call it, in which he waited until he knew by instinct that I had seen what there was to see and would see no more? Why else?" (115).

The Sex Arcade, Bocage proclaims, is a place where "There is forbidden life enough for everyone! There is a charade for each of us if we can but summon it to mind!" (200). His words echo those of Seigneur, who calls for "More life!" (102). His words also define the Sex Arcade as paralleling the purpose of Seigneur's *école des femmes*, which is to give life to his idea of the ideal woman. But whereas Seigneur institutes a regimen of exercises that are erotic metaphors for sexual life, Bocage gathers a group of people who play out their sexual fantasies as they please. Heide Ziegler comments that although Bocage does not dictate to the women in his establishment, "still their erotic experiences are not a result of free choice, but of random sexual encounters" ("Postmodernism as Autobiographical Commentary," 212). But it is this very randomness that highlights a crucial aspect of the two worlds in which Seigneur and Bocage function as authors: the production of meaning.

Hawkes comments on "the vastness of sexual ruin that, for me, summed up the Second World War. I found sexual death to be the only conceivable analogue to death itself, the only way to dramatize the power of death" (O'Donnell 125). In 1945 Bocage busies himself stopping up the signs of ruin in his chateau, "stuffing the emptiness of broken panes with rags and crumpled paper," creating a haven from the world Virginie looks out on, "all that invisibly frozen darkness from which we inside were safe" (116). The people inside the chateau have come there with their baggage of sexual ruin: the impotent Monsieur Malmort, the boastful temporarily crippled Lulu, Monsieur Moreau, wracked with suspicion of and desire for his teenage daughter, Monsieur and Madame Pidou with their sexless marriage, Clarisse who has known only one afternoon of passion which she had with a pair of strangers, Yvonne the prostitute who performs fellatio on her little brother, Sylvie and Minouche, whose ruin we can only guess at by the fact that they are there. In the light of Bocage's hearth they play out "charades of love," some perverse, some merely silly, but all finally a means by which they resurrect their humanity through the exercise of their imaginations.

In one charade Sylvie tries to awaken Monsieur Pidou's potential for love by helping him bathe little Déodat, Minouche's son. When Sylvie fishes the soap out of the water and offers it to Monsieur Pidou, Virginie realizes that once he takes the soap from the woman's palm "he would enter into a bargain with Sylvie defined not by what the soap actually was but by what it meant" (125). This investment of meaning characterizes much of the activity of the Sex Arcade, so that objects such as an old corset or a peacock pin excite their viewers and wearers and inspire sexual possibilities which themselves are meaningful as imaginative interactions with others. Investing objects with meaning constitutes the fictional process for Hawkes, who says, "I think of myself as a totemic or fetishistic writer. For me, every object, every fictional detail, becomes energized with its own meaning, its own life" (LeClair 28). The characters of the Sex Arcade thus share the work of authoring with Bocage by their imaginative transformation of objects, but they also act as authors in the stories they tell, which compose whole chapters. The stories they tell are from their pasts, from the time when there was "life beyond the Sex Arcade" (154). Although the details they relate are often rather sordid, Virginie can see them as "sad and beautiful" (200), suggesting that the act of telling and receiving confers this beauty. The telling of stories serves as a prelude to re-imagining them; the stories serve as the inspira-

tion for acting on the desires they express in a new way with the inhabitants of the Sex Arcade.

The women in Seigneur's establishment must also tell stories, these in
the form of their journal entries. Seigneur requires that these entries be
prose, never poetry, but the journal entries of the women that Virginie
records in her journal are—according to Seigneur—poetry in spite of
this. The stories the women write rely on metaphor, which is precisely
the vehicle Seigneur thrives on. He interprets what the women write,
dictating the meaning of their stories just as he dictates to them in all his
lessons what it means to be a woman. In all things, Seigneur is the arbiter
of meaning. Virginie's description of the beginning of Seigneur's days
illuminates this: "most of our days began in a chapel stripped of every
relic, every appropriate sign, and containing only Seigneur who always
stood where once the altar had stood. How strange that from such a
place, all the more devotional from having been rendered meaningless,
should come the conception that so determined the pain or pleasure of
our days" (52). Seigneur, who has put himself in the place of God, abolishes one order of meaning to replace it with another—his own, which
will be embodied in his own icons—the women he "creates."

Seigneur is the eighteenth-century author who sets himself up as the
origin dispensing meaning, and Bocage is the twentieth-century author
who speaks only as one voice among many. Yet meaning is plural in both
the 1740 and 1945 sections because Virginie is their writer. Virginie, calling the confines of Dédale (Seigneur's establishment) a labyrinth, says,
"Yet even inside the labyrinth, seeing only what was before my hand or
hanging on slender chains from the high ceiling above me, still I also saw
our chateau as if from without and afar. . . . Who but I could know what
occurred both within and without?" (51). She is the imaginative text,
able to see from any perspective, including Seigneur's or Bocage's, and
finally, the women's. She describes rising from her resting place, the dead
hearth of the kitchen: "the entire chateau lay around me like a labyrinth
that only I might explore. Straight-backed on my stool, drinking and eating, I experienced a moment of that curious pride when she who is assumed to have no consciousness knows, for one instant, that she herself
is the vessel brimming with all the world for whom, this instant, she does
not exist. Hence I saw them all in the mirror that was myself" (49). She
proceeds to describe the appearance of the chateau in the early morning
and what everyone in the domicile is doing so that it seems she is "actually" seeing all this. But she is simply sitting in the kitchen: "I sat in the
light and around me lay a labyrinth of light. What was it all if not the very
domain of my purity? . . . But then the still morning erupted into all the
fragments of its actuality" (50). The novel is very self-consciously com-

posed of fragments that are made to cohere through the domain of Virginie's voice, the mirror of the labyrinth.

Virginie uses the word "labyrinth" repeatedly and is careful to write that she does so deliberately. Seigneur explains the significance of the word when he delineates the map of the Land of Love. In the Land of Love the desired destination is the Citadel of the Desire to Please, and at the heart of this citadel is the labyrinth of Surrender All: "The garden of green confusion, which it initially appears to be, is in fact as orderly as the citadel itself; the greenness of the labyrinth determines all. Everything in the citadel is held in its proper place, attains its balance and hence its meaning" (100). It is "a labyrinth in which we cannot lose our way" (100). A woman's genitals are a labyrinth, Dédale is a labyrinth, the Sex Arcade Monsieur Malmort visits where skeletons travesty love is a labyrinth, the domain of Virginie's purity is a labyrinth, the text itself is a labyrinth. John Barth (inspired by the work of Jorge Luis Borges) uses the image of the labyrinth in his essay "The Literature of Exhaustion" to talk about the enterprise of contemporary art: "A labyrinth, after all, is a place in which, ideally, all the possibilities of choice (of direction, in this case) are embodied, and—barring special dispensation like Theseus'—must be exhausted before one reaches the heart. Where, mind, the Minotaur waits with two final possibilities: defeat and death, or victory and freedom" (34). Barth's essay addresses the position of the contemporary writer who must confront the corpus of intellectual and literary history in trying to create viable art. *Virginie: Her Two Lives* takes a path through the labyrinth that Barth summarizes as a possibility for the contemporary artist in his later essay, "The Literature of Replenishment": "artistic conventions are liable to be retired, subverted, transcended, transformed, or even deployed against themselves to generate new and lively work" (71). Complementing the use of parody in *Virginie* is the insistence on the self-renewing power of the imagination. The labyrinth in the novel and the labyrinth of the novel is what is most mysterious and most lucid, what is darkest and brightest, what holds life and death in the balance. "What could be more ominous than the death of this rhetoric?" Virginie asks (61). But the rhetoric does not die; phoenix-like, the wings of language (207) rise from the ashes like Virginie rising from the ashes of the hearth or from the fires that kill her.

The image of wings occurs more than once in *Virginie*. Before he is burnt at the stake, Seigneur reveals to Virginie the Tapestry of Love and she is filled with "the immensity of Seigneur's vision" (204). The tapestry consists of Seigneur's "scepter" (phallus) on a field of blue "so uniformly pale it might have represented the unchanging sky or even emptiness" (204–205). The scepter rises, "borne aloft by two great wings, the uncontested occupant of the blue space!" (205). The overawed Virginie exclaims that it is a "magnificent mirage" to which Seigneur agrees, adding "exactly as are the man, the woman, the labyrinth itself. The scepter is the emblem of them all! and just as indestructible! and as much a mirage!" (205). The tapestry is an emblem for Seigneur's project: transforming sexuality into art and transforming art into sexuality. It portrays this activity as phallic mastery. But the novel undercuts this mastery, working to show precisely that the authority of the scepter/phallus is *not* uncontested.

Seigneur, calling himself the artist, designates Virginie as his soul, a typical figuration of the female. This causes Virginie to question whether such an assignation denies her her own soul, but she determines it does not because she has (and for the reader, is) language. And because Virginie is innocent, the assertion seems to be that her language is innocent. Seigneur defines innocence as "the clarity with which the self shows forth the self" (206). Language, then, has the visionary status Hawkes claims for it: we are back to his definition of visionary fiction as "a fish bowl in which the clarity of the bowl is unique and you see the stream of fish, the gleam of fins" (Santore and Pocalyko 174). In *Virginie* all is a mirage, constituted by language and outlasted by it. Barthes writes:

It may be that men ceaselessly re-inject into narrative what they have known, what they have experienced; but if they do, at least it is in a form which has vanquished repetition and instituted the model of a process of becoming. Narrative does not show, does not imitate; the passion which may excite us in reading a novel is not that of a "vision" (in actual fact we do not "see" anything). Rather it is that of meaning, that of a higher order of relation which also has its emotions, its hopes, its dangers, its triumphs. "What takes place" in a narrative is from the referential (reality) point of view literally *nothing*; "what happens" is language alone, the adventure of language, the unceasing celebration of its coming. (*Image/Music/Text* 124; Barthes's emphasis)

Perpetually innocent, perpetually in the process of becoming what she will never be, Virginie resists the limits of Seigneur's or Bocage's world. Observer of erotic games, her performance as language is itself erotic in Barthes's sense. Language becomes not a matter of mastery but of process; Virginie becomes the text "eternally written *here and now*" (*Image/Music/Text* 145). This condition, however, coexists with the various parodistic qualities of her writing which make it a continual revisioning of the past, as her writing also is in terms of the "plot." *Virginie* stands as a postmodernist text in the sense that John Barth applies to Italo Calvino, who, Barth says, "keeps one foot always in the narrative past . . . and one foot in, one might say, the Parisian structuralist present" ("The Literature of Replenishment," 70). By using an innocent virgin girl as the narrator of events in an establishment of male fantasy, Hawkes is able to celebrate the innocent imagination while at the same time examining the loss of innocence in the imagination's inevitable recourse to power and embroilment in history.

## II

In *Adventures in the Alaskan Skin Trade* (1985) Hawkes pursues the possibilities engaged by a female narrator with the narration of Jacqueline Burne Deauville, nicknamed Sunny, a thirty-nine-year-old woman who explicitly negotiates the terrain of sex and death explored by an eleven-year-old-girl observing a master's instructions in eroticism and by the middle-aged male narrators driven by the need to articulate the conforming of reality to their desires. The critique of authorial power that is also paternal power elaborated in *Virginie* continues in Sunny Deauville's narration. Sunny develops a discourse that explores paternal authority from the viewpoint of one who has suffered its "seduction and betrayal" (92), as she counters the "masculine" confrontation with the wilderness with her own exploration of the boundaries of the known and unknown: "At an early age I knew that woman, not Alaska, is the last frontier" (16). But just as "the Alaskan dream" (344) proves to be a fiction, so too does the image of woman; the final frontier is fiction itself, both empty and excessive in its vastness, the locus of received "truths" and of produced meanings.[1]

In exploring the final frontier of fiction, *Adventures* remaps the cartography of all of Hawkes's past imaginary landscapes. The novel takes place in a world rife with all the desolation of Hawkes's darkest novels, while Sunny dreams of an alternate life in a world as rich and idyllic as any of Hawkes's most lyrical creations. *Adventures* engages Hawkes's persistent concerns with the issues of innocence and power, creation and representation, and fiction and eroticism, at the same time that it constitutes a dramatic stylistic break from his previous work. This late novel by an author who privileges repeated image and structure over plot, character, and theme has the traditional elements of story in its incarnations as tall-tale and adventure narrative, and has family and personal history as the central concern of its narrator.

The adventure tales that compose the novel are for the most part stories told by or about "Uncle Jake" Deauville, recounted here by his daughter whom he is responsible for nicknaming "Sunny." A man who lived in the hope of realizing a vision of conquest, discovery, and accomplishment in the harshness of a frozen wilderness, Uncle Jake is most notable for his unvanquishable innocence, a quality that translates to imaginative daring as well as sexual ignorance and a lack of self-knowledge. It is the frigidity, misogyny, and emotional cruelty implicated in his seductive innocence that caused the suffering of his wife, Sissy, and that has determined both Sunny's profession as the proprietor of the Alaska-Yukon Gamelands and the necessity of narration:

> But no matter the treachery of his innocence and misguided masculinity; no matter his Alaskan history of ever-increasing brutal flights of fancy that broke Sissy's spirit and caused her death; and no matter that his entire life was my seduction and betrayal—all this aside, Uncle Jake was a storyteller. He laughed and ranted and soared in his odd rhetorical fashion, extolling himself and maligning others, making jokes and moralizing and exaggerating all that was injurious. Generally he missed the point of his own stories, yet he held us in the thralldom of those endless stories. . . . No wonder at my late age I've embarked on telling his story and mine. No wonder I know his story so well and have the words for it. (92–93)

The reinscription of Uncle Jake's life through the voice of Sunny transpires because of the demands of her own dreams in which the continued presence of the dead father traps her in the past at the same time that her vision of a lyrical existence beckons her from the harsh, "masculine" world of her father's desire to a sunny France of sensual pleasure. Her dreams reveal and debunk the attractions and absurdities of her father and the paternal, hierarchical values for which he stands, and they also counter the mimetic and suspenseful elements of "story" through their recourse to anti-realism and their dependence on symbol and interpretation. Buried among the fictions constituted by the elaboration of Sunny's dreams, and buried among the fictions constituted by Uncle Jake's stories and reconstituted by Sunny's narration, lies the subtext of Sissy's journals, the minimal counter to the bombastic excesses of Uncle Jake and the ambivalence of Sunny.

The tall tales, the dreams, and the few recounted journal entries, all linked by Sunny's past and present "history" and that together compose her narration, serve as a means of incorporating and exorcising the father—and the mother and the dream, too. The fictional time frame of the writing of the novel is a matter of a year and some months, beginning with the imperatives of finding the father and envisioning a new life, a second skin, in France and taking us to Sunny's dream of three mornings before and the revelation, on that day, of Uncle Jake's distant suicide. Sunny's narration ends with her abandonment of her vision of herself in France and her acceptance of an inimical world, transfigured now through the process of narration itself. While the novel begins with Sunny saying, "Dad? . . . Where are you, Dad?" followed by a lyrical, disembodied response, Sunny's or Uncle Jake's, that places him ubiquitously in the harsh landscapes of the north and west, it ends with Sunny again saying, "Dad?" and receiving no answer. But then "Dad" has always been a word with no referent for Sunny, a longed-for name disallowed by her father, representing intimacy and relation denied. Sunny can list the names that denote her family—"John Burne Deauville. Cecily Flowers. Sunny"—for what persists in all the rambling excess that is *Adventures in the Alaskan Skin Trade* is the elusive substance of language. Instead of being the "Alaskan woman feeling good in her skin in France" (13) that she imagined herself to be in her vision, Sunny is, as her last line tells us, "an Alaskan woman feeling good in her skin in Alaska" (396). She accepts an identity composed by the "skin" of language, the seductive layers of history and image, symbol and story, rhythm and sound which she has constructed in these pages.

The first dream Sunny recounts establishes linguistically constituted identity as integral to its meaning. In the dream, she hears Uncle Jake calling her and follows his voice through darkness and desolation, "across the lunar ice" (17), to the edge of a crevasse which, in clear and crystalline icy depths, holds her strong and laughing father and the unbelievable brightness of the sun: "my name—nickname actually—is the joke of the dream. Sunny discovering the buried sun" (18). The dream stands as an obvious paradigm of the strata of meanings available in the translation of images into language in "dream work." The discovery of the buried father is the discovery of the buried sun/son; the discovery of each is the discovery of Sunny's self; the self Sunny discovers is an identity constituted by a name; the male-sounding name "Sunny" is her father's creation which covers over her "real" name, itself consisting of her father's family names.[2] The name also recalls a name from a buried textual past, *Second Skin*'s Sonny, the black messboy whom Skipper cherishes and relies on as a faithful second in his duel with a suicidal daughter and a hostile world, and as his man Friday in his new Eden, a tropical version of Uncle Jake's innocent wilderness. And the buried "hero" recalls the man mythically buried alive in *The Beetle Leg*, a world in which the imagination works upon an absence to vivify a dead landscape and spin a myth of innocence both lost and maintained. Sunny's dream entangles the imagination's unearthing of the father with a circular return to a linguistic source, though in the dream her father's appeal to her is mute and she refuses it. "I am not my own woman," says Sunny (109), for she is caught in the nightly web of images and words that compose her dreams of herself, driven as she is to know the father.

Uncle Jake's claim, as a storyteller, on language multiplies itself in the power he assumes over naming. Not only does he determine that his daughter shall have the feminine form of his name (which goes from being John to Jack to Jake) and his mother's and father's family names, thereby erasing Sunny's linguistic inheritance from her own mother, he renames his wife, Cecily Flowers, "Sissy," so that the two women in his life have names that have their ultimate referent in the male. When Sissy begins her journal the joke of it is her name, for she calls herself "the dead flower" (39). And this, too, recalls a buried textual past: *Virginie* ends with the entry, "Remember the ghosts of dead flowers." Unlike the lush descriptiveness of Virginie's journal, Sissy's writing is terse and "telegraphic" (162). In it, she chronicles the bare bones of Jake's adventures and mentions the details of food and ordinary quotidian events. She also conveys, minimally, the state of her emotions: "Last night cried myself to sleep as usual" (38, 162). For all its reticence, the journal is, nonetheless, a record of despair. Inspired by suffering and maintained in secrecy, the journal enacts the play of language with silence, that state to which Sissy is condemned by the effusive verbosity and domestic control of her husband. Because he would view her misery as traitorous, her writing transgresses her social bonds; its minimalism both reveals and denies revelation; its existence conquers her erasure as it simultaneously submits to silence. Communicating facts and rejecting embellishments, she plays in reverse Uncle Jake's excessive narratives of discovery and conquest.

While Virginie doubles as the innocent imagination and innocent text, Sissy's recourse to writing suggests a loss of innocence. Her journal reveals that she "was in life a person of courage, though she was ignorant of her strength, her courage. At any rate [Uncle Jake's] were the risks, hers the suffering" (39). Suffering, in the terms set forth by Martha Washington, the woman who strangely appears on the scene of Sunny's domain of pleasure, abolishes the state of being an innocent: "'An innocent,' she said steadily, 'is a woman who doesn't suffer. She has no commitments, no problems. Sex is easy. Her life is without drama and hence without interest to those other than herself'" (279). Not being an innocent, according to Martha Washington, does not preclude possessing innocence. Being an innocent, however, does exclude being a feminist; Sunny, she says, is an innocent. Resigned to submissiveness and agreeableness, Sissy yet exceeds what Martha Washington would have to consider Sunny's pseudo-knowledge of women and men ("Your experience is contemptible," Martha tells Sunny [279]). The qualification of suffering commits Sissy, who endures the sexual silence imposed by Uncle Jake's supreme innocence, his puritanical rigor, his deafness to the language of sex and harkening to an exclusively male world, to the parameters of the page. Her journal exerts a sad fascination for Sunny, yet its interest to those other than herself remains moot, since Sunny perpetuates the exclusionary position that prompted Sissy to write in secret by burying her words in a text devoted, even in its moments most critical of him, to the father. When Sissy dies what remains is "the silence of the lost voice" (241), the voice that was lost long before, when Uncle Jake embarked upon actualizing his vision of Alaska. Even as Sunny writes of Sissy's realization that "she was here in Juneau only to suffer, which no one but herself could know" (69), she breeches Sissy's silence at the same time that she inscribes it.

The recording of a life to which she becomes increasingly a witness marks Sissy's condemnation to the reproduction of her desolate circumstances and her distance from the creative vistas of the imagination. The "art" of her journal writing resembles the reduction even of her music to silence: Uncle Jake replaces himself for Sissy with the gift of a piano, and "she heard herself playing silent music for the rest of her days in Alaska, and knew that that was all she had—the piano—and that she was doomed to solitary enjoyment of the music she had once loved" (161). The arrival of the piano recalls the first appearance of Rock Castle in *The Lime Twig*: "Up from the dark hold of the ship came Sissy's prize, a single wooden crate shaped like a coffin and large enough to hold a horse . . . and trapped up there and swaying in a cargo net suspended by an iron hook from the end of the rusty cable" (158). Rock Castle embodies the burden of excessive fantasies turned lethal; the piano represents the death of the music of Sissy's own fantasies, an instrument that will commemorate absence rather than create joy. It is the consolation for Uncle Jake's own deadly fantasies, of which Sissy is the victim: "the piano represented all that killed her" (163). But, true to Hawkes's insistence on paradox, the cruelty inherent in Uncle Jake's pursuit of his fantasies is concomitant with innocence, and, although this innocence is complicit in destructiveness, it allows the expansion of the imagination.

The drama that inheres in Sissy's journal is the drama of slow death, the imagination's enslavement to circumstance. Her record of the undeniable facts of her Alaskan experience counters the reporting done by Uncle Jake after each of his adventures, for his stories that pretend to realistic accounting dispose of mimetic function in favor of the formal requirements of an exciting and suspenseful tale. In his telling of his adventures he depends on the embellishment of language and the manipulation of plot, the tools that make such events as his confrontation with a black bear a portentous clash of titans, enthralling his listeners and making himself and them experience the rhythm and import of his words more fully than life itself. Sissy, in contrast, lives day to day outside the bounds of fictively infused experience: "There were no stories to give saving color to Sissy's home or to the strings of widely spaced electric lights going down our steep hill to the docks, no aura of expectation to make the black and rain-drenched mountains rising behind us any the less awful. There would never be a storyteller to make this bleakness tolerable to Sissy, though tolerate it she surely did" (90). Uncle Jake, "an

artist in the life of adventure" (15), escapes frustration and disappointment in the artful adventure of storytelling, the body of language that
replaces experience. Relating one of his more dangerous escapades,
Uncle Jake says that he was "thinking of only one thing: that no other
man could have done what I was doing, if I lived to tell the tale" (348);
indeed, for Uncle Jake, telling the tale is what makes the adventure exist.
The representation replaces the experience it describes for Uncle Jake's
fellow-adventurers and audience, too, who listen "raptly, as if we ourselves had not been there" (360).

It is the power and seduction of a story, about Indians who were inspired by a story, that engendered Uncle Jake's desire to go to Alaska: "A
friend in Washington had told him that there existed somewhere in
Alaska a totem pole carved by Indians who had been so moved by a mis-
sionary's tale of the President who had freed the slaves that they had
carved a totem pole surmounted by Lincoln, stovepipe hat and all. It was
the totem pole that had lured my father to Alaska" (15). When he finally
does find this totem pole, it is in a sacred grove among other totem poles
that "tell the end of [the Sundown Indians'] unknown story"; the story
is unknown, for even Suslota John, the last of the Sundown Indians "has
forgotten what most of [the totem poles] mean" (368). Furthermore,
Suslota John never heard of Abraham Lincoln. The legendary Indian
artifact, which exists for Uncle Jake by virtue of layers and layers of myth
and fiction, rests finally in its status as image, detached from any referents, eluding meaning and the desire for narrative. When the Lincoln
totem pole crumbles upon human touch, thus foiling Uncle Jake's dream
of shipping it to the Smithsonian, his Alaskan saga also disintegrates. He
commits suicide with the knowledge only of Sitka Charley, whom he
swears to secrecy, thus creating a death that is wholly an absence, beyond
narrative and beyond image, until twenty-five years later when Sitka
Charley reveals the truth of Uncle Jake's disappearance to Sunny.[3]

Uncle Jake's obsession with the totem pole and its legend underlies his
identity as storyteller and "artist in the life of adventure" (15) in a way
that is similar to Hawkes's idea of himself as "a totemic or fetishistic
writer" whose writing is "an act of eroticizing the landscape" (LeClair
28). Indeed, all of Uncle Jake's sexual and creative energy is invested in
penetrating the frontier, and in acquiring the masculine accoutrements—from clothing to companions—that go along with the frontier
fantasy that he has both bought into and made his own. The image of
the totem pole, so instrumental, along with its alleged narrative genesis,
in eroticizing Alaska for Uncle Jake (who refers to the territory as "her"
[174]), is, obviously, a phallic image—so obviously as to represent a
parody of the phallic desire that impels his vision in particular and male

artistic vision in general. Since Uncle Jake's artistry is communicated to us through the artistry of Sunny as "author," this parody attains a multivalent critique of the erotic/artistic desire to dominate the scene of creation.

Sunny's own totem that stands at the archway of Gamelands parodies Uncle Jake's desire as it reinscribes that desire and offers an ambiguous alternative to his fetishistic fantasy:

It rose a full thirty feet into the air, and except for the traditional winged creatures of Indian lore which divided it into quarters, and except for the greater-than-life-sized figure surmounting it, the entire totem pole was entwined with the bodies of nude women. . . . [T]he women [spiraled] upwards like stripes on a barber's pole, reaching and clamoring up my wooden rainbow toward the noble bareheaded man who soared above us in the darkening night. He wore his wooden parka, held aloft his wooden gun. He was pointing north to adventure. (108–109)

This totem pole marks the introduction to the artifice of the pleasure-driven world, devoted to sex, which Sunny has designed as the antithesis to the rigor and sexual denial of Uncle Jake's chaste existence. Uncle Jake is the figure at the top of Sunny's totem pole because, as she says, "He was afraid of women" (109). But the institution of a glorified frontier bordello as the alternative to an ethos that excludes the female asserts the reality and the power of female sexuality at the same time that it puts this sexuality in the service of male fantasy. The Gamelands totem pole can represent phallic power, both asserted and denied by Uncle Jake and his likeness, being overcome by women; or it can represent women clinging to a phallic ideal, the pinnacle of which is represented by Uncle Jake.[4] Regardless of any symbolic critique, however, the effect of the totem pole on the customers of Gamelands is magnetic: "Our Willie is drawn to the totem pole; he wants to approach it facing the angry beaks and spread pairs of wings. So he walks through the archway and stands before the totem pole in homage. He can't help himself. The totem pole speaks to him as does the glacier" (26). Sunny's deliberate manipulation of a phallic code in her creation of "an ultra-artificial settlement that guarantees sex twenty-four hours a day, sex in all seasons" (26) parodies this code without necessarily overturning it. Her recreation of Uncle Jake and his stories and her creation of her own narrative incorporate ambiguities similar to those upon which Gamelands is based, for she institutes her father's legacy at the same time that she deconstructs it.

When the Lincoln totem pole, the source and conclusion of Uncle Jake's designs, crumbles beneath his hands and under his eyes, threatening to collapse into dust and debris, his Alaskan dream also falls into ruin. The disintegration of the totem pole—one emblem of "the insistent dreams of the West, of the frontier, of primitive innocence" (Laniel 243), "diseased through and through with rottenness," as Uncle Jake himself says (378)—enacts, again in Laniel's words, "a symbolic and parodic debunking of the colossal Myth of Lost Innocence" (243), as well as a symbolic and parodic debunking of phallic power. The novel concerns itself throughout with the problem of myth, starting with the myth of the family, which is itself inextricable from a myth of innocence. Describing her relationship with her parents, Sunny says, "I was the myth of our trio, the myth of their lives, the embodiment of the myth of the only child, and a girl as well" (49). She exists in the first place because of the foundation of myth upon which her parents' marriage was based. Sissy lived out a Cinderella tale, trapped in a home where she was victimized by two evil sisters, until finally her "prince" saved her. Uncle Jake courted Sissy because he watched her suffering on a tennis court, the victim of inappropriate shoes: "He wanted to rush after her, pick her up in his arms, carry her off, since only saving by a white knight, as he now thought of himself, could possibly atone for such a complete defeat" (33). The genesis of Sissy and Jake's marriage can be reduced to a few key words charged with the power of the culture's romantic myths: "Orphaned child, charmed bride. White knight, saviour" (38).

As a victim in her own right of Uncle Jake's pursuit of his myth-inspired dreams, Sunny rejects these dreams at the same time that she identifies herself, in her capacity as the proprietor of Gamelands, as "Sunny Deauville, or the woman behind the myths of Woman" (24). The significances of this are played out in Sunny's description of her attempt to seduce a young customer: "I got myself up like a woman insisting on satisfaction in a silent film, donning nylon stockings and my sheer negligee—no garter belt or black net stockings, nothing to suggest the glitter of old-time artificiality, just the modest negligee and ordinary stockings, achieving thereby the image of a real woman in need of love. And in fact I was nothing if not a real woman, image or no image" (101). Sunny's reality, however, cannot be separated from the images she invokes and the myths in which she participates, and these myths cater to phallic desire. She describes her private cabin as "a citadel of sex" (101), recalling the realms of the Land of Love mapped out in *Virginie* by Seigneur, that dictatorial man who schools women in anticipating and satisfying male fantasy. She also describes her cabin as a museum (another favorite image of Hawkes's), and concludes: "Alaskan lore and contemporary luxury— what a context for the oldest of male fantasies . . . what a world for a woman" (101). Sunny takes the operation of the symbolic order into her own hands but does not change it.

Gamelands is a place where men can find "girls, women, fetishism, the

comforts and surprises of technology in the wilderness" (23); the totemic fetish that fueled Uncle Jake's fantasy of the Alaskan wilderness has
become, under Sunny's management, the varied fetishes supplied by literature, photographs, film, and technology. The interest in the Alaskan
frontier has become an interest in the frontier of woman, but the explor-
ers are still men and the territory still exists in representations. The representation of sex in language, however, affords Sunny the possibility of
her own exploration of the territory of women and men. She writes a
long paragraph, part of which follows, about the reasons why "sex" is her
"favorite word":

its duration varies infinitely each time this word, my word, is voiced. Sex, the
word, goes its way without euphony, flees from euphony, is sweetness without
music, which is best of all. Not big with blood, not round, lacking the inwardness
of the sigh, the body of a word like passion, how could it be more unexpected for
what it means, what it arouses? And isn't sex the heart of the unexpected? It's
so short, that word, so small, with its vowel that hardly deserves the name, is so
purely of the mouth that it cannot be said without invoking the ear. The small-
ness and closeness of the ear is drawn to that sound as to no other. No sooner
does anyone say it—sex—than you want to put your ear to his mouth. Or
hers. (27)

Just as Uncle Jake is an artist in the life of adventure through his conversion of adventure into story, Sunny is an artist in the life of sex by virtue
of her attention to language, though her interest is in the magical and
efficacious power of words themselves rather than story. At Gamelands,
she and the other women "talk as well as perform our sex" (28); the
language is itself performative. Her project at Gamelands, then, recalls
Papa's in *Travesty*, for he also wishes to actualize the impact of his words.
Whereas Papa's muse is his absent wife, Sunny's muse is her absent father, whose denial of sexual life and ignoring of Sunny's gender (350,
for example) fuel Sunny's desire to "heed hedonism" and her claim that
she is "something of a man" (24). But in her adulthood pursuit of sex in
language, and in her present narration, language becomes for Sunny the
medium of representation in which she explores the possibility of becoming her own woman.

Uncle Jake's own preoccupations also are similar to Papa's, for Papa
delights in "the unseen vision." Gazing at bare cliffs that were once covered by glaciers, Uncle Jake says that he can still hear "the booming of
the ice": "And what about the towering firs and the mastodons big as
houses? The destruction of them makes them all the more real. . . . It's
easier to see what's invisible than what's standing right in front of your
face! Nothing like a dead world to teem with life, I've often thought"
(333). Sunny carries on this relishing of paradox: "I live for paradox,"

she says, "I've created my own brand of Alaskan elegance, striving all the time, no doubt, to simulate French rarities, French forms of indulgence" (99). She also lives, however, for the visible, from the nine Mastodon mobile homes that compose the landscape of Gamelands, a place that does teem with life, to the photographs and articles of clothing that are an integral part of her repertoire of seduction. Her haven of luxury in the wilderness offers the talents of a woman who is a sex photographer and a woman who is a clairvoyant, and so Gamelands can offer its customers "[t]he forgotten past, the secret future, as well as the fluids of the flesh, the music of the flesh recorded in a Mastodon mobile home equipped as no place they've ever seen, and played back" (24). Yet this hyperactivity of the image paradoxically contains its own death; the act of sex is buried amidst the technologies that simulate and re-create it. The reign of paradox extends further, however, since the forgotten past (of her father's life, as well as Sissy's and her own) and the secret future (an idyllic life in France, or a comfortable life in Alaska) are the subjects of Sunny's narrative, which ends with a dream of her father buried alive (an image of the past as both invisible and ever-present) and with the revelation of his distant suicide. This absent father who reveled in a dead world that Sunny is rejecting inspires and necessitates her bringing to life and to light family and personal history, including their bearing upon the conception of sex and gender, in the excesses of language and the rigors of narration.

In Sunny's dream of Uncle Jake's burial alive, her father participates in the ritual of the Sundown Indians and is pleased with his death: "There is nothing so terrible but what he must praise it in his childish delight, in his boundless innocence. Dupe of himself, dupe of half a dozen Indians in a dark and suffocating hovel . . . I too am an accomplice to his self-aggrandizement" (390). This realization extends beyond the dream and comes appropriately at the end of this narrative, for Sunny has commemorated her father's legendary legacy. Sitka Charley tells Sunny that when Uncle Jake decided to take his own life, "he thought he was leaving you Alaska" (395). But Alaska is Uncle Jake's lunar landscape; it is a territory composed in the imagination, a domain where the fictive impulse, including cultural myths and family romance, comes to bear against a harsh and implacable blankness. Through the process of narration Sunny abandons her dream of a distant, imaginary France for an Alaska that is just as much the product of vision and fictive manipulation. "All the life there is is in Alaska" (395), as Sitka Charley says, and, indeed, it is the imagination that makes any world teem with life. Sunny's dream of France included renaming herself Jacqueline Flowers: "not a single trace of Deauville. Father forgiven, Alaska purged, Sissy's family

name become my own" (115). (Ironically, France is Uncle Jake's ances-
tral land, even though Sunny sees him as having rejected the aesthetic
harmonies that it represents.) But she ends calling herself Sunny, the
name that holds her father's legacy and the many layers of meanings
accrued in her struggle with her identity as his daughter. And she ends
calling herself "an Alaskan woman"; far from being purged, Alaska has
been incorporated through the body of the text.[5]

In exploring the frontiers of history and fiction, myth and identity,
language and sexuality, Sunny abrogates at last the condition of being an
innocent which she rebelled against in her father and which she thought
she had obliterated in herself in her life devoted to hedonistic sex and
to "planes and men and fish and game" (278). Through suffering the
persistence and the pull of the past and of the magnificent and uncon-
sciously cruel dreamer who ruled it, she commits herself to the problems
of narrating a drama in which memory and desire, tall tale and dream,
autobiography and fantasy give birth to herself as an Alaskan woman in
a journal/novel meant for the eyes of an Other. She thus escapes being
the innocent that Martha Washington defines as having a life "without
drama and hence without interest to those other than herself" (278–
279); and she makes even more metaphorical Martha Washington's
claim that "Every woman remains a virgin . . . until she has borne her
first child" (269). This conception of creative experience stands in contrast to the dictum put forth in *Death, Sleep & the Traveler* "that a man
remains a virgin until he commits murder" (145). In this novel and in
*Travesty* the male narrators actually commit or desire to commit murder;
and while Cyril's and Skipper's narration are basically life-affirming, they
have in common with the other male narrators a deadly compulsion for
form, which comes to bear not just on the text but on the characters who
people their worlds. The loosely structured, anecdotal text of *Adventures
in the Alaskan Skin Trade* contrasts to the denseness of imagery and tight-
ness of form to which the other novels tend; and unlike the male narrators, Sunny desires not to impose her will on a recalcitrant landscape
and impenetrable Other, but rather to arrive at an understanding of
these things. Making creative paradigms distinct for each of the sexes,
however, implies an essentialism belied by the conclusions not only
of Martha Washington, but also by the in-depth, formulaic exploration of
gender in *The Passion Artist*. *Adventures* relies, of course, just as much on
the control of language and structure as any of Hawkes's works. Furthermore, Sunny's creation and re-creation of herself as an Alaskan woman
involves both the obliteration of the father, the knowledge of whose
death is necessary for Sunny's conclusions (about her identity and of her
text), and the simultaneous bringing of the father to life. The equation,

emphasized repeatedly in Hawkes's opus, of innocence with virginity, and of virginity with language, as that which both exists and does not exist, obtains in *Adventures*, too; the idea of paradox that fascinates both Sunny and Uncle Jake has its most far-reaching expression in the idea of innocence as that which underlies narcissism, obliviousness, and the assertion of control, as well as beauty and creativity. Innocence is both integral to creation and lost in creation.

The distinction Martha Washington draws between being an innocent and possessing innocence is a distinction between essence and construction; her opposing being a feminist to being an innocent conceptualizes gender and sexuality as constructions. When she effuses about "Alaska's effect on male potency," she says, "Of course I use that word in its broadest sense and on the assumption that it applies equally to women and men" (281). She pilots airplanes and hunts, activities Sunny considers her own forte, but instead of ascribing these activities to possessing a masculine component, as does Sunny, she asserts that they are an expression of herself as a woman. She recounts her battle with a she-bear and her cubs as a clash of titans; her story has all the bravado, hyperbole, and suspense of the stories Uncle Jake told. When she seduces and disappears with Hank, Sunny's friend and lover, Sunny says, "I have just lost a boyfriend to my own father reincarnated in the form of a woman" (303). With her open sensuality and her theorizing about sexuality, Martha Washington seems an extreme contrast to Uncle Jake's sexual deafness and silence, but the strength of her imagination's possession and transformation of a landscape and a self, in deed and in word, links her with Uncle Jake as storyteller and artist. "[E]very Alaskan man—every real Alaskan man—is a legend," says Martha Washington. "It's just that some are more legendary than others" (271). And the assumption of legendariness applies equally to women. Certainly it applies to the "mother of us all" (296), as Sunny calls Martha Washington, whose inscription by Sunny confirms her status as legend and whose very name holds the layered resonances of history.[6]

In her speech to the women who work for Sunny at Gamelands in which she tells them to end their exploitation, Martha Washington says,

Man in his lust . . . has regulated long enough this whole question of sexual intercourse. Now let the mother of mankind, whose right and duty it is to set bounds to his indulgence, rouse up and put an end to the sexual exploitation of women in marriage, in adultery, on dates, and, worst of all, in the long nights of prostitution. Never, never indulge in sex for money, protection, or security. Never have sex if you don't want to. Sometimes it's better to deny yourself in order to deny on principle some insistent male. You too are part of the universal motherhood. Be true to your sisters. Take back the bed. Help put an end to the universal rape. (288)

Martha Washington's invocation of "the universal motherhood" smacks of jingoism and precisely the insidious sort of mythologizing and recourse to delimiting archetypes that are so destructive in the texts of Hawkes's male narrators. At the same time, in the context of her other remarks the phrase calls for a redemption from a state of innocence which allows violence and oppression. She urges the women to take individual control; she urges the rewriting of the received text of sexuality, that domain in which Sunny has set herself up as an artist of artificiality. Martha Washington brings the artificial and constructed nature of sexuality more fully to light. In her powerful and nearly constant stream of language, she eroticizes the landscape of Alaska in a way that is just as domineering as Uncle Jake's and she employs a rhetoric of liberation that masks her own adoption of received images of (masculine) adventure; at the same time she illuminates the possibilities of self-creation and imaginative freedom. The words that come from this female form of the father, along with the narration given form by the daughter, compose a text of life on the frontier which explores the borders of identity, and of representation and creation, existence and nonexistence.

"The Alaskan skin trade" for which the narrative is named contains the flux of meanings enacted in the process of the text: the coveted hides of wild animals appropriated as the coinage of the "masculine" frontier are traded for the fetishized representations that grant value to the female body; the dialogue of the "masculine" and the "feminine" in the text occurs in the exchange of verbal representations; the frontiers of Alaska and of woman are exchanged for the frontier of fiction, the skin of language that trades upon absence and upon the complex play of innocence and power.

Along with *Virginie*, then, *Adventures in the Alaskan Skin Trade* engages the possibilities of critique and revision of the authorial role engendered by a female perspective and female voice. Virginie records the tableaux offered to her by Seigneur and Bocage; Sunny recounts the stories bequeathed to her by Uncle Jake; the male author figures draw upon culturally constituted images and narrative codes. Both texts thus specifically engage representation—its origin, its dissolution of origin, its refiguration. The female body that obsesses Hawkes's male narrators and artist figures becomes the body of the text; the female voice becomes the medium of meaning and its transformation.

# Chapter 7
## The Artist and His Subjects in *Whistlejacket*

Some dark secrets never come to light. Some riddles never submit to unraveling. Some mysteries remain unsolved. But not so the mystery of what occurred so recently at Steepleton. My lips, after all, are not sealed. Natural light and dark secrets are in the realm of innocence, the beat of a horse's hooves, the sounds of a silent photographer curling himself about his subject.
Remember?

—John Hawkes, *Whistlejacket*

The reinscription of male fantasy by female narrators in *Adventures in the Alaskan Skin Trade* and *Virginie: Her Two Lives* continues the exploration of sexuality and eroticism as language and spectacle that dominates Hawkes's novels from *The Blood Oranges* onward. *Whistlejacket* (1988) returns to male narration, but with an increased critical and analytical elaboration of visual aesthetics and the dynamics of reification. Michael, the narrator, differs from Hawkes's other narrators in being not only narrator-as-artist, but a professional artist, a fashion photographer who focuses much of his narration on the description of his art. The addiction to collecting or producing erotica or pornography, "the common man's art" as Hawkes would have it, shared by Hawkes's previous narrators and artist figures, becomes, in this novel, an obsession with seeing all women—and all of life—through the lens of a camera. Much like the previous male narrators, Michael considers his artist's vision paradoxically innocent in the purity of its aestheticism and transgressive in its violation of ordinary ways of seeing. But in the process of constructing a narrative in which he brings images to voice, the meanings Michael attempts to create and control become increasingly suspect.

The contemporary relevance of Michael's expression of artistry in fashion photography has its foil in *Whistlejacket*'s section of third-person narration about the eighteenth-century painter George Stubbs. This juxtaposition of eighteenth- and twentieth-century artists builds upon the issues raised by a similar juxtaposition in *Virginie*. And just as *Virginie* examines the idea of mastery in art and culture through its multiple levels of representation—rendering in language the making of women into art and sex acts into dramas and tableaux—*Whistlejacket* also addresses the cultural ramifications of the fascination with representation itself.

In his essay "The Discourse of Others: Feminists and Postmodernism," Craig Owens describes the modern age as the age of the master narrative and of representation. He quotes Heidegger, according to whom

> the transition to modernity was not accomplished by the replacement of a medieval by a modern world picture, "but rather the fact that the world becomes a picture at all is what distinguishes the essence of the modern age." For modern man, everything that exists does so only in and through representation. To claim this is also to claim that the world exists only in and through a *subject* who believes that he is producing the world in producing its representation. (66; Owens's emphasis)

Owens goes on to explain that "the transformation of the world into a picture and man into a subject" resulted in the mastering of phenomena (66). It is the idea of mastery that Owens says postmodernism questions. Feminist theory also, of course, examines the dynamics of mastery, and Owens addresses the conjunction of feminist theory and postmodernism, particularly in terms of the visual arts. "Modern aesthetics," Owens says, "claimed that vision was superior to the other senses because of its detachment from its objects" (70). He quotes Luce Irigaray's critique of such a view: " 'Investment in the look is not privileged in women as in men. More than the other senses, the eye objectifies and masters. It sets at a distance, maintains the distance. In our culture, the predominance of the look over smell, taste, touch, hearing, has brought about an impoverishment of bodily relations. . . . The moment the look dominates the body loses its materiality.' That is, it is transformed into an image" (70). As photographer and narrator, Michael exercises precisely this form of distancing and mastery in *Whistlejacket*, but the text itself functions as a critique of mastery.

There is little at stake for Michael, a man who is "generally fortunate enough not to feel strong emotions" (136). He is not trying to expiate guilt, recreate a lost paradise, or attain control of a life in which he finds himself a slave to chaos rather than master of his fate. He is neither the sex singer nor sex aesthetician we find in *The Blood Oranges,* he is simply an aesthetician. The language of the novel is the most lucid, but least exciting and least consciously performative of that in any of Hawkes's novels. It is the structure that is very consciously a performance, that is explicitly construction. Michael tells us in the first chapter, for instance, that the "photographic scenes that follow . . . are arranged chronologically" (4). Time will be contracted into images of time and these images will be arranged in a sequence. The novel is for the most part constructed by a series of photographs which Michael describes and explains. It is a novel in which even "love letters" are photographs, a novel in which language is put to use as almost a second-rate affair: words are subsumed by images, existing only to describe them. But in the process images are subsumed by words. *Whistlejacket* explores the tension between image and narration as they embody description and revelation, representation and creation.[1] In a novel in which characters transgress the law against murder and transgress against sexual taboos and gender roles, the transgression of primary interest for the narrator occurs when images are made to speak—and to mean. When Michael, the creator of images, becomes the interpreter of images, the innocence of his detachment is violated and he finds himself both implicated in the events around him and disempowered.

The double absence of Hal, a character who is not only dead but is murdered outside of—and prior to—the text, informs the text and is, in a sense, its reason for being. Alex, the dead man's widow, asks Michael "to re-create his life in photographs" (38). In constructing a "photographic biography" of the dead Harold Van Fleet, Michael is in the authorial position of filling an absence, of reconstructing not Hal's life, which would be impossible, but in creating the significance of that life. He is scornful of Alex's collection of photographs of Hal, which to him represent only Alex's naïveté and sentimentality; they betray the feeling that any moment of Hal's life, and by extension any person's life, is important and further, that the moment or the person represented takes precedence over the manner of representation. Michael reflects on the distinction between the family, personal, or amateur photograph and the artistic photograph to reveal his aesthetics and his modus operandi: "The photograph for which the artist strives has no story. Story is the anathema of the true photographer. Narrative, dull narrative, of interest only to those who sit or stand at the frame's center or lurk at its edges trying to squeeze themselves into the picture, is what the chronicler of the family hopes to preserve" (106). Such a claim echoes Hawkes's oft-quoted statement that he "began to write fiction on the assumption that the true enemies of the novel were plot, character, setting, and theme, and having once abandoned these familiar ways of thinking about fiction, totality of vision or structure was really all that remained" (Enck 149). Hawkes later, however, retracted this statement, citing his youth and his desire to avoid a pedantic and conventional way of talking about literature. He says that the terms he disparaged "are the simplest kinds of schemes with which to talk about fiction, and I don't like them. On the other hand, I will recant and say that plot is of course necessary" (LeClair, "Hawkes and Barth," 14). Michael's claims about photographs have the bravado of Hawkes's early claims about fiction. Yet it is precisely the "partially revealed narratives" (107) of certain of the photographs of Hal that fascinate Michael, and out of them he creates full narratives that reveal Hal's character. From a picture of Hal at a high school dance Michael constructs a traditional education story; the picture becomes a "narrative of youthful choices—aesthetic, moral, personal" (108). He goes on, forming an unacknowledged reversal of his former distinction between personal and artistic interest: the photograph is "one view of Harold's early decisiveness. But for Alex it was only a picture of Hal at a dance" (108–109). This denigrates Alex's interest in the photograph because she sees it just as image, not as story. Michael privileges his perception of the photograph because from it he constructs a narrative that gives him insight into Hal's character.

The irony of this reversal of aesthetic priorities is increased by its accompanying claim to knowledge. A picture of a young Hal and a young Buse, the woman who would become his mistress, prompts Michael to construct another lengthy narrative and to comment that "here, finally, was a Hal it had never occurred to me might exist. A man like the rest of us. Had Alexandra really known him? I thought not" (116). In fact it is Michael who had never really known Hal and Alexandra who had been living with a profound and difficult knowledge of him. When Michael takes his own photographs for Hal's biography, however, he does return to a less equivocal emphasis on form, on knowledge as pure photographic perception rather than knowledge of character. He photographs two of Hal's pipes: "Their final portraits—two—would have nothing to do with remembrance, unlike the pipe itself. One sight of the pipe and I smelled its rising smoke, saw the smoker. The camera, at least mine, did not admit the past. No matter what Alex expected, my photographs, especially those I took that week in Hal's room, would stand only for themselves" (131). The question is, what are the photographs themselves? The fact that they "stand" for anything, even if it is themselves, implies the mediation of perception which is external to the photographs. The photographs are formed by a dual construction: that of the photographer and that of the viewer; and as Michael's descriptions of the photos he takes and the ones he views demonstrate, viewing and constructing are inseparable. Despite Michael's emphatic championing of a pure imagistic aesthetics, it is precisely the image's autonomy and innocence that his narrative calls into question.

Michael tells us that when he was taking photos of Hal's personal belongings he "made no distinctions, could find no hierarchy of values among his furniture, his clothes, his effects. So I had no choice and could only exhaust the possibilities of what was there, giving importance to the large and small, the personal and impersonal alike. In the end nothing was impersonal" (132). Michael states his erotic and aesthetic theory that would eliminate hierarchies from both sexuality and art by comparing bodies to menus: Western menus stand for a goal-directed, climax-oriented erotics, as opposed to an Eastern menu in which there is an appreciation of every dish/part. He explains his theory to a woman he meets in a Japanese restaurant: "The person as menu . . . is not a hierarchical arrangement. We wouldn't concentrate on eyes before lips, lips before tongue, throat before hands" (49). He continues: "So the Western menu limits how we please our appetites. Imprisons the whole thing, makes it monotonous, dull, uninspired, uninteresting, banal, unarousing. Whereas the Eastern menu gives us free choice. Choice means variable, variable means discontinuity, discontinuity destroys hierarchy" (50). Michael's fashion photographs would seem to demonstrate this theory; he does a series of photographs in which lips are the erotic center, and later a series glorifying buttocks. The implication is that he will go on to glorify other body parts, and any of these parts will be aesthetically and erotically stimulating. The novel's narration also seems to demonstrate a destruction of hierarchy. Although the photographic scenes Michael describes are in chronological order (itself a temporal hierarchy), the scenes are juxtaposed with scenes concerning Steepleton and its inhabitants so that the exploration of the characters of these inhabitants is clearly not central to the novel. Moreover, not even Michael's voice is privileged; two chapters in the first section and the entirety of the second section have a third-person narrator. Yet hierarchies persist. When Michael's female auditor in the restaurant comments that the lack of hierarchy he develops in his erotic menu theory "doesn't sound very passionate" a surprised Michael insists that "[l]ogic is the way to erotic truth" (50). His professed interest in materiality is really a detached idealism. Michael does indeed adhere to hierarchies: to logic over passion, to the photographer as subject over the photographed as object, to the fetishized part over the whole.

It takes no great insight to see Michael as a fetishizer, and the fact that he is a fashion photographer, that his photographs are used to sell products, explicitly marks his aesthetics as producing a commodity fetish. Michael himself ends his chapter on his series of "rearview" photographs by describing one designed to sell shoes in which he positions the model so that the shoe is juxtaposed to her buttocks. He concludes:

> One fetish celebrates another.
> Women want to see what they think men want to see. Why not? (162)

The fetishes celebrated are standard ones in the culture's stock of images. Michael presents them not only without questioning what ends the valuing of these fetishes serve, but without questioning the authority of male vision. He maintains the hierarchy of the photographer as the director of the viewer's vision, structuring the picture so that the viewer must look at a certain point, so that in viewing the image the viewer duplicates the photographer's construction. Ironically, Michael deliberately refers to his models as "subjects, which is not the same as models" (16). Such a distinction seeks to emphasize the aesthetic rather than the commercial aspect of Michael's work. But the individuals whom he photographs no longer function as subjects; by becoming subject to the photographer, the individual becomes object. The only subject left is the viewing subject. Michael reveals the importance of the aggrandizement of himself as subject, as viewer and knower, when he discusses the power of the photographer who gives "visual shape to utter absence" (12).

The novel is, in a sense, a murder mystery, and Michael is, without knowing it, the detective. The process of going through Hal's belongings and photos, of rephotographing photos and taking "new" ones, culminates in Michael's pictorial reconstruction of the crime. The photographs of Hal's youth reveal facets of his character, the photographs of the rooms from which Hal is absent reveal something about his presence, and the photograph sets of trampling hooves, one set with Hal, one set without, reveal the nature of his death. Instead of "standing for themselves," the pictures are epistemological tools. And instead of being in the role he most likes, that of the watcher "among those who do not wish to be seen" (16), Michael is among those who very much want to be observed and who are observing him.[2] His detective work is entirely directed; he is a detective who doesn't know he is a detective and who is given all the clues by the crime's perpetrators who in fact will be best served by his "discovering" them. When Michael photographs Marcabru, the horse who trampled Hal to death, he photographs the stall including "some detail of the horse in each exposure" (123), pictorially dismembering a body in a way similar to the dismemberment he enacts in his fashion photography. He also photographs Marcabru in a simulated trampling, rearing up at the woman who has come into his stall and disturbed him with her scent. These pictures are replaced in his darkroom by pictures of the actual trampling of Hal, pictures with blurred figures and body parts. The reification enacted by Michael's photographs is doubled by photographs that reify a death. His own photographs are lost and the replacement photographs are scratched, their images obscured. But what is visible is enough to reveal the conditions of Hal's death, and Alex exposes the details of it by telling her story.

The verbal and pictorial exposure of Hal's life and death includes Michael's learning about, and subsequent learning from, Hal's "love letters." These love letters are neither letters nor about love as it is customarily connoted by such letters. They are Polaroids, each containing "A man, a woman. Nude. Variations on the familiar position of standing man and kneeling woman. . . . There was a full-length mirror, the man taking photographs by aiming into the mirror, though occasionally he had simply pointed the camera down at the top of the woman's head" (148). The man is Hal, the woman sometimes his wife, sometimes his mistresses. The image of photographs taken in a mirror is the representative image of the novel.[3] Hal's photographs constitute a complex reflection on the concept of photographs as mirrors of natures, documents of realism. For if photographs hold the mirror up to nature, Hal's photographs hold the mirror up to the mirror. They are mimetic of the artistic function itself. The image produced in the mirror's reflection is that of the photographer as the male and camera eye who views himself producing icons of his own dominance as male and as artist. If, as Heide Ziegler claims, "Innocence for Hawkes means either the non-existence or the dissolution of any power resulting from sexual dominance" ("Postmodernism as Autobiographical Commentary," 208), this imaging of the photographer, if nothing else, casts doubt on Michael's claim that he is "[a]n innocent though not entirely pure photographer" (3). One could categorize Michael and Hal as benign and malignant versions of the artist, much as Hawkes does in speaking of Cyril the sex singer and Hugh the puritanical pornographer of *The Blood Oranges*. It is easy to label Hal a malignant artist and malignant male. The novel dissects his character to reveal his need for power and self-aggrandizement, which expresses itself in misogyny, the very cause of his eventual defeat and death. Michael as benign artist is more problematic, for although he is anything but domineering (he is in fact malleable and insecure) in his relations with women—or men—the self-reflexive icons that are Hal's pictures are metaphorical figurations of Michael's position as artist.

Michael delivers his speech against erotic and aesthetic hierarchy looking into a mirror, at himself and at a woman who cannot see him. He enjoys the advantage this vision gives him, and the parallel to his position as photographer (he surveys the woman's features—"lips not full enough to hold my attention" [49]) is obvious. (Michael's dominance as viewer itself undercuts any of his proclamations against hierarchy.) The scene is a variation on the male and female positions in Hal's photographs, as is the scene that is the climactic one of the novel and of Michael and Alex's relationship. Michael and Alex have just made love (that scene itself is absent); Michael is on the bed, Alex at her dressing table. Looking at Alex in the mirror, Michael asks, "Who do you really love, Hal or Harry?" Alex smiles into the glass, replies, "You" (191). The affirmation or positive proof of the self as object of desire is one significance of Hal's photographs, and Alex here provides that affirmation for Michael. Significantly, Michael and Alex do not look at each other, only at images of each other. This is consonant with the way the body in this novel is repeatedly replaced with images of the body. A further significance of the scene is that Michael is there at Alex's will. Although Michael is the narrator, it is Alex who has a plot that has included using Michael to cover up the evidence of Hal's instigated death and which finally includes having him in her bed. Alex's plan to have Michael re-create Hal's life in photographs ends by implicating him not only in Hal's life but in Hal's death; Alex's lovemaking with Michael implicates him in the significance of Hal's death. Situated in the frame of the mirror, Michael is finally in "the frame's center," in the position of one for whom "Narrative, dull narrative" (106) is of interest.

In the image of Alex and Michael in the mirror there is no figuration of male hierarchy as there is in Hal's pictures. It is precisely the destruction of this hierarchy that Hal's wife and daughter, Virgie, worked to effect. That mirrors reverse the images they reflect mimics the reversal in the social order at Steepleton. Hal's lifelong fetishizing of horses and women, culminating in what turn out to be his last words—"Too bad women can't be more like horses"—brings about his own objectification in the finality of death (a death further objectified in photos). Alex, finally rebelling against Hal's treatment of her, maneuvers his murder by deliberately bringing her mare in heat into the enclosed space where Hal stands with his stallion. But it is the male and animal rage for sexual gratification before which nothing can stand in the way that literally kills Hal, who suffers a heart attack upon being trampled under the hooves of the horse he loves. Symbolically, it is Hal's own violence that kills him. The memorial fox hunt Alex stages demonstrates the destruction of the male order Hal represents. Alex is the Master of Fox Hounds, leading Hal's best friend (who will suffer a death that duplicates Hal's, victim of the violence of his horse mounting a mare while he is a rider) to exclaim, "A female MFH! . . . Travesty!" (164). Hal's riderless horse, recently gelded, looks on. The inhabitants of Steepleton all ride mares and Alex uses the "bitch pack," the hounds best at picking up scents. The hunt dissolves into straggling and dispirited riders, and the chapter concludes with the man who has met his demise in it quoting Oscar Wilde: "Fox hunters . . . foxes. The unspeakable in full pursuit of the uneatable" (181). The order represented by Hal is revealed as not only destructive but absurd.

Michael sympathizes with the women in this story and implies his rejection of Hal's behavior. Yet this rejection is never explicit nor uncomplicated, for although Michael is more timid than domineering in specifically sexual episodes, he reveals a need to dominate in the dictates of his camera eye. Within the parameters of his vision he maintains his position in a hierarchy that privileges him as the image maker objectifying women. His vision is the Origin; after that, individuals and objects, horses and women, are interchangeable, subject to the order he will impose on them. The childish sense of mischief that Michael experiences as a boy violating taboos with the Van Fleet girls becomes in the adult Michael a relishing of his ability to violate ordinary ways of seeing in his art. The photographer, he tells us, "sees what no ordinary person sees. . . . Sudden intimate speech and behavior is a rare gift. And the photographer, or the kind of photographer I have in mind, intrudes into convention in the same way except with sight, not speech, though sometimes both" (57). But within the novel Michael does not violate convention and attain intimacy without the shield of his camera lens until he is seduced by Virgie, who in turn sends him to Alex's bed. Virgie breeches Michael's timorous distance in a mating scene that echoes those of the horses, with the male who would overpower himself overpowered by the female's scent. Significantly, Michael's erotics of the visual have nothing to do with his immediate seduction, though once seduced he maintains his excitement by a reversion to vision. The momentary violation of Michael's visual erotics coincides with another violation; because Michael grew up in the Van Fleet household, he and Virgie are "sister and brother for all intents and purposes" (3), which means he and Alex are mother and son for all intents and purposes. In making love to both Virgie and Alex, Michael doubly violates the taboo against incest. But of course Virgie and Alex are not *actually* his sister and mother. Transgression collapses into its representation.

Michael's incest can only be symbolic. The symbolic or metaphoric is precisely what Michael disparages in his erotic and aesthetic theory. To view any part of the body as erotically interesting means to see it in itself, not attaching outside meanings or preconceived notions that would mark one part as intrinsically different from another. He applies the theory to photographs, which should "stand only for themselves." But as we have seen, photographs are unable to achieve this purity; their contexts coalesce about them. When describing his photograph series of rearviews, Michael laments that the word buttocks does not accurately denote the anatomical part to which it refers. He finds the word ugly but uses it because, he tells us, "I avoid metaphor. . . . I prefer the concrete" (159). Michael's avoidance is doomed to failure since language, as signifier, is necessarily metaphorical. Yet one need not split hairs to illustrate the impossibility of Michael's ideal; he explicitly denies it himself. On the first page of the novel he says, "Through the thick, transparent lens of my camera—cameras I mean to say, but one will do for the metaphor—I see woman." This follows immediately on his statement that "Woman is a field of vision, woman is her own landscape" (3). Michael not only clearly uses metaphors, the metaphor of the image structures his entire narrative. The erotic fashion photo itself is metaphoric in that it always must stand for something else, producing a desire to buy or to have by linking erotic possibilities with a product. The use of a menu to describe the body is an extended metaphor that images the body as a product for consumption. In his review of *Whistlejacket* Patrick McGrath refers to the "long discussion near the beginning on mouths and another near the end on buttocks, rendering the book a sort of body through which its own matter passes." The text, metaphorically a body consumed by the reader, is filled with images of the body which by their very nature absent the body and in its stead place embodiment.

The centerpiece of the novel, "The Horse Painter," compounds the use of images to structure the text. The rationale for the thirty-page excursus on the eighteenth-century painter George Stubbs is that his famous painting *Whistlejacket* is the centerpiece of the grand salon at Steepleton. The Van Fleet men are of course fond not only of horses but of representations of them. Stubbs "is remembered for the amazing accuracy of representation he achieved in a body of work largely devoted to horse portraiture; many of his anatomical drawings, generated from the corpses of horses he himself killed and then painstakingly dissected, have never been bettered" (McGrath). The section on Stubbs goes into detail not only about his dissection of horses, but his dissection of a woman who died in her eighth month of pregnancy. The work that is gruesome and repulsive for his wife and helpmate is fascinating, absorbing, and indispensable for Stubbs: "Early in his life Stubbs discovered for himself two simple laws, which were never to paint from anything but nature and never to paint what he saw from the outside unless he had seen the inside first" (73). Assumptions about reality and the representation of it commonly applied to photography are also commonly applied to realistic painting that takes nature as its model. Stubbs's patron, Lord Nelthorpe, asks Stubbs to paint Lady Nelthorpe and him "as in a mirror" (93). Yet clearly Stubbs's subjectivity makes this mirror at best a distorting one. Stubbs paints Lord Nelthorpe to look like a dull, unimaginative boor and Lady Nelthorpe to look like a lovely and vibrant presence—for these, after all, are the characters Stubbs has perceived in them. The portrait of Whistlejacket, informed by Stubbs's anatomical knowledge, is also informed by the transforming vision of his artistic eye. The painting does not so much mirror Whistlejacket as portray the essence of him. Stubbs paints a fantasy of Whistlejacket "attacking his invisible victim" (100), but the actual Whistlejacket poses before him calmly and peacefully. This is necessary: "Only a tranquil scene would allow for the creation of majestic terror" (99). Instead of the painting mirroring Whistlejacket, Whistlejacket mirrors the painting. He sees it and rears up, striving to trample it and eliciting Stubbs's choice to save his art before trying to save the stableboy who also might be trampled (a scene evoking the famous dialogue of Sartre and Beckett regarding whether, if they had to make the choice, they would save poetry or a child's life).

Whistlejacket's owner praises Stubbs for seeing "what no one else—including the horse's owner—had seen, namely that the living Whistlejacket was a bronze statue" (101). The making of the living horse into art immortalizes Whistlejacket. But more than that, it immortalizes Stubbs. The painting is, as the section's coda tells us, a "monument" to Stubbs; "By the number and quality of his works he raised a monument to himself that will vie with time. Valuable Man. Oh, Valuable Man. . . ." (102). Stubbs is an artist securely in the humanist tradition. But as feminist criticism demonstrates, "traditional humanism is in effect part of patriarchal ideology. At its center is the seamlessly unified self—either individual or collective—which is commonly called 'Man.' . . . In this humanist ideology the self is the *sole author* of history and of the literary text: the humanist creator is potent, phallic and male—God in relation to his world, the author in relation to his text" (Moi 8; Moi's emphasis). The authority that Stubbs has as an eighteenth-century artist serves as a foil to the contested authority of the twentieth-century artist represented by Michael.

Michael's position as the male camera eye, the photographer and narrator who narrates by explicating images, links him to the artistic authority of Stubbs. But whereas Stubbs creates monuments to himself, Michael as fashion photographer is the anonymous purveyor of seductive images that will be reproduced again and again as an enticement to consumerism. And Michael as photographic biographer re-photographs existing pictures, an activity similar to fashion photography in that the artist disappears behind a discourse of circulating images. Stubbs does not even sign his portrait of Lady Nelthorpe and her son, since every brushstroke of his is itself his signature. When Michael accidentally allows his shadow to slip into a picture he will destroy the negative, even though the shadow would not show in the finished photo. This act, in contrast to

Stubbs's, registers an absence of the maker consonant with Michael's insistence on the removal of context and absence of meaning in photographs.

The section on Stubbs readily suggests the application of the Hawkesian catchphrase "design and debris" that is so extolled by Papa in *Travesty*. Stubbs dissects creatures then reconstitutes the debris of corpses as art, and the suggestion is that this art is more than design: it is life-giving in terms of medical uses and in terms of the immortalization of the subject of the portraits and of their maker. Stubbs converts debris into design; Michael creates design by fixing debris. His photographs themselves are a form of dissection, with their emphasis on body parts and objects as opposed to the living personalities painted by Stubbs. When Michael shoots (a term he is careful to say he dislikes) his subjects, he imposes a form on them that is a metaphoric death. Susan Sontag in her book *On Photography* writes that "to photograph people is to violate them, by seeing them as they never see themselves, by having knowledge of them they can never have; it turns people into objects that can be symbolically possessed. Just as the camera is a sublimation of the gun, to photograph someone is a sublimated murder" (14).

Sontag also describes a photograph as "a view of the world which denies interconnectedness, continuity, but which confers on each moment the character of mystery" (23). The statement recalls Michael's insistence on discontinuity destroying erotic and aesthetic hierarchy, claiming a personal freedom derived from the freedom of focus. The eradication of values leads to an innocence of vision. But the power implicit in the gaze itself counteracts this innocence. Furthermore, the very fact of a photograph's discontinuity frustrates any eroticism it might represent.

Georges Bataille's erotic theory has death as its center, but his theory marks death as the opposite of the way it is registered in the discontinuity of photographs. Bataille suggests "that for us, discontinuous beings that we are, death means continuity of being" (13). This is true of physical, emotional and religious eroticism: "with all of them the concern is to substitute for the individual isolated discontinuity a feeling of profound continuity" (15). He applies this same desire for transcendent continuity to poetry: "Poetry leads to the same place as all forms of eroticism—to the blending and fusion of separate objects. It leads us to eternity, it leads us to death, and through death to continuity. Poetry is eternity" (25). It is the blending and fusion of separate objects that so distinguishes the "lunar landscapes" of so much of Hawkes's work. But *Whistlejacket* presents a narrator/artist who resists metaphor and seeks not to transcend but to construct and to capture, and who is finally captured by his own constructions.

The coda of the novel has Michael excited by his spying a man surreptitiously depositing a magazine in a streetside garbage can, one among many heaps of "trash and junk" (192). The man's guilty actions reveal exactly the desire not to be seen that excites Michael, so he retrieves the magazine, saving it "from some public dump and oblivion" (193). The man's need for secrecy, the guilty need to avoid observation, immediately becomes Michael's own. He hurries away to look at the magazine, an unprofessional publication of home pornography, and the novel ends with the words "Shall we look?" The question is put not only to Michael's companion, but to the reader. We are implicated along with Michael as carnivorous consumers of images. When Michael begins recounting the scene with the businessman trying to get rid of the magazine he implies that he will learn something about the man. But of course the man is not important except insofar as he is representative. Michael can refer obliquely to the sort of magazine he finds because of its very typicality; what is important is not what it tells us about one man in particular but about the culture at large.

It is the availability of such images that Hawkes would rescue from the junk heap. The project of his novels has been the refashioning of sordid materials into something rich and strange, and it is this trait that so marvelously creates the "unique world, separate and different from the world we live in despite surface semblances" that he deems necessary for visionary fiction (Santore and Pocalyko 174). *Whistlejacket* is a novel specifically about vision, its narrator a photographer concerned with revitalizing vision through art. But his vision is not visionary except as it constitutes the novel, which is an examination of vision and the written image. The "silent photographer," innocent in his love for beauty, his appreciation of form, loses his innocence as soon as he speaks as the narrator, the revealer of "dark secrets" (7). For he is no longer just a creator of photographs, he is their explicator, and his explication involves the expounding of a network of relationships—of the artist to his subjects, of the artist to those he lives with, of the artist to his art, and of this art to its consumers. These relationships reveal the domination of his subjects by the artist's vision, but also the domination of the artist, along with everyone else, by images. The images in the pornographic magazine, the fashion photographs Michael takes, or the pictures of Harold Van Fleet's life and death all finally exist on the same level of signification. Rather than being mirrors of nature, recording "reality" as it is, they record the nature of their own construction and their uses. A novel that registers the social revolution that occurs in one household ends with a return to the stasis of an image that represents the ojectification this revolution overturned and invites the image's passive consumption.

The image the ending invites the reader to look at is an image which, like all the others in the novel, must remain absent to him or her. The situation is similar to the one Jan Gorak speaks of in his discussion of *Travesty*: "By participating in the masculine hunt for a disembodied icon, a fox and grapes chase begun by Adam himself, the reader is forced to taste the most bitter illusion of all, the possession of mere vacancy" (141). *Whistlejacket* contains the paradox of images that assert a reality by their own materiality while registering the absence of what they depict and while being absent to the reader. But an even more significant absence is the absence of the all-powerful artist creating *ex nihilo*. The novel dissects the deployment of artistic power to reveal Michael, photographer and author, in a disempowered middle ground between the poles of the authorial self—cruelty and innocence—which Hawkes designates. For the "murder" he performs is on the level of representation, and his innocence as "silent photographer curling himself about his subject" (7) is violated when he becomes the interpreter and consumer of images, determined as much by them as they are by him.

# Conclusion: The Domain of Purity, the Fragments of Actuality—*Sweet William: A Memoir of Old Horse* and the Imagination's Prism

What [the writer] has finished in one book, he starts over or destroys in another.

—Maurice Blanchot, *The Space of Literature*

Inner and outer life were assuming a single shape as if to conform with one of his theories.

—John Hawkes, *The Passion Artist*

[W]omen are both inside and outside gender, at once within and without representation.

—Teresa de Lauretis, *Technologies of Gender*

In *The Passion Artist* Hawkes most explicitly explores what he says he has decided are "the three most important subjects . . . consciousness, the imagination, and the nature of woman" (LeClair 29), but certainly all of these subjects have been his concern from the beginning, with "woman" increasingly becoming the prism through which consciousness and the imagination are refracted. *Travesty*'s Papa, for instance, formulates the dynamics characterizing the triangulated relationships of the sex triad when he speaks of experiencing "the gift of love as seen through the prism, as I may call it, of another woman" (64). Even in the early *Lime Twig*, it is William Hencher's narration of his perversely intimate and claustrophobic relationship with his mother, serving as prologue to the story, that seems to spawn the ensuing nightmarish pursuit of horses and sex—of fantasy.[1] Hencher avidly, ravenously consumes and regurgitates the image of his mother in the process of ingesting a piece of "bleeding meat," bringing it up to her mouth that is a "round stopper of darkness" (9); "Love is a long close scrutiny" (8–9), he tells us. In his startlingly visual prose Hawkes adumbrates a love of language that celebrates the image by virtue of its excesses and lingering attention. The image—and idea—of woman remains the most elaborated, coming under close scrutiny in multiple and echoing portraits of the distant mother, the impenetrable love object, the self-renewing virgin, the underside of the writing self's consciousness. Through this focus, Hawkes explores the plenum of imagination that is at once sexual, creative, artistic. He also explores that aspect of the sensual, sensuous imagination that is totemic or fetishistic. "The language of love," as *The Blood Oranges*'s Cyril calls it, is the investment of objects, actions, people, words, with meaning that both reveals and transfigures them. In *Virginie* for the first time the object of erotic and artistic fascination becomes not just the body of the narrative, but the speaking body; four years later, in *Adventures in the Alaskan Skin Trade*, a woman is again the narrator. (Significantly, Virginie is a woman as child, and Sunny is in many ways an autobiographical figuration of this male author.) Each of these narratives transgresses the border between subject and object. In each, the "nature of woman" remains the focal point, but now seen through the simulation of a perspective that is both within and without, and which thus newly foregrounds issues of the innocent artistic imagination exerting its power in grappling with the unknowable self and unknowable Other and imposing its order. In *Sweet William: A Memoir of Old Horse* (1993), the horse, that image which embodies the powerful and fearful sexuality both attributed to and exercised upon the image of woman, is transmuted into consciousness; in this novel, again, Hawkes inscribes the transgression of the object of fascination becoming the voice of the narrative: this is a story that comes straight from the horse's mouth, and that more than ever returns us to the problems of the page.

*Sweet William* itself can be viewed as a prism through which all of Hawkes's work is refracted. Hawkes has said, "I see my work as a continuum of recurrent images, obsessive thematic concerns, repeated form" (Ziegler 174), and indeed, his *oeuvre* enacts a complex intertextual play that constitutes the later novels as palimpsestic or layered, and engages veiling and unveiling, repetition and transformation, and the shifting and crossing of boundaries. *Sweet William* further complicates this intertextual web, not only continuing the crossing of boundaries between texts but transgressing the boundary of the formerly represented object to simulate self-representation. The novel carries on Hawkes's obsession with paradox that problematizes the oppositions between male and female,[2] the ideal and the material, creation and representation, the imagination and its objects, interior and exterior.

It is precisely the flux of interior and exterior, of inner and outer life that has imbued Hawkes's lunar landscapes with much of their power. Hawkes has often spoken of the "psychic leakage" that informs his fictional worlds, and of his desire "to find all the fluid, germinal, pestilential 'stuff' of life itself as it exists in the unconscious" (O'Donnell 125). In one of his earliest interviews, he discusses the structure discovered in the writing process, saying that "[t]he success of the effort depends on the degree and quality of consciousness that can be brought to bear on fully liberated materials of the unconscious" (Enck 149). Tony Tanner's remarks on *The Cannibal* engage this dynamic of inner and outer life intermingling within the fictive world: "Among other things, the book is about all kinds of incarceration. The figures wandering or pursuing or fleeing through this land of 'lost architecture' are really prisoners, not only of this or that building, but of delusion, fear, brutality, their own and other people's obsessions and fantasies, so that there is little difference between inside and outside the institution" (206). In *Travesty*, Henri, the poet and alter-ego of Papa, has been released from a psychiatric institution and Papa considers the possibility of entering one himself. In the confines of his sportscar, Papa roams the terrain of his inner life, binding Henri to himself in the prison-house of language that would more logically be an interior monologue but is spoken to an audience of two and that means to be efficacious. Indeed, whether in third-person or first-person, Hawkes's novels inscribe the terrifying and beautiful potentialities of a poetic voice that comes from and speaks out of a world, or that creates a world and speaks to it. *The Passion Artist* most self-reflexively formulates this process, as Konrad Vost undergoes "the crossing of public axis and private axis" (42, 121) in an interior and exterior journey that is his crossing over to the world of women. *Virginie* goes on to problematize any conception of inner and outer world. "Mine is an impossible story" the book begins, and we are thrust into a consciousness and a world that exists and does not exist, into the life of an eleven-year-old girl who has two lives and no life, who observes and records, imagines and remembers, the pages of her journal written and consumed, read and relinquished.

*Virginie* (along with many of Hawkes's other novels) both enacts and thematizes the relation between interiority and exteriority. It is a novel that portrays eroticism as specular and verbal, as the externalization of an inner condition and as the self's response to externality, and thus the ideal subject for the visionary writer. Virginie, of course, is not only the writer but the embodiment of innocence who serves as the model for the innocence of sexual generosity for the women she watches in their charades of love. When Seigneur attempts to instruct one of his students that "[t]here can be no womanhood without the inner child" (183), it is Virginie who demonstrates this tenet by allowing a hive of bees to swarm all over her naked body. She even receives the bees inside her mouth: "Was there another accomplishment to compare with holding inside one's poetic orifice a mouthful of bees? What had the bees become if not my voice?" (186).[3] For Virginie there is no separation to be made between herself and things in the world, even while she remains perpetually excluded from participating in the events around her, and there is no distinction to be made between her inner self and her outer self; she is the artist, and Seigneur's most perfect creation. The interpenetration of inner and outer finds harsher expression in *Whistlejacket*, seven years after the publication of *Virginie*. George Stubbs, the horse painter and dissector of cats and dogs, of cadavers, of a pregnant woman, and of horses, made it a rule "never to paint what he saw from the outside unless he had seen the inside first" (73). The novel elaborates a calculus of images, of surfaces from which the narrator—and sometimes other characters—alternately desire superficiality and depth, concealment or revelation.

*Whistlejacket*, most explicitly of all Hawkes's novels, makes the image into fetish. The fetishized objects, horses and women, end up turning on the man who would master them by killing him.[4] "Too bad women can't be more like horses!" Harold Van Fleet says before he is trampled to death by his horse made frantic by a mare in heat (139), but in effect he has reduced horses and women to a reified sameness in his acting out of mastering fantasies. Following upon *Whistlejacket*, whose artist narrator, while desiring transgressive technique and content, instead of achieving any real transgression in his life or his art ends up only representing transgression, *Sweet William* has a narrator whose consciousness and voice as the realization of the unknown and impossible are transgressive from the start. Moreover, *Sweet William* echoes Harold Van Fleet's comparison of women to horses in its presentation of Orville, a man who is the stern owner and trainer of the horse Sweet William and even sterner father and trainer of Sweet William's jockey, Mary. Sweet William overhears Orville "telling little Mary that horses are like women. In a crisis, he said, a woman screams, a man thinks. Horses and women are screamers, he said . . . not thinkers" (109). Sweet William decides that "[t]he man who could speak such words . . . is precisely the man who could dispose two Thoroughbreds to a shady fellow bent on horse killing" (109). Sweet William is a self-proclaimed misanthrope, a term that includes women but a stance that is at least in part a rejoinder to the misogyny of the men in *Whistlejacket*. More than this, the term functions as a rejoinder to the imposition of language on beings transformed into seductive images;[5] yet now, the object given subjectivity, this "equine aesthetician" (58) inscribes and enacts a narrative viewpoint that is both different from *and* the same as the narrative perspective we have seen again and again in Hawkes's texts. The horse as misanthropic authorial voice recasts Hawkes's belief that the writer "has to become an outcast, an outsider" (LeClair 27).

In *Sweet William* we have a narrator who violates ordinary ways of seeing in yet another impossible narrative. (One thinks of *Virginie*, or of *Travesty*'s defiance of the possible as Papa in his speeding car slowly unfolds an accounting of his own suicide.) The novel begins with a prologue titled "A Gentle Warning" spoken by a disembodied voice, ambiguously coming from author or horse, warning away all but those readers who are prepared for the unsettling of their familiar world;[6] it is these readers who are invited to "persist, walk on, ride to the end, and in the adversities of this horse's life find yours." And this narrative that takes us up to—and beyond—the death of our horse narrator ends with the words "Ride on! Ride on through it!" This horse narrator beset by the stupidities, frailties, and cruelties of people unleashes language that is an invocation of abjection and an invitation to identification, language in which the boundaries between author, narrator, and reader are always shifting and often invisible. The book is a memoir, a narrative written in recollection under the hand of a master within the text and without it. The second half of Old Horse's account of his life in fact is largely this horse's relaying of the stories told by Master and Ralph (Master's tutor and his subject, and, in many ways, his master). It ends at the moment of Old Horse's death, with Master's lengthy story of a remembered horse turned into art, its skull disinterred, plated with silver, hung on a wall. The final words, "Ride on! Ride on through it!" return us to an ambiguous realm of language without origin that elicits a return to the narrative's beginning and invokes a movement outside or beyond it.

In its nearly encyclopedic echoing, reworking, layering, and revisioning of all of Hawkes's past work, *Sweet William* is indeed a return to origins, and also a terminal. From the first page of Sweet William's narrative we embark on a parody of the picaresque as he introduces us to a Master and his sidekick who are reincarnated and reduced versions of Don Quixote and Sancho Panza, and whose significance he displaces by relating his own torturous equine adventures; he speaks the unacknowledged life endured by a "dumb" beast become picaresque hero. "[T]he comic brutalities of the early Spanish picaresque writers," says Hawkes, "is where I locate the beginnings of the kind of fiction that interests me most" (Enck 141–142).[7] In parodying the corpus of Hawkes's work and his fictional origins, *Sweet William* engages a postmodernism which, writes Patricia Waugh, "is nearly always parodic, acknowledging its implication in a preexisting textuality, creating through decreation, displacing that secure perspective of a stable vantage point from outside" (11). (The implication of the self in preexisting textuality, or as palimpsestic text, emerges in such images as Master's "parchment covered hands" [154].) Picaresque fiction itself displaces a stable vantage point from outside, involving, for Hawkes, the confluence of inner and outer worlds; it has, along with other types of fiction Hawkes admires, "a quality of coldness, detachment, ruthless determination to face up to the enormities of ugliness and potential failure within ourselves and in the world around us" and at the same time allows the author "to bring to this exposure a savage or saving comic spirit and the saving beauties of language" (Enck 143). Sweet William performs just such paradoxes. He is a horse as genteel and idealistic as he is cynical and primitive; a horse capable of speaking (of writing?) in graceful, formal, highly structured sentences; a horse tied to the primary importance of eating, attached to its own excrement, periodically overpowered by airborne pheromones; a horse mostly desiring bodily pleasure, always insisting on aesthetic harmonies, often and increasingly wracked by bodily pain. The problems and impossibilities of a horse as narrator serve to highlight the problematic sources of language and its literary use.

Through allowing the exploited and voiceless Other to speak, Hawkes engages the dynamic of language's relation to the world that Kristeva describes in *Powers of Horror:*

There would be a "beginning" preceding the word. Freud, echoing Goethe, says so at the end of *Totem and Taboo:* "In the beginning was the deed." In that anteriority to language, the outside is elaborated by means of a projection from within, of which the only experience we have is one of pleasure and pain. The non-distinctiveness of inside and outside would thus be unnameable, a border passable in both directions by pleasure and pain. Naming the latter, hence differentiating them, amounts to introducing language, which, just as it distinguishes pleasure from pain as it does all other oppositions, founds the separation inside/outside. And yet, there would be witnesses to the perviousness of the limit, artisans after a fashion who would try to tap that pre-verbal "beginning" within a word that is flush with pleasure and pain. They are *primitive man* through his ambivalences and the *poet* through the personification of his opposing states of feeling—but also perhaps through the rhetorical recasting of language that he effects. (61)

Hawkes's use of a horse for a poetic recasting of language foregrounds a revelation of what, in Kristeva's terms, are the conditions of narrative literature: "On close inspection, all literature is probably a version of the apocalypse that seems to me rooted, no matter what its socio-historical conditions might be, on the fragile border (borderline cases) where identities (subject/object, etc.) do not exist or only barely so—double, fuzzy, heterogeneous, animal, metamorphosed, altered, abject" (*Powers of Horror* 207).

At the beginning of his narrative Sweet William says, "Distant sounds and long shadows swim inside this head of mine, and clear sights and filmy scenes drift across my large and flickering eyes" (13–14). This is a speaker hovering on a border, both within and without himself, presenting himself as consciousness and image. (But after all, this is the kind of self-description in which narrators like Skipper and especially Cyril indulge.) As readers of *Sweet William* we experience endlessly the movement back and forth across a border: we become horse, the horse becomes human, and, in their base cruelty, humans become animals.

As with a number of Hawkes's narratives (*The Lime Twig, Second Skin, Death, Sleep & the Traveler, The Passion Artist, Virginie*) *Sweet William* concerns the narrator's psychic incorporation of the mother, of her death and her replacement or reappearance. Sweet William describes the death throes of his mother, the incomparably beautiful Molly-Long-Legs, as "the violent effort to eat her way inside herself to find the pain and devour it" (21). Willy,[8] too, will eat his way inside himself, exploring his inner life, consuming his pain and expelling it in narrative. The mother, buried before she was actually dead because of the pronouncement of a careless vet, awakes in the aftermath of steady rain beneath earth turned to mud, and Willy witnesses her violent resurrection from the muck (a parody of the buried Mulge Lampson whose rebirth the characters of *The Beetle Leg* await). "I was the secret witness to the eruption of secrecy," says Willy (29). His words echo Seigneur's words to Virginie when she questions why she may not be "visibly present" in the salon, why she had to conceal herself in a confessional box while he stood in the open watching one of his students ravish a pig. "Life's first principle is love," he says, "But the first principle of love is secrecy. In the salon . . . you are my secret" (113). The idea of the secret, of that which is hidden, informs the text of *Sweet William* throughout. Master longs to regain Hidden Hall, the locus of his youth and of his most meaningful family romance, and the metaphor for the imagination. Narration from a horse's point of view in itself constitutes an unveiling of the unknown, a revelation of the imagination, but within the text the complexities of Willy's inner life remain hidden from the people around him. And the buried core of Willy's inner life is his image of the mother from whom he was torn asunder but who lives on, transmuted into the stuff of dreams and rage.[9]

From the start, language in *Sweet William* both reveals and conceals. Reviewing the time of his mother's death, Willy says, "Even in that distant past I stopped short in my grief and thought of my name, Sweet William, and then and there decided to deny the faith that my poor dam must have had in me and to become a fullgrown horse who would be anything but sweet, a horse whose name would be only the bitterest of ironies" (23).[10] While the death of his mother determines Sweet William's willful construction of identity, he is also the victim of identities that are imposed on him. He recounts his own birth, his emergence from the mother's body and emergence from the afterbirth that surrounds him like a second skin; just three weeks later he is covered by yet another second skin, the afterbirth of a stillborn colt whose mother will now feed the orphaned Willy, so that he feels turned into an imposter and a ghost (24). And indeed, Willy does come to be a ghost of his former self; and this former self is but a shadow of the horse who tells his story. "I put no stock in the promise of youth," he says, "in retrospect I do not admire the young horse that I once was" (57). A thoroughbred who was in his youth a magnificent winner of races, Willy in his old age says, "I do not admire those who race, and would not race again if I could" (57). Even when young he "discovered that the *one horse, one race* adage was nothing but the deceptive rhetoric of dull and mediocre oldsters, that it concealed rather than exposed the truth, that it reeked as strongly of conventional morality, which is no morality at all, as a poorly mucked-out stall reeks of ammonia" (56–57). As authorial voice, Willy carries out Hawkes's often voiced opposition to conventional morality. He rejects false "truths," though his own exposure of the truth of his life is the unconventional exposure of complicated "truth"—of actions, thoughts, and desires which also, insofar as they exist only as language, do not exist. They reveal and conceal simultaneously. The metaphorical permutations of his mother's burial and resurrection enact just such complicated veiling and unveiling. The second skin of his mother's body is replaced by accretions that put distance between that original unity or wholeness, accretions of disguise, deception, and cruelty. He stands abject in his old age at the Metacomet ranch: "My own filth and the filth of others caked me in a hard and crusty second skin" (117).

The repeated metaphorical use of "second skin" in *Sweet William* relates, of course, to Skipper's use of second skin, and, indeed, Willy is as concerned as Skipper with forging an identity that will redeem adversity and with coming to flourish through artful narration. *Sweet William* also shares with *Second Skin*—and with *The Blood Oranges*—an engagement of the pastoral; Willy, Skipper, and Cyril all invoke a verdant world and "time of no time." For Willy, his young life at Millbank is a "timeless time" (35), "the timeless time of my youth on that flourishing farm" (236) where he leads a pastoral life in which the care of substitute mothers—both horse and human—and beautiful, harmonious surroundings contribute to what he will later call feeling good in his "horse's skin"

(85). This language also of course recalls Sunny's description of herself at the end of *Adventures in the Alaskan Skin Trade* as "an Alaskan woman feeling good in her skin in Alaska." Sunny has achieved this unity of inner and outer aspects through her narration in which she reconciles past and present through incorporating the life of her mother and, most importantly, her father. Willy, too, seeks wholeness, last experienced by him in his earliest days. Just as Master aspires to regain Hidden Hall, Willy longs to return to his origins: "there is no horse alive who does not expect to come full circle, to find that this or that new barn where he is to be stabled is in fact the barn of his birth," that "this or that next horse farm . . . will prove to be our first and our last" (130). The idea of circular return is particularly reminiscent of *The Blood Oranges* where Cyril, having replaced one woman with another (and the women having exchanged roles as mother and lover), insists on the ever-renewing quality of his paean to love. Moreover, circular return in *Sweet William* self-reflexively suggests the novel's return to all of Hawkes's earlier work.

The return to the place of birth in *Sweet William* significantly emphasizes a metaphorical return to mother. In *Over Her Dead Body: Death, Femininity and the Aesthetic* Elisabeth Bronfen writes,

> Freud has termed "death" and "femininity" as the two most consistent enigmas and tropes in western culture. Within psychoanalytic discourse itself the anatomy of the feminine body serves two diametrically opposed moments—extreme confirmation and extreme destabilisation of the self. The maternal body is experienced by the child as a site of wholeness and stability. . . . Even though this sense of wholeness is illusory, precariously constructed over a post-natal lacuna, with one of its occulted signifiers precisely the loss it tries to assuage, the "phallic mother" can be seen as a model for culture's privileging of the feminine body as a figure for unity and timelessness; for the triumph over disseverment and facticity. (11)

But Bronfen goes on to say that "[t]he female genitals have, however, also served as a privileged trope for lack, castration and split and by metonymic association, as a trope for decay, disease and fatality" (11). This multiple and ambiguous conception of the mother plays itself out in general in Willy's desire for wholeness throughout his subjection to dissolution, and in particular in his reaction to Trixy, a sort of painted horse, a onetime circus performer, "insufferably standoffish" (101) and the favorite of Paul J. Goossen, owner of the miserable urban riding school where Willy and his friend London Bobby have the misfortune to be incarcerated. Willy calls Trixy "Mother Horse"; "Mother Horse's Brood, as we thought of ourselves" (102). When London Bobby, making an escape with Willy, is shot to death by the police, Willy has a vision in which London Bobby's dead body turns into "a monstrous immensity of another horse, a white horse, yes, Mother Horse herself, consuming the scene of the accident, displacing grief, drawing closer to where I stood amazed, affronted, readier than ever to pursue revenge. . . . But the great white haunch that she was now swinging as if into my very face, was it a mockery or a matriarchal offering or both?" (108). Willy bites into Mother Horse's "snowy haunch," then stands back to admire "the imprint of my sharp teeth, the horseshoe shape of my resolve to remain and be at any cost myself, my own horse" (109).

Willy's leaving his mark on Mother Horse's skin corporeally duplicates his assertion of self in marks on the page that become the textual second skin that preserves and creates his selfhood. But the narrative that comes from his abused and decaying body records a life that is his own and not his own, just as his stories are his own and those of others. Wholeness is belied by the discontinuities of the narrative's episodic structure, along with the discontinuous perception of the self. Willy's story ends with the symbolic reunification with the mother embodied in the return to the farm of his birth and the woman who, as a girl, raised him, in addition to his friendship with the nurturing Clover. "Birth was the death of me," says Willy at the start of his narrative; "Birth was the death of her" reads the epigraph from Beckett at the start of *Virginie*.[11] Virginie and Willy both exist and do not exist, inscribing presence and absence in creating a textual identity.[12] Life in the text—in language—is continual self-generation and continuously reenacted death; wholeness is re-presented only in death, in the silver-plated horse skull on the wall in Master's final story. (The final words, however, belie this closure, extending beyond the end of the story.)

Having first, at the age of three weeks, spied on his mother's death, resurrection, and second death, Sweet William next, before the age of two, spies on his father's copulation in the covering yard (a term suggestive of a dynamic of veiling and unveiling). His mother's death engenders his misanthropy; his father's sex engenders his loss of innocence. Knowledge of the father itself delivers the loss of innocence: "In retrospect I have no idea how I managed to preserve my innocence for as long as I did. How, to the very brink of maturation, I was able to remain oblivious to the fact that I, like every other horse, had been sired as well as carried and dropped. How it was that I had not given a thought to the stallion to whom I owed my life" (36). Prior to this, he had been "more susceptible than most to the vulnerability of innocence. So much for my resolve to live by my wits and willed restraint. So much for my faith in consciousness. At least my losses of self-control were short-lived" (37). His innocence collapses at his acknowledgment of the power of the father. Watching in horror the animal urgency of his sire, Harod,[13] Willy identifies with him: "The sounds he made might have been coming from my own silent and constricted throat, so keenly did I feel the pain of his lonely trumpeting" (41). But his identification is multiple, for he also says, "how I suffered the plight of the mare" (42). He is soon both metaphorically and literally hobbled, as Kate is hobbled for insemination; he is recalcitrant with the farrier and therefore must be restrained: "Thus momentarily I was no better off than Kate herself had been" (43). More significantly, he is captured—and disempowered—by the conflict of innocence (or ignorance) and force: "Insipid innocence, despicable desire—that day I was caught between the two" (43). Put under before gelding, Willy dreams of Oedipal triumph, but with a mother replacement—Kate—as Harod watches, excluded. It is this sort of reversal that the novel effects in giving the power of narration to the horse that has formerly figured as part of the mastering fantasies of men, of fathers and sons. Willy's castration signifies a demasculinization and disempowerment that in some sense abolishes the progression of time: "Between my hind legs hung no future, but a void" (81).[14] The void is filled by the progression of language.

Willy's castration marks just the beginning of the twenty years of abuse he will suffer at the hands of humans. But his series of picaresque misadventures end when he is rescued from the Metacomet Ranch, where he has become Old Horse, by Master, Harry of Hidden Hall, and his Irish horse trainer, Ralph. (The Metacomet Ranch, somewhere in New England, is a ranch that parodies ranches, just as the novel is a novel about, or that parodies, Hawkes's previous novels, tracing a cometlike trajectory of journey and return.) Now Sweet William/Old Horse relates his struggles in the pain and decrepitude of his old age to disprove Ralph's condemnation of him and to embody Master's dream of him. The long awaited return to a semblance of good fortune marks Old Horse's translation into the vehicle for the stories of Master and Ralph. In these stories, which multifariously echo images and themes of Hawkes's earlier work, the issue of innocence is what is most at stake. Willy compares himself to Master thus: "THE DIFFERENCE BETWEEN MYSELF AND MASTER WAS THIS: THAT I WAS FORTUNATE ENOUGH TO LOSE MY INNOCENCE, WHILE HE WAS NOT" (34); Master has "the friendliness of purest innocence" (122). Master, who in his old age is still a virgin, shares the sexual ignorance, the rampant idealism, and the transforming innocence of Uncle Jake in *Adventures in the Alaskan Skin Trade* (and its spinoff, *Innocence in Extremis*). Like Uncle Jake, Master's grandfather was the head of an estate[15] (for Master, this estate is the original Hidden Hall), the sire of nine sons, and, like Uncle Jake's grandfather and like Harold Van Fleet, a fox hunter, a commanding horseman, and the initiator into a world of masculine pleasure. Master, who calls himself Harry—the name that he reveals in the last pages of the novel was his grandfather's—longs to recreate his grandfather's Hidden Hall, and so it is necessary to, for the first time in his life, own and ride a horse.

As Master studies the row of horses in which Old Horse stands at the Metacomet Ranch, Ralph tells Josephine, the Ranch's owner and ruler, "His name's not Harry. There is no Hidden Hall. He's daft, you see. He's never been on a horse in his life, he doesn't know a thing about horses except for what he's got from books. It's the reading that's turned his head" (124). Ralph then says of Josephine's horses, "I'd send the lot of them to the knackers if I were you. Of course I don't mean a word of it. Just joking" (124). These sentences inscribe not just the intertextual evocation of Quixote, but, through Ralph's language play, a dissolution of the border between truth and fiction. The text foregrounds radical subjectivity when Master praises Old Horse and Ralph ridicules him; "'We're not looking at the same horse,' said Ralph. 'Perhaps not,' said Master" (127). Master's particular subjectivity is not only idealistic, but specifically aesthetic; he studies the horses "as if scrutinizing masterpieces hung on a wall" (123). Indeed, Master tries to master the waywardness of reality by transforming it into a series of aesthetic correspondences.

Just as "Harry" may or may not be the name of this man trying to imitate and re-embody his grandfather Harry, "Master" does and does not correspond to the incompetent Harry who whispers to his horse that his "role is Master and [Ralph's] the groom" (194) and who listens to Ralph say that *he* is the authority and Master is "no more . . . than that horse's turds" (146). But in Old Horse's tale that transmutes into old man's tale the horse gives the man his chosen identity by always calling him Master (a tribute Master can never know). And Master asserts the importance of linguistically conferred reality when he renames Old Horse, which Old Horse/Sweet William considers "the restoration of my dignity" (149). Master names him Petrarch and discourses on the virtues of poetry:

"Purity, Ralph, purity!" exclaimed Master. "Petrarch believed in writing the page of eternity! He believed that the eternal poem is achieved only at the cost of the poet's own natural life. The poet's vitality must be metamorphosed into words. To put it more simply, just as Petrarch transformed Laura into the living tree that bears her name—or perhaps it was vice-versa—so the poet both dies and lives in the poem he writes! And thereby lives on in eternity!" (152) [16]

In this conception, the poet and his subject become transcendent through the poem; the world becomes word, life becomes text. (For Petrarch, the unattainable Laura/laurel is attained in art.) Ralph analogizes from Master's formulation: the horse can be seen as the poet and Master, the "prospective rider," as the horse's verse, which would mean that "this horse is going to give his life for your fulfillment," by which Ralph means Petrarch will die; or, casting the analogy in terms of Master's perspective, Ralph says, "riding is nothing more nor less than writing poetry," which, he concludes, means that "riding shall be the death of you!" (153). Or, to translate further, *writing* shall be the death of you, just as birth—becoming text—was the death of Virginie. Language's purity and power consists in its simultaneous rendering of absence and presence; it is, in Blanchot's words, "that deferred assassination which is what my language is" (*The Gaze of Orpheus* 43). "Goodbye Sweet William! Goodbye Old Horse! Petrarch I was and always would be!" says our narrator (154). But of course he is and is not Petrarch, and he is and is not Sweet William, he is and is not Old Horse. The time shifts of the narrative compound the layering of names, the second skins of language that veil and unveil the narrator's self. What is left of the narrator, who is put to sleep at the end, is *Sweet William: A Memoir of Old Horse,* a title whose compound names signify the complex correspondence between words and the things they embody.

The conflation of man, horse, and woman in Master's and Ralph's formulations of the poet and his subject further attests to the appropriation of the objectified and fetishized Other. Master reveals that his conceptions of horse and of woman are inextricably bound. "[N]o man consumed by interest in a woman can think of his horse!" (194), he exclaims; later he will say, "no man may respect a woman, young or old, unless he respects his horse" (201). The horse becomes the privileged starting point, the ultimate signifier because of its more easily appropriable status as a voiceless being to be owned and tamed. Master's words suggest the necessity for respecting the ultimate Other, but they also suggest that both horse and woman have equal status as that which is given meaning by the Master. Both horse and woman signify, among other things, the regaining of Master's past and the actualization of a boyhood dream.

At the age of seventeen Master went to his grandfather's Irish estate for his grandparents' Golden Wedding. The grandfather felt young Master had no aptitude for riding horses and so would not allow it, a fact that excluded him both from riding and from joining the fox hunts. For fear that Master would alarm or injure the horses, the grandfather would not even allow him in the stables, which "in design and construction resembled a temple" (199). This is the one prohibition of his grandfather's that he transgresses; he enters this temple, and in it he sees "the vision . . . in which I still live" (200). He sees his favorite serving girl, regal and self-possessed atop a bay horse very much like Petrarch, a similarity Master realizes only in recounting his story to Petrarch. He watched the girl "in shyness that was all but self-consuming and desire as pure as the smile on that young rider's face." While still stationary she called to him, saying, "I am riding your horse! . . . Do I not ride him well?" then rode out of the stable "forever" (201). "Once seen, could any boy or man recover himself from the power of that slim creature, hardly more than a child, who so erectly sat her horse that day in my grandfather's stable? I glimpsed her, I must glimpse her again, and shall. How like I am to your namesake, Petrarch!" (201). It is, then, the image of this remembered woman that propels Master's idealistic quest, and his idealism that engendered the initial fascination. The horse becomes the object through which he will repossess this image, and through which he will merge with his image of his grandfather, the original possessor of horse and serving girl alike: "I adored my grandfather and wanted nothing more than to grow in his image, as I have done" (199). Master has purchased a horse and named him Petrarch so that he can become "a true horseman" "for the sake of Hidden Hall, about which I say little but which I always seek. Not the original Hidden Hall, of course, not the Hidden Hall of Golden Wedding fame. But that other Hidden Hall on our side of the waters and of which I am Master. Oh find that second Hidden Hall again I must! And shall—through my horse! Through you, Petrarch" (194). It will be through becoming a "stationary traveler," [17] through the exercise of his imagination, that Master will attain his dream of Woman and become master of a world of images.

It is the grandfather who warned Master to avoid "the three inflammatory topics as he called them: money, religion and womanhood" (209). These three things typically are sites of worship and in some sense relegated to the sacred in Western culture; they are, indeed, terms that frequently exist in a system of metaphoric and metonymic exchange. (It is fitting that Master has his vision of ideal woman in a "temple.") The grandfather's desire, in his position of multifarious privilege, to make these things invisible is consonant with the austerity of the family motto: "*Ne quid nimis* . . . Nothing too Much" (238). The grandfather discussed the ambiguity of the motto with Master: "He told me that only the black sheep of the family chose to believe that our family motto gave them the license to pursue the unattainable, no matter the cost to themselves or others. Whereas the family at large did nothing, thought nothing, said nothing in or to excess, which is the other meaning of our motto. Grandfather told me that I too must avoid excess. And so I have" (208). The idea of behaving in accordance with a representative set of words again foregrounds the problematic relation of the word to the world, the problematic nature of writing and of interpretation. Master's words become unreliable, their interpretation undecidable. He has given his entire life to the pursuit of the unattainable—unless, that is, we grant a new meaning to attainable, a meaning that would be metaphoric and aesthetic, accomplished only in Master's fictive constructions and in *Sweet William: A Memoir of Old Horse*. The multiplicity of possible meanings marks literary language as excessive. Furthermore, it is the "problem" of "womanhood" as it relates to the creation of meaning, the expression of sexuality, and the concept of innocence that is involved with the overdetermined excesses of language in *Sweet William* and in all of Hawkes's work.

In *Innocence in Extremis* (1985) the Deauville family motto is also "Nothing Too Much" (55). The grandfather, called the Old Gentleman, explains the meaning of this motto to an audience that will soon see the event he has orchestrated of eighteen naked village "virgins" stomping grapes: "regarding the horse, the honored woman, and the grape, ours is a morality of excess. 'Without the Sun I am Nothing,' as I myself have written, but the true meaning of my single line of verse lies in its unwritten corollary: 'In My Birth I am All.' Excess, my dears, excess" (55).[18] The status of *Innocence in Extremis* is itself excessive: it is a short novel written in the third person in which Uncle Jake of *Adventures in the Alaskan Skin Trade* makes a boyhood visit to his grandfather's French estate, an event that would exceed the bounds of the novel in which Sunny narrates her own experiences and repeats the Alaskan adventure stories that Uncle Jake chose to tell. *Sweet William*'s permutation of Uncle Jake's family structure (and the permutation in each of Hawkes's own lineage) rewrites the grandfather as enforcer of repression rather than proponent of excess, and this distinction rests largely on the grandfathers' differing attitudes toward women. While Master's grandfather—at least in Master's version of him—silences the contemplation of woman, the Old Gentleman, who keeps a mistress and utilizes any number of other females, displays his women as well as his horses, visually and verbally elaborating on their erotic significance. (He is something of an artist of eroticism, believing that "artificiality not only enhances natural life but defines it" [45].) For both men, Woman is the site of erotic fascination subject either to repression or expression—both on the part of the male.[19]

Ralph, who provides a lusty, earthy, rational counterpoint to Master's idealism, engages the ideas of innocence, excess, and sexuality through his series of stories about his sister Carrie (perhaps a deliberate revisioning of Dreiser's heroine). As a girl in Ireland, Carrie scorns her parents and their religion, hates clerics for their vow of celibacy and their secret indulgences, and satisfies her own desire by accommodating the desires of all the young men at the local pub, the Tank and Tit. According to Ralph, she taught him what it meant to be a man, for she revealed her own desire and engendered desire in him.[20] Ralph's friend, Coreen Mulcahy, who comes to stay at the stable where Ralph and Master live, exhibits the same healthy desire as Carrie. Ralph calls her "as innocent in the true meaning of the word and as lively as was my sister," and adds "what I mean by innocence in a girl is generosity" (187–188). This formulation of innocence suggests that it is played out in the body of the sexually generous woman who reciprocates and accommodates the innocence of male desire. But Ralph's potentially mastering conception of woman co-exists with a potentially empowering acknowledgment of women: he says that Carrie's glorious singing voice came from her mouth but also "from between her legs! . . . Or perhaps I should simply say that whatever the origins of Carrie's singing voice, that voice came from the sweetest spot in all the land of Ireland—and was the sweet spot of woman herself" (164). He allows for the interrelatedness of sexuality and voice in a way that seems to be a response to the "silence" of the female genitals as they have been conceived in a masculine tradition of, for instance, art and psychoanalysis.[21] When Master expresses his horror at Ralph's "vulgarity," Ralph responds, "you've no ear for poetry" (164). Indeed, Ralph addresses and redefines Master's idea of poetry as transcending—and absenting—real life. Significantly, however, the poetry is in *Ralph's language*; he, then, is the poet, and the glorious Carrie remains a subject. The exchange continues the problematic relationship between body and embodiment, between the bodies of people and the body of the text; innocence exists and does not exist, affirmed and compromised in its formulation.

Master expresses his horror at any but an idealized relation to a woman when he refuses to stay in the rooms he shares with Ralph while Coreen Mulcahy is there. In his self-imposed exile he sleeps in Petrarch's stall (an act reminiscent of Konrad Vost's night spent in a horse's stall where two women "rape" him). While Master considers the woman "blameless" (194), he speaks of himself as having made a moral choice. For Petrarch, the innocent Coreen Mulcahy appears as a full-bodied ghost from his past: she is the girl he hates for making him watch his copulating father, thus destroying his own innocence. The combination of Master's and Petrarch's reaction to Coreen Mulcahy returns the text from the conception of innocence as generosity and desire to innocence as idealism and ignorance. Petrarch revenges his past by biting Coreen, and has the reward of believing that she understands his motive, that she gains knowledge of his inner life; that she, in other words, has lost that aspect of innocence that would, in Hawkes's words, "make one the lyrical fool without the fool's wisdom" (O'Donnell 124).

The body of this woman is just one way in which Petrarch's past returns to him. It is Master's rescuing him from the Metacomet Ranch that returns Petrarch's memory and turns him into a storyteller—or a poet. In this sense it is only fitting that Petrarch tells the stories of others along with his own, for the awakening of memory is also the awakening of desire and imagination, and imagination includes the effort to portray—if not enter—the Other. In spite of his continued misanthropy, Old Horse loves Master, even while this idealistic dreamer exhorts nearly impossible physical tasks of the broken horse and comes close to killing him. Sweet William/Old Horse/Petrarch's efforts to conform to Master's vision of him proves to be the redemptive restoration of his dignity. The last part of the novel celebrates the mutual compassion of horse and man; it also inscribes the fluidity of the border between master and subject, played out in the realms of imagination and inscription.

Sweet William recovers his origins in the surprise and fortuitous return to Millbank, the farm of his birth, as he and Clover, Master and Ralph, escape a plague of rats (a suggestively Petrarchan event) in their stable. Millbank is a ruin, like Old Horse, and like him it gets renamed; it is, proclaims Master, Hidden Hall. Precisely why Master decides this remains mysterious, except that it seems he has come to the end of an interior journey; he has reconciled the imagined and the real. The conferring of beauty on a ruin occurs for Petrarch, too, in a visionary experience in one of Millbank's fields. The decrepit horse comes upon a creature covered with nuggets of shining gold; but the sun shifts, and it is revealed to be a goat covered with pustules and close to death. The image recalls Skipper's creation of beauty out of ugliness and death in his triumphant final chapter, "The Golden Fleas." And the goat recalls the many goats that populate the hillsides in *The Blood Oranges* and which become material for Cyril's mythmaking when he reconstitutes them as satyr figures in his "tapestry" of sexual love. The transfiguration of the ugly affirms the moment of vision as truth. Ralph urges that the dying goat be put to sleep, and in trying to convey his point relates a story of being a member of the Irish Fusiliers assigned to the "company Padre's staff" and coming upon a dead horse which the priest raves about as "a vision of pure gold" that blankets the creature and moves in waves. The priest says "no one has ever seen what we are seeing. A poor abandoned horse destroyed in a field by random fire and now blinding as a glory we cannot hope to explain" (239). But Ralph can explain it, for the gold is maggots. The priest says, "The point is that what we saw at first is the truth. The maggots, mortally unpleasant when seen through eyes such as yours, will return this white horse to the very earth he lies upon. The maggots are sacred. . . . No matter how dead white they may now look to you, they are still as golden as they first looked to us both" (240). Nonetheless, they remain maggots to Ralph, always the rational pragmatist. But all of Hawkes's texts again and again engage the visionary experience that transforms and transcends the material. (In Ralph's story, the analogy lends itself to the modernist conception of the writer as priest.) In his interview with Patrick O'Donnell, Hawkes relates an anecdote of a man he once met who had been stationed in the South Pacific during World War II on an island covered with corpses; "He told me how, at one moment, he looked at a corpse, and he noticed that the maggots inhabiting the corpse were golden. To me, that was immediately the statement of an artist" (124–125). Sweet William/Old Horse/Petrarch is the death-ridden horse who is art and artist.

The conflict between the material and the ideal informs all of Hawkes's novels. Repeatedly we see artist figures who in their will to transcendence exert their power over an Other (women, horses, men who will be subjects). In *Sweet William* the idea of mastery is travestied, as the man who is called Master exerts his power over nothing and no one, not even his horse, but does gain control of himself through his artistic vision of life. This vision is simultaneously life-enriching and life-denying; it is not until the end of Old Horse's memoir that Master's dream of his past and future acknowledges the realities of the present. His compassionate identification with Petrarch's pain and immanent death causes him for the first time to lose "his usual innocent self-concern"; he "had no thought even of Hidden Hall" (262). The reality of life and death intrudes on his dream. He offers bruised, shrunken crabapples and carrots and rotting potatoes to Petrarch and his companion Clover the afternoon before Petrarch is to die, and the horses eat desultorily until Master himself reaches for a rotten potato and chews it, which gives Petrarch "Relief! Release! For it was then that I threw off my imminent future . . . and reverted to the horse I was" (262). (He returns to the horse he was when he is soon, like Konrad Vost, to discover what it is to be nothing.) He eats ravenously, consuming in the face of death that will consume him. (The novel is, in many ways, about hunger.) Master's gesture of eating the horses' food reveals him as in his dream and out of it; he becomes animal at the same time he becomes most humane. The opposition between self and Other collapses.

The breech in Master's innocence is also the assertion of innocence. In *The Passion Artist* we are told that "[i]nnocence leads inevitably to ice and iron: to bones that become iron, to skin that freezes gradually into a blue and glittering transparency, and then cracks and refreezes until the entire surface of the body is encased and encrusted in scales and broken mirrors of ice, frozen in place" (145). But the rigidity and frigidity of this conception coexists in Hawkes's body of work with the fluidity of the innocent Virginie's description of herself, as she sits drinking and eating in the labyrinth of the chateau and the labyrinth of light that are "the very domain of [her] purity," experiencing "a moment of that curious pride when she who is assumed to have no consciousness knows, for one instant, that she herself is the vessel brimming with all the world for whom, this instant, she does not exist. Hence I saw them all in the mirror that was myself" (*Virginie* 49). In *The Passion Artist* and *Virginie*, as in all of Hawkes's novels, the worlds of the novels reflect a consciousness and unconsciousness, and the consciousness and unconsciousness construct a world; innocence and power, dream and nightmare find simultaneous and paradoxical expression.

Of the dream, Blanchot writes: "The dream touches the region where pure resemblance reigns. Everything there is similar; each figure is another one, is similar to another and to yet another, and this last to still another. One seeks the original model, wanting to be referred to a point of departure, an initial revelation, but there is none. The dream is likeness that refers eternally to likeness" (*The Space of Literature* 268). Interestingly, Hawkes's description of the dreamlike world of his novels as "lunar landscapes" uses the image of the "feminine" luminary and figure of reflection as representative of fictive worlds in which artist figures attempt to represent the self and the Other. In Hawkes's novels we again and again find halls of mirrors that endlessly reflect the images of the self and of the Other through the endless reflectiveness and reflexivity of language. But in this specular realm there always remains an aspect of hiddenness—the hiddenness of what language is meant to represent beyond the ambiguous materiality of words on the page.[22] The final words of *Sweet William*, "Ride on! Ride on through it!" suggest this dynamic as they send us back to the beginning of the text and through all of the mirroring, echoing texts Hawkes has written at the same time that the floating signifier "it" sends us outward, beyond the text. This movement within and without the text engages the question of what is at stake in the processes of fiction.

The words on the page are always, in Hawkes's texts, asserted as the innocent realm of the imagination realized in language. But it is through the imagination's desire to achieve wholeness or unity between vision and matter, word and world, that Hawkes maintains "the truth of the fractured picture" (Enck 144). And it is through the imagination's negotiation of creation and representation that there is an excess of possibilities for the conceiving and enacting of innocence and power. The various formulations of innocence and power never solidify into a unified, monolithic definition but remain variously and actively produced in the complex multivoicedness of texts. The shifting of borders between master and subject that occurs in *Sweet William* is yet another example of the possibility of the imagination's will to power engendering its own critique. This writer whose novels have repeatedly elaborated the claustrophobic potentialities of a single viewpoint paradoxically opens the field of his texts to other voices—to opposition that would dissolve opposition. Faithful to the paradoxes of the visionary imagination, Hawkes's novels inscribe the innocence and power of giving the unspeakable voice.

# Notes

## Introduction

1. All citations of Hawkes's interview with Patrick O'Donnell ("Life and Art: An Interview with John Hawkes") will be given in the text as "O'Donnell," along with the page number. Citations of O'Donnell's book *John Hawkes* will be given as "*JH*," and of his essay "Self-Alignment: John Hawkes' *Travesty*" in *Passionate Doubts* as "*PD*."

All other interviews will also be cited by the interviewer's name. Thus, Heide Ziegler's interview, "John Hawkes," will be cited as "Ziegler"; citation of her essay "Postmodernism as Autobiographical Commentary: *The Blood Oranges* and *Virginie*" will be indicated by title. Robert Scholes's interview, "A Conversation on *The Blood Oranges* between John Hawkes and Robert Scholes," will be cited as "Scholes"; citation of *Fabulation and Metafiction* will be indicated by title. Thomas LeClair's interview "The Novelists: John Hawkes" will be cited as "LeClair"; LeClair's "A Dialogue: John Barth and John Hawkes" will be cited as "Barth and Hawkes."

2. In a 1971 interview with John Kuehl, Hawkes responds to Kuehl's query about being "lumped" with surrealists: "I appreciate being identified with the surrealists, but at the same time resist that identification because I don't think it's very applicable. There's nothing merely murky or dreamlike about my fiction, and it's not a matter of unconscious flow or automatic writing. I'm interested in highly shaped and perfected works of art in which the language and everything in the fiction have to achieve a certain intensity and rightness. The prose in *Charivari* is highly poetic and that short novel is, I guess, the closest to surrealistic writing that I've done" (Kuehl 180).

## Chapter 1. Textual Image, Authorial Vision, Narrative Voice in *The Cannibal, The Beetle Leg, The Goose on the Grave,* and *The Owl*

1. The novels were published together in 1954 as *The Goose on the Grave and The Owl* and reprinted in *Lunar Landscapes: Stories and Short Novels, 1949–1963* (1969). In 1994 Sun & Moon Press reissued the novels as *The Owl and The Goose on the Grave.* All references in this text are to the *Lunar Landscapes* edition of the novels.

2. Hawkes draws upon Winthrop's "A Modell of Christian Charity." My source

for this text is *The Puritans*, volume 1, edited by Perry Miller and Thomas H. Johnson (New York: Harper & Row, 1963), pp. 195–199.

## Chapter 3. Writing the Self: *Second Skin*, the Second Sex, and the Second Take

1. *Second Skin* can be considered a "narcissistic narrative" in the sense in which Linda Hutcheon uses the term in her book *Narcissistic Narrative: The Metafictional Paradox*. Hutcheon's interest is not with the psychological suggestiveness of the term, but rather with an "ironic allegorical reading of the Narcissus myth" which yields a loose, suggestive paradigm for a strong current in contemporary fiction, sprung from the tradition of the novel that has indeed always "nurtured a self-love, a tendency toward self-obsession" (10); "the text is its own mirror" (14). The metafictions, or narcissistic narratives, she discusses foreground fiction as process over fiction as product. "Overtly narcissistic texts reveal their self-awareness in explicit thematizations or allegorizations of their diegetic or linguistic identity within the texts themselves. In the covert form, this process is internalized, actualized; such a text is self-reflective but not necessarily self-conscious" (7). The erotic or sexual metaphor sometimes serves the metafictional end of articulating the author's—and the reader's—relation to the fictive language or subject (85–86).

2. In his interview with Patrick O'Donnell, Hawkes describes the image of the ship as "fetal: it is dead but full of potential" (122). This recalls the fetus that serves as a key metaphor in *The Beetle Leg*. In *Second Skin*, the image reappears when Miranda announces that Cassandra has left behind a fetus in a jar.

3. A passage from Julia Kristeva's "*Stabat Mater*" is suggestive here: "Man overcomes the unthinkable of death by postulating maternal love in its place—in the place and stead of death and thought. . . . It is only 'normal' for a maternal representation to set itself up at the place of this subdued anguish called love. No one escapes it. Except perhaps the saint, the mystic, or the writer who, through the power of language, nevertheless succeeds in doing no better than to take apart the fiction of the mother as mainstay of love, and to identify with love itself and what he is in fact—*a fire of tongues*, an exit from representation. Might not modern art then be, for the few who are attached to it, the implementation of that maternal love—a veil over death, in death's very sight and with full knowledge of the facts? A sublimated celebration of incest?" (*Tales of Love* 252–253; Kristeva's emphasis).

4. Mary F. Robertson quotes this passage as suggesting "not only that our fancy is not our own but that neither is our identity, since it is shaped by such fancy; our personal voice and expression are already streaked through at their origin with 'writing,' here literally writing from the Greeks" (436).

5. Skipper says, "there was no mistaking me for anything but the leader now, and they were faithful followers, my entourage" (166). His words recall the fascistic Zizendorf of *The Cannibal*, the Leader who will give birth to the Nation. Hawkes again ironically recalls Zizendorf in Skipper's benedictory words to his dead family: "what else can I say to Father, Mother, Gertrude, Fernandez, Cassandra, except sleep, sleep, sleep?" (161). *The Cannibal* ends with Zizendorf ordering the child, Selvaggia, to "go back to sleep," a command with lethal implications for a world in which people numbly succumb to the rule of force and the reign of nightmare.

6. Skipper repeatedly attributes rosy colors to Catalina Kate. In his first description of her, for example, he describes her skin as "some subtle tincture of eggplant and pink rose," and he calls her "this mauve puff of powder" (49).

7. In *A Lover's Discourse*, Roland Barthes writes, "What wounds me are the *forms* of the relation, its images; or rather, what others call *form* I experience as force. The image—as the example for the obsessive—is *the thing itself*. The lover is thus an artist; and his world is in fact a world reversed, since in it each image is its own end (nothing beyond the image)" (133; Barthes's emphasis).

## Chapter 4. Dreams of Wholeness, Nightmares of Dissolution: Aspects of the Artist in the Triad

1. Another passage from Foucault's *The History of Sexuality* is relevant here: "By creating the imaginary element that is 'sex,' the deployment of sexuality established one of its most essential internal operating principles: the desire for sex— the desire to have it, to have access to it, to discover it, to liberate it, to articulate it in discourse, to formulate it in truth. It constituted 'sex' itself as something desirable. And it is this desirability of sex that attaches each one of us to the injunction to know it, to reveal its law and its power; it is this desirability that makes us think we are affirming the rights of our sex against all power, when in fact we are fastened to the deployment of sexuality that has lifted up from deep within us a sort of mirage in which we think we see ourselves reflected—the dark shimmer of sex" (156–157).

2. Cyril is "spectacular" also in that he wears glasses, with golden rims, which he mentions frequently. This can be seen as a pun on the deficiency of his vision, or as a gilded variation on the cliché of looking through rose-colored glasses.

3. For a detailed reading of the ways in which this scene confirms Cyril's vision, see Steven Abrams's essay "*The Blood Oranges* as a Visionary Fiction," particularly pages 100–103.

4. The use of "halter" is one small testament to the richness of Hawkes's imagery; a halter conceals, restrains, or enforces, and is used on women, on animals, and on the necks of the condemned.

5. Cyril extols the beauty of virgin shepherdesses, but this beauty redounds to Cyril's aestheticization of the girls. Implicitly, they cannot know their own beauty.

6. When Cyril first talks about the Virgin and child at the beginning of his narrative, he uses the name Mary once (18) and not again.

7. Roland Barthes, in *A Lover's Discourse*, speaks of language as constitutive of love relationships: "In the lover's realm, there is no *acting out*: no propulsion, perhaps even no pleasure—nothing but signs, a frenzied activity of language; to institute, on each furtive occasion, the system (the paradigm) of demand and response" (68; Barthes's emphasis).

8. An interesting aside: in discussing a fragment of his youth with interviewers, Hawkes says, "My mother had to learn to give me injections for my asthma—I remember she used to practice on an orange to give me the injections which I didn't like at all" (Santore and Pocalyko 172).

9. In an interview with John Kuehl, Hawkes says, "Hugh doesn't mean to kill himself. He means to undergo a partial hanging in order to experience sexual release, but he slips and thus accidentally dies. I meant the death of Hugh in a sense to trick the reader into thinking of it as a moral judgment on the multiple relationships—but to me it is not. Hugh's death is thoroughly absurd" (169).

10. For example, in his interview with Santore and Pocalyko, Hawkes states his unequivocal opposition to suicide and violence, but says, "The irony is that I'm not appalled yet by the privileged man's murder/suicide in *Travesty*. This is because I think of it as so purely a work of art that he assumes responsibility rather than commits an outrage against life itself" (181).

11. This is suggestive of Said's remark that "Freud [in *The Interpretation of Dreams*] likens the dream to corpses lying on a battlefield (p. 467). His interpretive task is thus to make the battlefield come alive again" (167).

12. C. J. Allen discusses Allert's homosexual desires in his essay "Desire, Design, and Debris: The Submerged Narrative of John Hawkes' Recent Trilogy."

13. Charles Baxter's "In the Suicide Seat" cogently addresses this issue.

14. Jane Gallop writes: "If the father were to desire his daughter he could no longer exchange her, no longer possess her in the economy by which true, masterful possession is the right to exchange. . . . So the father must not desire the daughter for that threatens to remove him from the homosexual commerce in which women are exchanged between men, in the service of power relations and community for the men" (76).

15. In an interview with Paul Emmett and Richard Vine, Hawkes says, "I discovered those two lines, by the way, in *Parade's End*. A friend of mine told me they were actually written by Christina Rossetti. I rearranged them slightly" (167).

16. See Jane Gallop's *The Daughter's Seduction: Feminism and Psychoanalysis*, particularly chapter 5, for a discussion of oculocentrism and univocity in terms of Lacanian and feminist theory.

## Chapter 5. The Artist in the World of Women: The Imagination and Beyond in *The Passion Artist*

1. In his interview with Thomas LeClair, for instance, Hawkes says, "The work that is deeply and truly moral violates conventional morality" ("The Novelists," 27).

2. The passage is reminiscent of a description of Miss Lonelyhearts in Nathanael West's novel of that name: "He knew now what this thing was—hysteria, a snake whose scales are tiny mirrors in which the dead world takes on a semblance of life" (9).

3. Hawkes here parodies his own belief "that we're all islands—inaccessible, drifting apart, thirsting to be explored, magical" ("Notes on Writing a Novel," 113).

4. Vost's similarity to Papa manifests itself throughout the novel, quite strikingly in other of his viewpoints listed in the passage on page 20 of the novel. Like Papa, Vost finds himself both ordinary and exceptional, and he shares Papa's obsession with deformity and incongruity: "How many men were capable of knowing, as he full well knew, that the artificial limb, the imitation of a hand in a black glove or the replica of a missing foot in a real boot, adds splendor to the body presumed to be merely maimed? . . . Or could suffer the understanding, as could he, that smashed glass is preferable to the pure plane?"

5. Hawkes's words about himself are suggestive here: "I find it very difficult to cope with the notion of being alive, being human; I'm not able to accept *us* very easily. I think we are all unaccountable. Life is also a constantly terrifying mystery as well as a beautiful, unpredictable, exfoliating, marvelous thing" (O'Donnell 122; Hawkes's emphasis).

6. Because the names listed include "Honorine," "Ursula," and "Ariane," female characters from *Travesty* and *Death, Sleep and the Traveler*, they are also a storehouse of an intertextual past.

7. Two events related in the novel happen on "a Sunday in summer": Vost's witnessing of a woman held captive at the train station who would later be taken to La Violaine, and Eva Laubenstein's childhood experience in which her much older brother viciously spanks her and she feels intense love for him (161–163).

8. Vost's words recall God's words to Moses in *Exodus* (significantly, a text of liberation): "And God said to Moses, 'I Am who I Am.' " *The Jerusalem Bible* (Garden City, N.Y.: Doubleday & Company, Inc., 80) glosses the line thus: "it may be that Yahweh is used here to imply the impossibility of giving an adequate definition of God. In semitic thought, knowledge of a name gave power over the thing named; to know a god's name was to be able to call on him and be certain of a hearing. The true God does not make himself man's slave in this way by revealing a name expressive of his essence." The formula "I am who I am" thereby contains a "refusal to reveal" (81).

## Chapter 6. The Labyrinth, the Wilderness, the Female Voice: *Virginie: Her Two Lives* and *Adventures in the Alaskan Skin Trade*

1. Hawkes, born in Stamford, Connecticut, at the age of ten moved with his parents to Juneau, Alaska, where they lived for five years before returning to the East. The harsh landscape of these Alaskan years provided him with images of desolation and extremity. While his father pursued adventure, his mother, who loved tennis, music, and singing, made the best of this alien life which Hawkes calls "the very antithesis of the kind of world my mother should have been in" (O'Donnell 107–108).

In the sidebar interview with Caryn James that accompanies the review of *Adventures* in the *New York Times Book Review*, Hawkes remarks of his writing a novel inspired by his Alaskan experience that he "couldn't use a male narrator because I'd get too close emotionally. I needed a narrator very different from myself. I tried to imagine the kind of woman I would want to be."

2. See Patrick O'Donnell's "Stories My Father Never Told Me: On Hawkes's *Adventures in the Alaskan Skin Trade*" for a discussion of the ways in which Hawkes plays on autobiography in this novel.

3. Uncle Jake's suicide stands in contrast to his brother Billy Boy's in 1929. Billy Boy drives his Stutz Bearcat onto the family tennis courts and shoots himself: "There was no blood. . . . [T]here wasn't even a bullet hole. . . . Only his dearly loved younger brother arrested in an unimaginable tableau that no one but Billy Boy himself could have created and that no member of the family could have thought him capable of creating. . . . [I]t was not just madness as the local paper claimed, it was stunning. It was inexplicable. It was a scene that no one who saw it ever forgot" (321). Billy Boy's suicide recalls Papa's in *Travesty*, since it defies meaning; but the compensation for this defiance which lies in the drama of the tableau recalls the repeated emphasis throughout Hawkes's texts on the tantalizing desire to bring images to voice.

4. That the carved women are "spiraling upwards like stripes on a barber's pole" alludes to Hawkes's "The Nearest Cemetery," the short work in which a barber murders a woman to preserve his idealized image of her and in which

*Second Skin* had its genesis. The image has the dark overtone of associating women with the blood the stripes on the barber's pole represent.

5. While *Adventures in the Alaskan Skin Trade* stylistically most differs from Hawkes's other works, it also widely alludes to them, both thematically and imagistically. Some of these allusions have been referred to above. All of the allusions would be too numerous to list here, but range from the reference to a dentist who installed a dentist's chair in "an ancient airplane and flew around the Territory pulling and repairing teeth" (324) — (reminiscent of *The Beetle Leg*'s Cap Leech), to direct quotes from other works ("All won, all lost, all over" [286], which appears in *The Lime Twig*), to the dream of a man hanged for his innocence. The abundance of intertextual references contributes to the conception of textually constituted identity. See Patrick O'Donnell's "Stories My Father Never Told Me: On Hawkes's *Adventures in the Alaskan Skin Trade*" for an excellent discussion of Hawkes's use of intertextuality.

6. Martha Washington's last husband's name was George, a fact which compounds the parodistic aspect of her own name, and which also recalls George (who, like the George of *Adventures in the Alaskan Skin Trade*, is an unsuccessful professor) and Martha from *Who's Afraid of Virginia Woolf?*, a couple who live in their own sad land of games.

### Chapter 7. The Artist and His Subjects in *Whistlejacket*

1. W. J. T. Mitchell writes that, "The presentation of imagistic elements in texts, textual elements in images, is a familiar practice which might be 'defamiliarized' by understanding it as a transgression, an act of (sometimes ritual) violence involving an incorporation of the symbolic Other into the generic Self" (157).

2. Michael's position recalls that of Michael Banks in *The Lime Twig*. And indeed, *Whistlejacket* can be seen as parodying that earlier novel, which is itself a parody of a mystery thriller. *The Lime Twig*'s elaboration of personal and cultural fantasies and their representations, its investment of glamour and sexuality in horses, its more and less powerful author figures, its engagement of the thwarted desire to exceed limitation, suggest intriguing intertextual links to violence and fantasy and their images in *Whistlejacket*.

3. In contradistinction to words, "The image is the sign that pretends not to be a sign, masquerading as (or, for the believer, actually achieving) natural immediacy and presence" (Mitchell 43). Susan Sontag writes that "A photograph passes for incontrovertible proof that a given thing happened. The picture may distort; but there is always a presumption that something exists, or did exist, which is like what's in the picture" (5). Photographs are commonly thought of as a "'natural' code" transmitting empirical information (Mitchell 60). Mitchell disputes this naive conception by elucidating the conventional aspects of all images. He states that "the notion of the image as a 'natural sign' is, in a word, the fetish or idol of Western culture" (90).

### Conclusion: The Domain of Purity, the Fragments of Actuality— *Sweet William: A Memoir of Old Horse* and the Imagination's Prism

1. In her book *Gynesis: Configurations of Woman and Modernity*, Alice Jardine uses *The Lime Twig* and *The Passion Artist* (along with Pynchon's *V.*) to illustrate

the "thematization of gynesis" in contemporary American fiction. (Jardine defines gynesis as "the putting into discourse of 'woman' as that *process* diagnosed in France as intrinsic to the condition of modernity; indeed, the valorization of the feminine, woman, and her obligatory, that is, historical connotations, as somehow intrinsic to new and necessary modes of thinking, writing, speaking. The object produced by this process is neither a person nor a thing, but a horizon, that toward which the process is tending: a *gynema*. This *gynema* is a reading effect, a woman-in-effect that is never stable and has no identity" [25; Jardine's emphasis].) These Hawkes novels, says Jardine, "clearly represent how the maternal body is both the beginning and the end of the son's *narrative*, both the source and receptacle of his *desire*—without problematizing either one" (253; Jardine's emphasis). (I would disagree with Jardine's last clause.)

2. Hawkes engages the tenuous border between male and female in many ways, not least of which is through metaphor. He says, for instance, "Somebody once told me that he thought all of those images—airplanes, ships, lighthouses—are images of sexual fear, sexual destruction, the lighthouse in particular being a ruined, gutted phallus. It's hard to tell whether the ship or airplane—they're all the same, I'm convinced—is male or female; it may shift back and forth" (O'Donnell 122). This metaphorical technique, along with many of Hawkes's thematic concerns, can be allied with feminist concerns. Jane Gallop, for instance, writes that the "problem of dealing with difference without constituting an opposition may just be what feminism is all about" (93).

3. The scene perhaps alludes to the swarming of bees on the mouth of the young St. Ambrose, which was said to prefigure his career as a great speaker; what is further suggestive for *Virginie*, Augustine credits St. Ambrose with being the first person to read silently. John Barth plays on these significances for the character/narrator Ambrose in *Lost in the Funhouse*.

4. Horses appear, either fleetingly or significantly, in nearly all of Hawkes's work, as powerful embodiments of dreams, fears, sexuality. "I have certain obsessive themes or subjects that I keep returning to," says Hawkes. "I'm obsessed with horses, birds, destructive sexuality, death, children" (LeClair 28). In *The Passion Artist* we have an example of a recurring association of horses with women: the child Konrad Vost is in love with a woman (his caretaker) named Anna Kossowski and with a horse he calls Anna Kossowski. In *Adventure in the Alaskan Skin Trade*, Sunny describes her father's family as "a family of men . . . in which women were at best only prized like horses" (20).

5. Steven Shaviro's discussion of Blanchot in *Passion and Excess* bears interestingly upon the dynamics of representation in Hawkes's texts. Shaviro quotes from Blanchot's *The Gaze of Orpheus*: " 'I say, "This woman". . . . A word may give me its meaning, but first it suppresses it. For me to be able to say, "This woman," I must somehow take her flesh and blood reality away from her, cause her to be absent, annihilate her. The word gives me the being, but it gives it to me deprived of being. The word is the absence of that being, its nothingness, what is left of it when it has lost being—the very fact that it does not exist. . . . My language does not kill anyone. But if this woman were not really capable of dying, if she were not threatened by death at every moment of her life, bound and joined to death by an essential bond, I would not be able to carry out that ideal negation, that deferred assassination which is what my language is.' ( [*The Gaze of Orpheus*], 41–43)."

Shaviro comments on Blanchot's underscoring of "the actual price of aesthetic idealization": "Signification is never neutral; it always bears the marks of particular relations of power. Herbert Marcuse, commenting on this same conjunction of Hegel, Mallarmé, and Blanchot, asserts the necessity of a 'language of negation': 'the absent must be made present because the greater part of the truth is in that which is absent' (*Reason and Revolution*, x). Blanchot suggests, rather, that the aesthete's or dialectitian's claim to universality is always founded on the violence of an exclusion. The one thing that is forever omitted from the totality, never represented in the dialectical process of linguistic symbolization, is precisely—that which is being represented. Literally speaking, 'My language does not kill anyone.' But the power of death inherent in the word insures that speech is never merely literal. Thus, for instance, a 'deferred assassination,' a making absent of women, is necessary in order that (as psychoanalysis, among other institutions of discourse, claims) the 'truth' of 'woman' be revealed as 'lack'" (17–18).

6. In a ventriloquism of Blanchot, Foucault writes, "Thought about thought, an entire tradition wider than philosophy, has taught us that thought leads us to the deepest interiority. Speech about speech leads us, by way of literature as well as perhaps other paths, to the outside in which the speaking subject disappears" (*Maurice Blanchot: The Thought from Outside* 13).

7. While *Don Quixote* is standardly considered to contain elements of the picaresque, Hawkes disagrees with its being designated as such. "*Don Quixote* uses so much the tone of the romances it is parodying," he says, "and is, after all, so tender, generally speaking, so sweet, that I don't think of *Don Quixote* as picaresque at all. I mean the brutalities of it are psychological, not rendered physically. Don Quixote will never fear for his life, will never be dismembered, will never lose a hand, will never starve to the extent that his mouth will be trying to eat his nose. I would think that *Don Quixote* stands alone in the history of literature. A picaresque novel is savage, marvelous, but marvelous in a different way from *Don Quixote*. I think the ideal is never very visible in the conventional Spanish picaresque novel" (Ziegler 182). In *Sweet William*, Master's story provides the engagement with the romance and the ideal, and Sweet William's story the engagement with the picaresque. The fact that in creating a multivalent parody Hawkes plays off of *Don Quixote*, itself a parody, complicates the web of textuality constituted in the novel.

8. Sweet William is called Willy by the girls and women who love him and whom he loves. Willy harbors a lifelong love of small women—and of small horses; this predisposition recalls Papa's similar fascination in *Travesty* with the small-bodied female. Willy (who, like Papa, considers himself a "privileged" being) echoes Papa's feeling when he says, "The smaller the girl or woman, filly or mare, the more startling her capacity for thought as well as passion" (57). The fact that women call him "Willy" recalls the women who work at Sunny's Alaskan Gamelands calling their customers "Willies."

9. Elisabeth Bronfen's *Over Her Dead Body: Death, Femininity and the Aesthetic* speaks interestingly to Sweet William's anguish over the death of his mother. Bronfen writes, "Over representations of the dead feminine body, culture can repress and articulate its unconscious knowledge of death which it fails to foreclose even as it cannot express it directly. If symptoms are failed repressions, representations are symptoms that visualise even as they conceal what is too dangerous to articulate openly but too fascinating to repress successfully. They repress by localising death away from the self, at the body of a beautiful woman, at the same time that this representation lets the repressed return, albeit in a disguised manner" (xi).

10. The fact that "dam" (etymologically related to "dame") denotes the female parent of a domestic animal provides a convenient allusion to the dam under which Mulge is buried in *The Beetle Leg*. Moreover, it puns on the conception of being damned by being born of dam.

11. "[I]s not my entire life a paean to paradox?" asks Willy (47), echoing the obsession with paradox in all of Hawkes's work, though most emphatically in *Travesty* and *Virginie*.

12. Bronfen writes: "Freud implies that what also disrupts and decentres human existence, producing both nostalgia for a previous state (the complete unity of the child with the maternal body) and a directedness toward detour and creation in the form of symbolic play, are the many inscriptions of death that mark the human body from birth on" (21).

13. The name lacks only one letter to be Harold, the name of the head of the household, lover of horses, and exploiter of women in *Whistlejacket*.

14. Bronfen writes: "What is put under erasure by the gendered concept of castration is the other, so often non-read theme of death, forbidden maybe because far less conducive to efforts of stable self-fashioning than notions of sexual difference. To see the phallus as secondary to the scar of the navel means acknowledging that notions of domination and inferiority based on gender difference are also secondary to a more global and non-individuated disempowerment before death. In the midst of all this aporia, it is no coincidence that this other theme, the theme of death, would be tied to the forbidden maternal body" (35). In this context, one might think of *Death, Sleep & the Traveler*'s Allert, absorbed as he is with death and the putrescence of his unconscious life, in thrall to his earth mother wife, and afflicted by a rash around his navel.

15. This estate was in Ireland, not the France of the Deauville estate. Interestingly, however, Uncle Jake's mother is Irish. The grandfather's mistress in *Innocence in Extremis* suggests a vast distinction between the French and the Irish (85). This distinction seems to play itself out in terms of (Irish) repression and (French) expression.

16. This description recalls Virginie's status as writer and text; eternal child, she is "the insubstantial voice of the page that burns" (11).

17. There are a number of allusions in *Sweet William* to the idea of stationary travel. Petrarch says, for instance, that "Master sat astride me and smiled, as I could feel, and without moving a single step enjoyed his ride" (169). And he says, "Clover [agreed] that my day's journey had been as far as hers, though she had grazed for miles while I, in fact, had gone nowhere" (169).

18. The Old Gentleman also says, "Our horses are famed for their hot blood; our women are justly famed for the number of sons they are capable of bearing in a lifetime" (55).

19. Discussing the use of women in the work of male avant-garde artistic practice, Susan Rubin Suleiman asks, "Why is it a woman who embodies most fully the paradoxical combination of pleasure and anguish that characterizes transgression—in whose body, in other words, the contradictory impulse toward excess on the one hand and respect of the boundary on the other are played out?" (82–83). She concludes that much of the work of male avant-garde artists is not finally subversive, but instead complicit with the ideology of dominant culture, which is bourgeois and patriarchal. Suleiman notes, however, that the fictions of many of these transgressive writers go "a long way toward providing the necessary commentary on themselves" (84).

20. One of Ralph's fond memories is of Carrie's pleasure when he lost control of the horse he was riding and the horse crashed through the window of the corset shop where Carrie worked, emerging with its great bulk bedecked with corsets. The image juxtaposes two fetishes.

21. See the discussion of Cyril's response to the male and/or female statue in Chapter 4.

22. In *Maurice Blanchot*, Foucault writes: "fiction consists not in showing the invisible, but in showing the extent to which the invisibility of the visible is invisible" (24).

# Works Cited

**Primary Sources**

*Novels*

Hawkes, John. *Adventures in the Alaskan Skin Trade*. New York: Simon and Schuster, 1985.
————. *The Beetle Leg*. New York: New Directions, 1951. Paperback reprint. New York: New Directions, 1967.
————. *The Blood Oranges*. New York: New Directions, 1971. Paperback reprint. New York: New Directions, 1972.
————. *The Cannibal*. Norfolk, CT: New Directions, 1950. Paperback reprint. New York: New Directions, 1962.
————. *Death, Sleep & the Traveler*. New Directions, 1974. Paperback reprint. New York: New Directions, 1975.
————. *Humors of Blood & Skin: A John Hawkes Reader*. New York: New Directions, 1984.
————. *Innocence in Extremis*. Providence: Burning Deck Press, 1985.
————. *The Lime Twig*. With an Introduction by Leslie A. Fiedler. New York: New Directions, 1961. Paperback reprint. New York: New Directions, 1961.
————. *Lunar Landscapes: Stories and Short Novels, 1949–1963*. New York: New Directions, 1969. Paperback reprint. New York: New Directions, 1969.
————. *The Owl and The Goose on the Grave*. Los Angeles: Sun & Moon Press, 1994.
————. *The Passion Artist*. New York: Harper and Row, 1979.
————. *Second Skin*. New York: New Directions, 1964. Paperback reprint. New York: New Directions, 1964.
————. *Sweet William: A Memoir of Old Horse*. New York: Simon and Schuster, 1993. Paperback reprint. New York: Penguin, 1993.
————. *Travesty*. New York: New Directions, 1976. Paperback reprint. New York: New Directions, 1977.
————. *Virginie: Her Two Lives*. New York: Harper and Row Publisher, Inc., 1981. Paperback reprint. New York: Carroll & Graf, 1983.
————. *Whistlejacket*. New York: Weidenfeld & Nicolson, 1988. Paperback reprint. New York: Macmillan, 1989.

Hawkes, John. *Fiasco Hall.* Cambridge, MA: Harvard University Printing Office, 1943.
————. *The Innocent Party: Four Short Plays.* Preface by Herbert Blau. New York: New Directions, 1967. Includes "The Innocent Party," "The Questions," "The Undertaker," and "The Wax Museum."

Hawkes, John. "Flannery O'Connor's Devil." *Sewanee Review* 70 (1962): 395–407.
————. "*The Floating Opera* and *Second Skin.*" *Mosaic* 8 (1974): 449–461.
————. "Notes on *The Wild Goose Chase.*" *Massachusetts Review* 3 (1962): 784–788.
————. "Notes on Violence." *Audience* 7 (1960): 60.
————. "Notes on Writing a Novel." *TriQuarterly* 30 (1974): 109–126.

Emmett, Paul, and Richard Vine. "A Conversation with John Hawkes." *Chicago Review* 28 (Fall 1976): 163–171.
Enck, John. "John Hawkes: An Interview." *Wisconsin Studies in Comparative Literature* 6 (Summer 1965): 141–155.
Fielding, Andrew. "John Hawkes Is a Very Nice Guy and a Novelist of Sex and Death." *Village Voice*, 24 May 1976, 45–47.
Graham, John. "John Hawkes on His Novels: An Interview with John Graham." *Massachusetts Review* 7 (Summer 1966): 449–461.
James, Caryn. "Protected Like a Daughter." *New York Times Book Review*, 29 September 1985, 9.
Kuehl, John. "Interview." In *John Hawkes and the Craft of Conflict*, 155–183. New Brunswick, NJ: Rutgers University Press, 1975.
LeClair, Thomas. "The Novelists: John Hawkes." *New Republic*, 10 November 1979, 26–29.
LeClair, Thomas, ed. "Hawkes and Barth Talk About Fiction." *New York Times Book Review*, 1 April 1979, 7, 31–33. Reprinted, with editorial commentary by Thomas LeClair, as "A Dialogue: John Barth and John Hawkes" in *Anything Can Happen: Interviews with Contemporary American Novelists*, 9–19. Edited by Thomas LeClair and Larry McCaffrey. Chicago: University of Illinois Press, 1983.
Levine, Nancy. "An Interview with John Hawkes." In *A John Hawkes Symposium*, 91–108. Eds. Santore and Pocalyko. New York: New Directions, 1977.
O'Donnell, Patrick. "Life and Art: An Interview with John Hawkes." *Review of Contemporary Fiction* 3 (Fall 1983): 107–126.
Santore, Anthony C., and Michael Pocalyko. "'A Trap to Catch Little Birds With': An Interview with John Hawkes." In *A John Hawkes Symposium*, 165–184. Eds. Santore and Pocalyko. New York: New Directions, 1977.
Scholes, Robert. "A Conversation on *The Blood Oranges* between John Hawkes and Robert Scholes." *Novel* 5 (Spring 1972): 197–207.
Ziegler, Heide. "John Hawkes." In *The Radical Imagination and the Liberal Tradition: Interviews with English and American Novelists*, 169–187. Edited by Heide Ziegler and Christopher Bigsby. London: Junction Books, 1982.

**Secondary Sources**

*Reviews*

Beatty, Jack. "Uncle Jake and the Mosquito-Crazed Prospector." Review of *Adventures in the Alaskan Skin Trade. New York Times Book Review*, 29 September 1985, 9.

Didion, Joan. "Notes from a Helpless Reader." Review of *The Lime Twig. National Review*, 15 July 1961, 21–22.

Halliday, Bob. "Father and Daughter." Review of *Adventures in the Alaskan Skin Trade. Washington Post Book World*, 29 September 1985, 5–6.

Hyman, Stanley Edgar. "The Abomination of Desolation." Review of *Second Skin. New Leader*, 30 March 1964, 24–25.

McGrath, Patrick. "Violent Horses and Violent Dreams." Review of *Whistlejacket. New York Times Book Review*, 7 August 1988, 11.

Sale, Roger. "What Went Wrong?" Review of *The Blood Oranges. New York Review of Books*, 21 October 1971, 3–4, 6.

Sontag, Susan. "A New Life for an Old One." Review of *Second Skin. New York Times Book Review*, 5 April 1964, 5. Reprinted in *The Merrill Studies in Second Skin*, ed. John Graham, 3–5.


*Books and articles*

Abrams, Steven. "*The Blood Oranges* as a Visionary Fiction." *Journal of Narrative Technique* 8 (Spring 1978): 97–111.

Allen, C. J. "Desire, Design, and Debris: The Submerged Narrative of John Hawkes' Recent Trilogy." *Modern Fiction Studies* (Winter 1979/80): 579–592.

Barth, John. "The Literature of Exhaustion." *The Atlantic* 220, 2 (1968): 29–34.

———. "The Literature of Replenishment." *The Atlantic* 245, 1 (1980): 65–71.

Barthes, Roland. *Image/ Music/ Text*. Trans. Stephen Heath. New York: Hill and Wang, 1977.

———. *A Lover's Discourse*. Trans. Richard Howard. New York: Hill and Wang, 1978.

Bataille, Georges. *Erotism: Death & Sensuality*. Trans. Mary Dalwood. San Fransisco: City Lights Books, 1986.

Baxter, Charles. "In the Suicide Seat: Reading John Hawkes's *Travesty*." *Georgia Review* 34 (Winter 1980): 871–885.

Blanchot, Maurice. *The Gaze of Orpheus*. Trans. Lydia Davis. Barrytown, New York: Station Hill Press, 1981.

———. "Michel Foucault As I Imagine Him." Trans. Jeffrey Mehlman. In *Foucault/Blanchot*. Trans. Jeffrey Mehlman and Brian Massumi. New York: Zone Books, 1990.

———. *The Space of Literature*. Trans. Ann Smock. Lincoln: University of Nebraska Press, 1982.

Bronfen, Elisabeth. *Over Her Dead Body: Death, Femininity and the Aesthetic*. New York: Routledge, 1992.

Busch, Frederick. *John Hawkes: A Guide to His Fictions*. Syracuse, NY: Syracuse University Press, 1973.

Carter, Angela. *The Sadeian Woman and the Ideology of Pornography*. New York: Pantheon Books, 1978.

Chénetier, Marc. "'The Pen & the Skin': Inscription and Cryptography in John Hawkes's *Second Skin.*" *Review of Contemporary Fiction* 3 (Fall 1983): 167–177.

Coleridge, S. T. *Biographia Literaria.* Volumes I and II. Edited by J. Shawcross. Oxford: The Clarendon Press, 1907.

Crump, R. W., ed. *The Complete Poems of Christina Rossetti.* A variorum edition, vol. 1. Baton Rouge: Louisiana State University Press, 1979.

de Lauretis, Teresa. *Technologies of Gender: Essays on Theory, Film, and Fiction.* Bloomington and Indianapolis: Indiana University Press, 1987.

Fiedler, Leslie A. "The Pleasures of John Hawkes." Introduction to *The Lime Twig.* New York: New Directions, 1961.

Foucault, Michel. *The History of Sexuality, Volume I: An Introduction.* Trans. Robert Hurley. New York: Vintage Books, 1980.

———. "Maurice Blanchot: The Thought from Outside." Trans. Brian Massumi. In *Foucault / Blanchot.* Trans. Jeffrey Mehlman and Brian Massumi. New York: Zone Books, 1990.

Fowler, Roger, ed. *A Dictionary of Modern Critical Terms: Revised and Enlarged Edition.* New York: Routledge & Kegan Paul, 1987.

Frost, Lucy. "The Drowning of American Adam: Hawkes' *The Beetle Leg.*" *Critique* (Atlanta) 14, no. 3 (1973): 63–74.

Gallop, Jane. *The Daughter's Seduction: Feminism and Psychoanalysis.* Ithaca, NY: Cornell University Press, 1982.

Gass, William. *Habitations of the Word.* New York: Simon and Schuster, 1985.

———. *On Being Blue.* Boston: David R. Godine, 1976.

Gorak, Jan. *God the Artist: American Novelists in a Post-Realist Age.* Chicago: University of Illinois Press, 1987.

Graham, John, ed. *The Merrill Studies in Second Skin.* Columbus, Ohio: Charles E. Merrill, 1971.

Greiner, Donald J. *Comic Terror: The Novels of John Hawkes.* Memphis: Memphis State University Press, 1973.

———. *Understanding John Hawkes.* Columbia: University of South Carolina Press, 1985.

Guerard, Albert. "Introduction to the Cambridge Anti-Realists." *Audience* 7 (Spring 1960): 57–59.

Hassan, Ihab. "Toward a Concept of Postmodernism." In *Postmodernism: A Reader,* 146–156. Edited by Thomas Docherty. New York: Columbia University Press, 1993.

Hawthorne, Nathaniel. *The Marble Faun.* Columbus: Ohio State University Press, 1968.

———. "The Custom House." In *The Scarlet Letter.* New York: Signet, 1959.

Heineman, Alan [Charles]. "'It Is a Lawless Country': Narrative, Formal, and Thematic Coherence in *The Beetle Leg.*" *Review of Contemporary Fiction* 3 (Fall 1983): 136–148.

Hryciw-Wing, Carol. *John Hawkes: A Research Guide.* New York: Garland Publishing, Inc., 1986.

Hutcheon, Linda. *Narcissistic Narrative: The Metafictional Paradox.* Waterloo, Ontario: Wilfrid Laurier University Press, 1985.

Irigaray, Luce. *This Sex Which Is Not One.* Ithaca, NY: Cornell University Press, 1985.

Jardine, Alice. *Gynesis: Configurations of Woman and Modernity.* Ithaca, NY: Cornell University Press, 1985.

Klein, Marcus. "Hawkes in Love." *Annals de la faculté des lettres and sciences humaines de Toulouse: Caliban* 12, n.s. 11 (1975): 65–79.

———. "John Hawkes' Experimental Compositions." In *Surfiction: Fiction Now . . . and Tomorrow*, 203–224. Edited by Raymond Federman. Chicago: Swallow Press, 1975.

———. "The Satyr at the Head of the Mob." In *A John Hawkes Symposium: Design and Debris*, 154–164. Edited by Anthony C. Santore and Michael Pocalyko. New York: New Directions, 1977.

Knapp, John V. "John Hawkes." In *Critical Survey of Long Fiction: English Language Series*, v. 4, 1303–1313. Edited by Frank N. Magill. Englewood Cliffs, NJ: Salem Press, 1983.

Kristeva, Julia. *Powers of Horror: An Essay on Abjection.* New York: Columbia University Press, 1982.

———. *Tales of Love.* Trans. Leon S. Roudiez. New York: Columbia University Press, 1987.

Kuehl, John. *John Hawkes and the Craft of Conflict.* New Brunswick, NJ: Rutgers University Press, 1975.

Laniel, Christine. "John Hawkes's Return to the Origin." In *Facing Texts: Encounters Between Contemporary Writers and Critics*, 215–246. Ed. Heide Ziegler. Durham, NC: Duke University Press, 1988.

Le Vot, André. "From the Zero Degree of Language to the H-Hour of Fiction: Or, Sex, Text, and Dramaturgy in *The Cannibal.*" *Review of Contemporary Fiction* 3 (Fall 1983): 185–192.

Lyotard, Jean-François. "Answering the Question: What Is Postmodernism? In *The Postmodern Condition: A Report on Knowledge.* Trans. Geoff Bennington and Brian Massumi. Minneapolis: University of Minnesota Press, 1984.

———. "The Sublime and the Avant-Garde." In *Postmodernism: A Reader*, 146–156. Edited by Thomas Docherty. New York: Columbia University Press, 1993.

Marcuse, Herbert. *Reason and Revolution: Hegel and the Rise of Social Theory.* Boston: Beacon Press, 1960.

Mitchell, W. J. T. *Iconography: Image, Text, Ideology.* Chicago: University of Chicago Press, 1986.

Moi, Toril. *Sexual/Textual Politics: Feminist Literary Theory.* New York: Routledge, 1985.

Morrow, Bradford, and Patrick McGrath, eds. *The New Gothic: A Collection of Contemporary Gothic Fiction.* New York: Random House, 1991.

O'Donnell, Patrick. *John Hawkes.* Twayne's United States Author Series, TUSAS 418. Boston: Twayne, 1982.

———. "Self-Alignment: John Hawkes' *Travesty.*" In *Passionate Doubts: Designs of Interpretation in Contemporary American Fiction.* Iowa City: University of Iowa Press, 1986.

———. "Stories My Father Never Told Me: On Hawkes's *Adventures in the Alaskan Skin Trade.*" In *Critical Essays on John Hawkes.* Ed. Stanley Trachtenberg. Boston: G. K. Hall & Co., 1991.

Owens, Craig. "The Discourse of Others: Feminists and Postmodernism." In *The Anti-Aesthetic.* Ed. Hal Foster. Seattle, Washington: Bay Press, 1983.

Reutlinger, D. P. "*The Cannibal*: The Reality of Victim." *Critique* (Atlanta) 6 (Fall 1963): 30–37.

Robertson, Mary F. "The 'Crisis in Comedy' as a Problem of the Sign: The Example of Hawkes's *Second Skin." Texas Studies in Literature and Language* 26 (Winter 1984): 425–454.

Said, Edward W. *Beginnings: Intention and Method.* New York: Columbia University Press, 1985.

Scholes, Robert. *Fabulation and Metafiction.* Urbana and Chicago: University of Illinois Press, 1979.

Shaviro, Steven. *Passion and Excess: Blanchot, Bataille, and Literary Theory.* Tallahassee: The Florida State University Press, 1990.

Singer, Alan. *A Metaphorics of Fiction: Discontinuity and Discourse in the Modern Novel.* Gainesville: University Presses of Florida, 1983, 79–114.

Sontag, Susan. *Against Interpretation.* New York: Farrar, Strauss and Giroux, 1966.

———. *On Photography.* New York: Farrar, Straus and Giroux, 1977.

Stevens, Wallace. "The Man with the Blue Guitar." In *The Collected Poems.* New York: Vintage, 1982.

Suleiman, Susan Rubin. *Subversive Intent: Gender, Politics, and the Avant-Garde.* Cambridge, MA: Harvard University Press, 1990.

Tanner, Tony. *City of Words: American Fiction, 1950–1970.* New York: Harper & Row, 1971, 202–229.

Trachtenberg, Alan. "Barth and Hawkes: Two Fabulists." *Critique* (Atlanta) 6 (Fall 1963): 4–18.

Trachtenberg, Stanley, ed. *Critical Essays on John Hawkes.* Boston: G. K. Hall & Co., 1991.

Waugh, Patricia. *Practising Postmodernism / Reading Modernism.* New York: Edward Arnold, 1992.

West, Nathanael. *Miss Lonelyhearts* and *The Day of the Locust.* New York: New Directions, 1962.

Wilde, Alan. *Horizons of Assent: Modernism, Postmodernism, and the Ironic Imagination.* Baltimore, MD: Johns Hopkins University Press, 1981.

Ziegler, Heide. "Postmodernism as Autobiographical Commentary: *The Blood Oranges* and *Virginie." Review of Contemporary Fiction* 3 (Fall 1983): 207–213.

# Index